Hozho:
Walking in Beauty

Hozho: Walking in Beauty

Native American Stories of Inspiration, Humor, and Life

Edited by Paula Gunn Allen and Carolyn Dunn Anderson
Foreword by Mark Robert Waldman

Contemporary Books

Chicago   New York   San Francisco   Lisbon   London   Madrid   Mexico City
Milan   New Delhi   San Juan   Seoul   Singapore   Sydney   Toronto

Library of Congress Cataloging-in-Publication Data

Hozho: walking in beauty: Native American stories of inspiration, humor, and life/edited by Paula Gunn Allen and Carolyn Dunn Anderson; with a foreword by Mark Robert Waldman.
     p.   cm.
     ISBN 0-7373-0585-1
     1. Short stories, American—Indian authors.   2. Indians of North America—Fiction.   I. Allen, Paula Gunn.   II. Anderson, Carolyn Dunn.

PS508.I5 H69   2001
813'.0108897—dc21   00-067392

Contemporary Books

A Division of The **McGraw·Hill** Companies

1 2 3 4 5 6 7 8 9 0   DOH/DOH   0 9 8 7 6 5 4 3 2 1

ISBN 0-7373-0585-1

This book was set in Adobe Caslon
Interior design by Anna Christian

McGraw-Hill books are available at special quantity discounts to use as premiums and sales promotions, or for use in corporate training programs. For more information, please write to the Director of Special Sales, Professional Publishing, McGraw-Hill, Two Penn Plaza, New York, NY 10121-2298. Or contact your local bookstore.

This book is printed on acid-free paper.

◆ CONTENTS ◆

MARK ROBERT WALDMAN

Looking at Indians Through White-Tainted Eyes

I AM AWAKENED IN THE MIDDLE OF THE NIGHT BY A HAUNTING suspicion of truth, for I fear that somewhere inside, I—like so many others—am unconsciously racist and blind. Ignorant of what it is like to be different and colored, near-dead. I am prejudiced, biased, and unkind simply because I am white. And because I am white, my eyes have been tainted by the stereotypes of life.

I grew up in Phoenix, in a town surrounded by some of the poorest people in the land. Negroes, Indians, Mexicans—that's what they were called in the 1950s when I was a very young boy. My mother, by contrast, was a fighter of hate, an advocate of civil rights, particularly for Jews, Hispanics, and blacks. But she too was blinded by the color of her skin—not out of hatred or choice, but just by a lack of awareness of how pervasive prejudice can be. A prejudice that everyone carries from birth. We may not be able to abolish such feelings from our soul, but we can certainly become more aware.

My mother, out of naive kindness, chose to hire a girl from the local Indian school to clean our house once a week, and thus a primitive conception was formed: a "native" woman who was sensually quiet and withdrawn; a lower-class servant for middle-class whites. But my first visit to a local reservation rattled this simplistic view. I had never seen such poverty before: homes made of mud sitting on dusty lots with rusting cars on the street. I did not know that I was standing on one of the poorest and tiniest reservations in America.

I also saw something else, for it was a day of celebration, with drumming and dancing and costumes and masks. For a ten-year-old boy it was a scene of magic and awe, a stereotypical view that stayed with me for years.

In the 1970s, more stereotypes emerged. Fostered by the New Age movement, hundreds of writers and dozens of movies offered thousands of seekers a hipper vision of Indian life: the noble "breed," an endangered species, keepers of the Great American Spirit. A young, naive, and essentially white generation of seekers donned feathers and beads. Navajo blankets were placed lovingly on the floors, and the walls were adorned with Russell or Curtis prints. With a proud or lonely Indian staring blankly into their homes, the insult went unseen.

Today, new stereotypes are stirred by the reservation quarrels over gambling and land. From Drunken Indian to Noble Savage to Red Profiteer, the prejudice never abates. Of all the colors in the world, red is the least understood, I fear.

That is why this book was created: it is an *essential* anthology for anyone seeking a deeper appreciation of a culture that is still under siege. A culture that is more rich and diverse than I ever expected to find. A culture whose writing competes with the best in the world, capturing the spirit, the humor, and the lives of a people enmeshed in the fabric of "white."

This book will shake the stereotype inside. It will make you laugh and sometimes cry. And maybe, just maybe, it will help you grasp the inner core of humanity when it is balanced between extinction and life. Through tainted eyes and wounded hearts, come walk in the beauty of this world.

PAULA GUNN ALLEN

May It Be Beautiful All Around

HOZHO—ANYONE WHO HAS READ ONE OF BEST-SELLING AUTHOR Tony Hillerman's Joe Leaphorn and Jim Chee detective novels will imme-diately grasp what it means: it is the Navajo word for walking in beauty, walking in a sacred manner, walking with a peaceful heart, living daily life "seated in the midst of the rainbow." Hozho is the heart of the Native American spirit, which is so directly involved with the beauty and living awareness of the land, and thus the stories contained in this anthology will be filled with indigenous people's traditional sense of natural awe.

What makes this anthology unique, however, is its inclusion of humor, for in this country, the stereotypical view of Indians lacks wit. Native wisdom, yes. Respectful serenity, yes. But never satire, teasing, or fun. Indians don't laugh, the stereotype says, but in reality Native life is filled with laughter and joy. Just meet a coyote on your path, and you will see what I mean. In Indian Country the sense of play, of humor, satire, irony, and wit plays as central a role in ceremony as it does in day-to-day life. Wherever Native people gather, laughter reigns. Nor is the humor confined to jokes—though there are plenty of them. Mostly it rests on pun, on irony and ambiguity that several centuries of occupation and genocide occasion. It's a matter of laugh or die. So we laugh. At ourselves, at our situation, at the ludicrous circumstances in which we live and move and have our being.

Our laughter is sometimes unabashed hilarity, sometimes bitter cynicism, sometimes embedded in a complexity of observation and tradition. Of necessity, Indian humor must reside alongside rage and grief. At the end of the day, whatever it is that is human pushed to the extreme edge of survival informs these stories, and more: for they are shot through with the glinting skeins of the great spiritual traditions from which they spring, from which All That Is ever arises and into which All That Is ever falls—ordinary sounds and activities of every day, love, death, loss. Each of the stories in this collection shows us how to transcend our circumstances while being firmly connected within them. Each, in that way, follows the way of Hozho, demonstrating how transcendence arises from the exigencies of daily life and informs it.

Perhaps there's something profoundly funny about spitting in the eye of death. After all, the Native nations of the Americas have looked extinction in the eye, and survived to tell the tales. In Indian Country it's been nuclear winter for centuries. We know all about survival, including the fact that without a wry view of history, survival itself is impossible. And that is a history that goes back thousands of years, long before the most recent challenges to our endurance and our sense of humor began.

There's a joke in Indian Country in which some folks are standing around outside the local tribal administration offices having a smoke, and to their amazement a flying saucer whirls into view and lands in front of them. "Here we go again," one of them quips. We are also all agreed that we're glad the Spanish-Portuguese ships hadn't sailed for Turkey!

This anthology, which contains a sampling of well-known and up-and-coming Native American writers, also depicts the reality of Native American life in exile-in-one's-own-home, the poignant and sometimes painful life of living in invisibility, revisioning, and chronic public humiliation. Thus these stories also exemplify how one of the world's major culture systems has managed to survive, to transcend, and to inspire. These are particularly American stories, for what are Americans but a society of people of diverse language and cultural strains caught alive between two worlds— the old, whether Indian Country or lands across the seas, and the new, which is still in the making.

I can't think of separate world views that are more divergent than that of the Native world and Western civilization. Rudyard Kipling, the bard of the Raj, rhymed: "East is east and west is west, and never the twain shall meet." And whatever truth there is in his observation about diverse Old World civilizations, the difference is magnified tenfold between a world fundamentally grounded in Hozho, and one fundamentally based on progress. *Hozho* means we walk in Beauty, in the Rainbow House of Dawn of balance, spirit, and the All That Is; *progress* means we pit ourselves against what is, and exert every effort to fix, change, and solve it.

And nowhere is this difference more evident than in our literary traditions. Given that fundamental difference (a difference so profound that one wonders how the two cultures can coexist), offering texts that spring from what we call "Hozho" to a readership that has been divorced from its immanent dynamic place seems all but futile. Let me give you an example of the extent of the gulf between the two. I was working with a colleague on a collection of biographies of American Indian leaders in various walks of life, and we suggested the title "Walking in Beauty." Our editor, quite rightly, pointed out that readers would think the book was about cosmetics.

The Hindi-Western doctor and writer Deepak Chopra writes about this difference. He tells a story about a Westerner walking in the country somewhere in India. The traveler comes upon an old man in a *dhoti* who is talking to someone. But as the Westerner looks around, he sees that the old man in the clearing is quite alone. After watching for a time and unable to restrain himself, the traveler says, "Pardon me, but what makes you converse all alone?" The old man looks up. "Pardon me," he replies. "What makes you think I'm alone?"

The divergence between Western and Native modes of consciousness is one of the basic themes in American Indian fiction, as in "The Problem of Old Harjo," by Cherokee journalist and fiction writer, John M. Oskison. Oskison's complex story explores the two-way nature of transformation. Old Harjo converts to Christianity, although church rules prevent him from being baptized, because his conversion is of the spirit and mind, not one of cultural mores. While the old Indian is undergoing a spiritual transformation, a young white missionary, Miss Evans, undergoes a parallel transformation of consciousness. She encounters a different sense of the meaning of "spiritual life" from the old pagan, to whom *spiritual* implies respect for the dignity and integrity of human codes of decency. The plot Oskison hangs his deeper insight upon is ubiquitous in Indian Country. There is an old joke about an elderly chief with three wives who was ordered by the newly arrived Indian agent or missionary, depending on the locus of the tale, to send two of the women away. The Native man thought about the demand for a time. "You tell them," he said at last. "And you say which one will stay."

The dynamics—the pain, the humor, the great gulf in perception and values—of Indian-White relations are best captured in stories like "The Problem of Old Harjo." The title itself is an ironic comment on what the U.S. government and Anglo-European settlers were wont to call "the Indian Problem." In fact, according to historian William Brandon in his wonderful study *The Last Americans*, the first item of business on George Washington's first presidential agenda was "the Indian Problem." His hawkish idea was that all Native people should be exterminated. The liberal view, held by leaders such as Thomas Jefferson, lay in two parallel courses. One counseled cultural extinction, assimilation of the sort that the federal- or church-controlled education system spent nearly a century attempting to implement, along with economic, religious, and political methods they also used. The other strategized removal to regions beyond the then borders of the United States of America. Over the course of the nineteenth and twentieth centuries, varying combinations of these three approaches were implemented with tragic consequences and mixed results. As the new century dawns, a fourth possibility is emerging, one that more closely resembles that suggested in most of the stories in this collection: a kind of peaceful and creative coexistence that itself may be as new as the American experiment.

At any rate, a multitude of implications lurk within that phrase, "the Indian Problem." One of them constitutes a major theme in American literature, both literary and popular, and can be summed up as a cultural identity problem. As a polyglot people, who are not really what we were, we find ourselves at a loss to define who we are. Neither Old World nor American Indian, a new society without land- and blood-connected traditions, we are faced with the necessity of making sense of our transitional collective nature. It was a problem, and still is, and there have been many like the fictional Mrs. Rowell who have had what they believed or believe to be a simple solution. Old Harjo's story reveals the grace of humor as well as the saving grace of faith, while addressing both the complexity of our situation and the place of humor in leavening it.

One of the more amusing effects of the biculturalism of the modern Indian story, as well as modern Indian lives, is captured in the hilarious satire by Charles A. Eastman (Ohiyesa), "The Singing Spirit." Like "The Problem of Old Harjo," "The Singing Spirit" was published in 1907, penned by a writer who was a physician sent by the U.S. government to gather medical evidence at the site of the Wounded Knee massacre of 1892 (about which he elsewhere recorded his horror). "The Singing Spirit" merges the heroic adventure story based on nineteenth-century revisions of the Scottish narrative tradition popularized by Sir Walter Scott with the beliefs about Native people and wilderness current among non-Indians in Dr. Eastman's time. This merger makes for a slyly hilarious narrative that is nonetheless not without its pointed commentary on biracial relationships. The story poses a question about the nature of wilderness, and responds, "It depends on who is doing the reporting," suggesting that like beauty, meaning is mostly in the eye of the beholder. Conflating the surreal with the factitious, Dr. Eastman lets us perceive how identity slips and changes as readily in a short story as it does in the oral tradition, and how humor lends texture and depth to both. Stories of the Little People abound in the oral tradition from many Native Nations in the western hemisphere, as they do among modern-day descendants of the Celts of Ireland, Scotland, and Wales. In "The Singing Spirit," Dr. Eastman combines the two traditions into a bifurcated narrative, adding a couple of trickster twists of his own.

We have followed the Oskison and Eastman stories from early in the twentieth century with one by Lorenzo Baca, "San Lorenzo Day in Laguna." While this story is as contemporary as tomorrow's news, it is timeless in its close connection to ancient ways at a modern Pueblo, Laguna, which is in New Mexico. Baca's story puts a very Native spin on the identity question explored by his early twentieth-century predecessors.

Although we have included only two selections from early twentieth-century fiction, let us not forget that that icon of American humor, Will Rogers, was Cherokee. His humor was singularly American Indian, and it struck a resonant chord with the larger body of the American people. It was Rogers who quipped, "I belong to no organized political party. I'm a Democrat." His on-the-spot commentaries, blistering and deadly funny, made him a celebrity and drew fire from every side of the political aisle. Like Native writers who would follow him in the later years of the century, Rogers's commentary was biting, pointed, and leavened with dry Oklahoma cowboy wit.

Rogers was an advisor to presidents and himself a short-lived candidate for that office. At the 1924 Democratic Convention, two delegates from Arizona favored him for the nomination. In his final Convention dispatch column, Rogers thanked the men for their "unwavering support during the entire fifteen minutes which they stuck so staunchly by me." In the 1928 presidential election, Rogers gleefully accepted the tongue-in-cheek nomination for president by the humor magazine *Life*, creating campaign promises and rhetoric in the finest political tradition. He was the presidential candidate for the Anti-Bunk Party, a position for which his columns and commentaries on the lecture circuit showed him to be well-suited.

In 1932, Rogers was given twenty-two votes from the Oklahoma delegation when Alfalfa Bill Murray released his delegation to "that sterling citizen, that wise philosopher, that great heart, that favorite son of Oklahoma...." As recounted in her book about her husband, Betty Rogers quotes Will's later column about this event:

> *Politics ain't on the level.... I was only in 'em for an hour, but in that short space of time somebody stole twenty-two votes from me. I was sitting there in the press stand asleep and wasn't bothering a soul when they woke me up and said Oklahoma had started me on the way to the White House with twenty-two votes. I thought to myself, "Well, there is no use going there this late in the morning," so I dropped off to sleep again, and that's when somebody touched me for my roll, took the whole twenty-two, and didn't even leave me a vote to get breakfast on.*

The editors of *Hozho: Walking in Beauty* made our selections for this collection with an eye to giving readers a sense of the complexity of Native writing in the twentieth century. We hope to reveal the range of experience and reflection upon it that Native writers command, while providing you, our readers, with a book of rousing good stories. We think we have accomplished our goals. Certainly there was no lack of short stories to choose from. We have collected twenty-five stories that demonstrate the dexterity of thought and style and the diversity of talent and voice that, taken together, provide a tapestry of American Indian life in the contemporary world.

Living within traditions as old as the hills and creating lives as untraditional as those of every American, Native writers have long been and remain singularly American writers. Both editors of this volume have functioned as instructors, writers, and anthologists, and in these capacities we have found that readers of whatever cultural background relate to American Indian fiction with surprising fervor. It is our thought that the reason for this powerful response is not due to the "exotic" nature of American Indian life outside of Indian Country, but rather to the basic shared experience embodied in these tales. Americans are, at base, hybrid people. One way or another we find ourselves in a world none of our forebears could have imagined, yet we must locate a common sense of coherence in that world, one within which our lives as individuals and as social beings makes sense. It is the act of revealing the inner coherence of American life, with all of its vicissitudes and affronts to every kind of sensibility, at which American Indian writers excel.

Just read how a young Native man tries to locate coherence in the gulf that yawns between his Native world and his life as a university student, lover of a woman who has never seen the rez, in D. Renville's stunning "Siobhan La Rue in Color." Or wait and watch with two frightened Native women in a modern condominium outside of Santa Fe as the sky opens and reality wavers before their frightened eyes, as that noted teller of tales, Anna Lee Walters, chronicles in "Bicenti." The boundaries between the real and the supposed are not fixed, these stories tell us, and this is an idea that is as much a part of the old traditional, ritual way of seeing the world as it is the shocking reality of life in modern America. As Vickie L. Sears, in the narrative voice of first a small child and then a woman, reminds us, deciding what is real, what is true, and what clarity means, exactly, are decisions not easily come to.

It seems that Old Coyote is alive and swinging in these stories. Carter Revard, whose day job as a professor of Medieval English Literature enhances his Ponca wit and quirky humor, as his wry "Never Quite a Hollywood Star" proves; and in his print-media debut Suleiman Russell gives us an eye-opening peek into the true machinations of good and evil on the superhighway of our time. Extrapolating on his riff, one might see that Old Man Coyote is alive and kicking in the White House, enlivening the Cherokee President William Jefferson Clinton's administration, much to the delight of comics, and to the dismay of Old Man Missionary in his many incarnations at this time.

Russell's delightful "How Old Man Coyote Lost His Manhood" is a satire on not only middle-class mores but on ethnographer's interpretation of old Indian "pourquoi" narratives. These are stories from the oral tradition that seem to explain how some feature of land or creature came about. "Pourquoi," which is French for "why," is a term that works to trivialize and diminish ancient knowledge. Such labeling recontextualizes traditional knowledge systems, lending a tint of childishness to stories from the oral tradition. Russell, like other writers whose work appears in this collection, reminds us that the boundaries within the world as defined by lateral-mindedness are far more fuzzy than Western thought believes.

Carolyn Dunn reminds us that the fuzzy boundaries extend not only around us, but in realms above and beyond. Navajo mother Patty Burns, who for a time embraced the Mormon faith of her childhood, had gone back to her father's house and spoke the language of the Old Ones once again. But there was something still that spoke to Patty through the stars. She listened to the instructions she received from "the angel Moroni and Changing Woman," a major supernatural figure among the Dine (Navajo). Here again the usual boundaries ascribed to the external and the inner worlds blur. In "Fishing," Dunn reminds us that culture-bound borders are fragile indeed, that dream is as factual as talking on the phone, and that what is dissolves and reforms around us as a matter of course.

In "Loaves and Fishes," Dawn Karima Pettigrew reminds us of the brittle humor of miracles, and the twists of spirit that composes them, while rapping a riff on old Harjo's problem and Eastman's spirit solution.

The Spirits come in many guises, some more life affirming than others, as Pettigrew wittily—and defiantly—reminds us. In "Loaves and Fishes," we encounter Mrs. Rowell in another guise, and old Harjo is morphed into a young woman and her charge. The situation is no less dreadful in this recent story than in its predecessors, and the solution, while charged with irony, is a point-blank statement of defiance. Trading booze for food may be a unique response, but the willingness of the community to care for the destitute is as old as Indianna—not the state, but the state of consciousness and community.

In many of the stories that follow Pettigrew's, spirits in alcoholic form play a major role. They star in "Six O'Clock News," free little Alyssa and her patroness, and lead a bourbon-soaked would-be swain into dimensions poorly mirrored by booze-induced altered states.

Lynda Martinez Foley takes us south of the U.S. border to explore the relationship between alcoholic spirits and the other kinds, a relationship that can be disastrous no matter which way it's sliced, and M. L. Smoker hits us again from another region in Indian Country. "Twins' Story" offers a commentary on the ancient sacred stories about the Little Twins, replete as they are both in legend and in our modern world. Like their mythic counterparts, August and Austin are blessed—and cursed—with the gifts of timing and intuition received from their mother, and a kind of reckless-ness and carelessness garnered from the intercultural conflict that swirls around them.

On the other hand, Emma Lee Warrior gives us another look at the sort of thing that drives a Native to drink. This time old Harjo is several characters, all of whom have resorted to alcohol in a doomed attempt to avoid the ubiquitous intrusion of tourists—some of whom have "gone Native," unfortunately to a Native tradition other than their own. "Com-patriots" is another trickster twist on the old identity question, only this time the conversions are going the other way.

No question about it. Identity issues are at least as tricky as Old Man Coyote, his southern cousin, Rabbit, or his northern counterparts, Raven and Iktomi (Spider Boy). In "Jules Bart, Giving Too Much—August 1946," we see how tricky self-definition, like social definition, can be. One thing that is indigenous to Native and Western literary traditions alike is that transformation of some sort powers a good story. Sometimes transform-ative events come disguised as personal trauma, in circumstances where one must face one's truth. Unmasking the false personality to reveal the true one beneath it is the theme of Debra Earling's story, another example of the old trickster narrative. Her story takes as its familiar theme the explor-ation of boundaries: where they are located and how they pertain to issues of integrity and significance.

The borderlands of sexual identity directly address the larger issues of our time; those hardy citizens of the crossroads, bisexuals and "closet" homosexuals and lesbians, are in a state of perpetual liminality, much as the Changer Coyote is perceived as being. For it is on the threshold between one set of realities and another that the most sacred events are likely to occur. Like the transitional states of childbirth, near-death, puberty, and dying itself, sexual liminality—between two worlds—is a state in which the most profound transformations can occur. There is a deep sense of humor operating in this trickster tale, one that is as challenging as the dilemma it embodies.

Following the theme of transformation and transition states, Mary Randle TallMountain stitches a pastiche story about life in the Tenderloin, a neighborhood in San Francisco inhabited by impoverished elderly, street people, down-and-out alcoholics, poets, and saints, their identities interchangeable. In TallMountain's "Tender Street," we observe how the brutal, dehumanizing streets help souls make significant crossings, leading them to safety, into all that is unknown but otherwise okay. There is someone to pick up where we leave off, however desperate our situation. Given the right kind of mind, we see, anyone can find the pure joy of open spaces. It turns out that the joke is on the guy who hit old Bilijohn—in that way driving him home, maybe jump-starting the Indian's Thunderbird.

Maybe Bilijohn made it through the "Door in the Mountain" that is the focus of Anita Endrezze's powerful story. This time we are in a city north of San Francisco, and the characters speak Spanish as well as English. That's because the national boundaries of the Western world's present aren't the ones the First Nations recognize. Here, location in space and matter is the borderland, where what should be one place is actually another. No matter, the point is transformation, and walking into the mountain on the way back home. It's a matter of the shimmer of thin air, which is how reality appears to the traditional-, ritual-minded viewer. As the late Lakota medicine man John Fire Lame Deer tells us, Indians don't have symbols. They think that material reality, stuff, is the symbol, and the reality is behind the stuff. It is this difference in point of view that gives short stories from the Native world their characteristic of humor in the midst of everyday life, whatever its cast. For what can be funnier than the difference between one set of assumptions and expectations and another, particularly when you hold both with equal intensity in your head?

It is this idea that Joanelle Redhawk and her little band of pilgrims to Sacred Mountain drive so far to discover in Gary Robinson's tale. From a state of terminal dismay generated by the day-to-day differences between expectation and attainment, Joanelle and her friends stumble on the truth of reality, which is that it isn't as inscribed in concrete as Old Man Missionary would have us believe. It is good to remember, as Leslie Marmon Silko has the old Laguna medicine man instruct, the earth is fragile, fluid, forever in a state of transformation. This is the reason that traditionals think of Earth as sacred, and of All That Is as part of the sacred hoop of being. It is also why one has to laugh often, as the changes go down before one's bemused and sometimes amazed eyes.

Perhaps Grandmother Wolverine, the predator that hunts the hunter, really is possessed of a cunning intelligence, and perhaps the horses share it. Perhaps humans are the truly ignorant and backward members of our planetary community, except for a few like old Sam. We can certainly make that surmise as we read S. Bruised Head's "An Afternoon in Bright Sunlight." The title tells a narrative that comments on the story and on modern assumptions about fact—we say, "It's as clear as day!" when we believe something to be incontrovertible, cold, hard fact.

There are a number of ways of looking at difficult times, and each of the stories has suggested one. Irvin Morris gives us some ideas, including the place of humor in the midst of sorrow and rage, and the deep intelligence that underlies our delusions about the nature of intelligence. "The Hyatt, the Maori, and the Yanoama" addresses two of the big issues of our times: what to do about aging family members, and how to live in a world of hurt and hate. "We walked a razor's edge," the narrator tells us. "What else could we do? Every day we faced the thefts, the lies, and the hate."

> "It's a dirty shame," said Frank. "In the old days, old folks stayed with family to the end."
> "That's the old days," sighed Grace.
> "Dead and buried," said Frank, shaking his head.
> "Gone with the buffalo," I said.
> Frank looked at me. He grinned. "Belly up," he said, holding out his hand and wiggling his fingers.
> "A raw deal," I said.
> "A bum steer."
> "A crying shame."
> "Honestly, you guys," Grace said.
> "Just awful," said Frank, and eyed her sideways.

Grace made a funny sound and her shoulders began to jerk up and down. I thought she was crying, but she wasn't. "Utter tragedy," she gasped, and her throaty laugh swept us up. Soon we were whooping and snorting at the absurdity of us flopping helpless as hooked fish in the language.

And so it goes. The absurdity of our situation, of all our situations, is indeed worthy only of whooping and snorting. In the face of an unforgiving death sentence, levied on us all, what are we *but* helpless as hooked fish?

Another significant thought in "The Hyatt, the Maori, and the Yanoama" is continued in Larry Littlebird's "The Hunter." It is a story about a boy learning to become a true hunter, and it is a parallel to the transformation of *Shimasani*, grandmother, returning in mind and body to the real world, the world where deer spirit runs forever, where history and legend continue on. "The Hunter" reminds us of an older, truer world that keeps on keeping on, that is coexistent with the one we think we live in, and that we might at last be free to know directly what it is to walk alive in the All That Is—someday, when we are all grown-up. Until then, one of the things we can do is laugh as we live, laugh at our clumsiness, at our help-lessness, at our indefatigable, inextinguishable, continuous efforts to learn true innocence, to see with truly clear eyes.

In honor of that goal, we end our collection with a wry and witty reminder of who we are, we indigenous writers. There is a way to write that is in keeping with the traditional rules for living in balance, walking in beauty. Vee F. Browne's commentary is a fit finale for all that has been said in the stories held in this volume. Despite centuries of living dispossessed in our own homes, Native people have survived, and more than merely surviving, endured.

———◆◦✦◦◆———

One may well wonder how so much humor can coexist with so much pain. Ask as well how so much belief in social mirage that enmeshes us all can coexist with the clear evidence of life far outside the borders of Horatio's philosophy. Clear enough, the latter explains the former, and the stories collected in this small volume go a long way to exploring and instructing us on the nuances of that response.

At the end of the day, the materialism of contemporary Western civilization, which denies the validity of such beings as Wolverine, Deer Spirit, Sacred Mountains of the inner planes, crystal caves, and basketball magic, and casts them off as superstitions or functions of primitive imaginations that can't quite grasp the subtleties of science and psychology, is missing the point.

It is the editors' profound hope that readers of this and other works by American Indian writers will use the stories as instruction manuals. They provide far better guidance into the intricacies of human/spirit (supernatural as well as deceased grandmothers) coexistence. There are truths about the nature of reality that go far beyond popular facts. And that's the real joke, what makes the whole situation so damned funny. Really. The gulf between the two points of view, logical positivism and spiritual vision, is so great, so dichotomous, you gotta laugh. Life is a lot like San Lorenzo Day at Laguna, generous, conventional, bloody when the limits are not observed, but all in all, it's fun.

JOHNNY RUSTYWIRE

Riding to the Shiprock Fair

RIDING ON TO SHIPROCK, SHE IS WITH ME AND WE COME WITH six horses. We left early this morning, twilight was gone and the pink of Dawn came to greet us and we rode out together. We ride with six horses to trade and race; my woman rides with me to Natani Nez (Shiprock). It beckons me to the North, I see it in the distance.

I turn and see she is riding close behind, even in the faint light she glows and the silver glistens. She sits in the saddle and glides along the ground. Her long hair catches in the breeze and it blows through it softly. Silver she wears, a concho belt, silver buttons, a fine heavy bracelet with turquoise from Cerillos, spiderweb it is. Jaclo (turquoise beads with red orange coral) hang gracefully from her neck. She glows with light of a new day. Hozhogo, our travel is with beauty.

We go on to race with those at the gathering by the river by Shiprock. On the bank we will camp and she will make me coffee and corn stew.

She rides as if she was born on a horse, her velvet shirt shines yellow gold in the dawn, the morning dew softens her face, her dark eyes shine with early morning light.

Yasho, it feels good to be alive. Let me wander these lands, my land, let me know that I am Navajo forever. Oh, how nice it is to ride this way, past Table Mesa and on toward Shiprock. Many join us and we travel together, there will be races, games and silver to trade. We will talk, sing and dance on the soft ground, drink cool water and share stories to tell over the winter nights. In the distant far off horizon a bonfire glows, a blazing light beckoning me to come.

I will sing with the Yei-Be-Che's and watch them move in the twilight. Let me go quickly and let them know I come. That she rides with me and my six horses. Let all our days be like this, that we shall be together forever and so we ride on to the Shiprock Fair . . . let the Holy People know . . . we are here in the light of Dawn and so it is with beauty I go and she rides with me.

Tonight when the sky is dark and trees very still and no sound is made I will be standing at the place near Shiprock and you will hear the sound of whistles blowing and the hooting of a sound far off. Yes, it is the sound of dancers singing and moving in the night. I will stand with the old, the young, Navajo men and women watching the story unfold as told many winters time and again. We will dance, sing, and laugh and do so all night.

Monster Slayer and Born for Water and the Holy People will watch us as we go about and they will say it is time to put away summer things and bring out winter, the frost has come and gone. They will taste fresh melon and delight in us remembering them and their stories in the Navajo Way.

Look closely. We shall be dancing and sing together this night. I will stand, just one of the people there, and I will watch them sway to the music, and listen to the laughter and talk once more. Join me tonight; we will dance till dawn. So look to the night sky and you will see a shooting star flick on by; it is the journey of the Holy People as they catch a shooting star to come way over by Shiprock in Navajoland to hear the songs that make my heart sing. . . .

To Vickie L. Sears

In Memoriam

JOHN M. OSKISON

The Problem of Old Harjo

THE SPIRIT OF THE LORD HAD DESCENDED UPON OLD HARJO.
From the new missionary, just out from New York, he had learned that he
was a sinner. The fire in the new missionary's eyes and her gracious appeal
had convinced old Harjo that this was the time to repent and be saved. He
was very much in earnest, and he assured Miss Evans that he wanted to be
baptized and received into the church at once. Miss Evans was enthusias-
tic and went to Mrs. Rowell with the news. It was Mrs. Rowell who had
said that it was no use to try to convert the older Indians, and she, after fifteen years of work in Indian Territory missions, should have known. Miss
Evans was pardonably proud of her conquest.

"Old Harjo converted!" exclaimed Mrs. Rowell. "Dear Miss Evans, do
you know that old Harjo has two wives?" To the older woman it was as if
someone had said to her "Madame, the Sultan of Turkey wishes to teach
one of your mission Sabbath school classes."

"But," protested the younger woman, "he is really sincere, and—"

"Then ask him," Mrs. Rowell interrupted a bit sternly, "if he will put away one of his wives. Ask him, before he comes into the presence of the Lord, if he is willing to conform to the laws of the country in which he lives, the country that guarantees his idle existence. Miss Evans, your work is not even begun." No one who knew Mrs. Rowell would say that she lacked sincerity and patriotism. Her own cousin was an earnest crusader against Mormonism, and had gathered a goodly share of that wagonload of protests that the Senate had been asked to read when it was considering whether a certain statesman of Utah should be allowed to represent his state at Washington.

In her practical, tactful way, Mrs. Rowell had kept clear of such embarrassments. At first, she had written letters of indignant protest to the Indian Office against the toleration of bigamy amongst the tribes. A wise inspector had been sent to the mission, and this man had pointed out that it was better to ignore certain things, "deplorable, to be sure," than to attempt to make over the habits of the old men. Of course, the young Indians would not be permitted to take more than one wife each.

So Mrs. Rowell had discreetly limited her missionary efforts to the young, and had exercised toward the old and bigamous only that strict charity which even a hopeless sinner might claim.

Miss Evans, it was to be regretted, had only the vaguest notions about "expediency"; so weak on matters of doctrine was she that the news that Harjo was living with two wives didn't startle her. She was young and possessed of but one enthusiasm—that for saving souls.

"I suppose," she ventured, "that old Harjo *must* put away one wife before he can join the church."

"There can be no question about it, Miss Evans."

"Then I shall have to ask him to do it." Miss Evans regretted the necessity for forcing this sacrifice, but had no doubt that the Indian would make it in order to accept the gift of salvation which she was commissioned to bear to him.

Harjo lived in a "double" log cabin three miles from the mission. His ten acres of corn had been gathered into its fence-rail crib; four hogs that were to furnish his winter's bacon had been brought in from the woods and penned conveniently near to the crib; out in a corner of the garden, a fat mound of dirt rose where the crop of turnips and potatoes had been buried against the corrupting frost; and in the hayloft of his log stable were stored many pumpkins, dried corn, onions (suspended in bunches from the rafters) and the varied forage that Mrs. Harjo number one and Mrs. Harjo number two had thriftily provided. Three cows, three young heifers, two colts, and two patient, capable mares bore the Harjo brand, a fantastic "HH" that the old man had designed. Materially, Harjo was solvent; and if the Government had ever come to his aid he could not recall the date.

This attempt to rehabilitate old Harjo morally, Miss Evans felt, was not one to be made at the mission; it should be undertaken in the Creek's own home, where the evidences of his sin should confront him as she explained.

When Miss Evans rode up to the block in front of Harjo's cabin, the old Indian came out, slowly and with a broadening smile of welcome on his face. A clean gray flannel shirt had taken the place of the white collarless garment, with crackling stiff bosom, that he had worn to the mission meetings. Comfortable, well-patched moccasins had been substituted for creaking boots, and brown corduroys, belted in at the waist, for tight black trousers. His abundant gray hair fell down on his shoulders. In his eyes, clear and large and black, glowed the light of true hospitality. Miss Evans thought of the patriarchs as she saw him lead her horse out to the stable; thus Abraham might have looked and lived.

"Harjo," began Miss Evans before following the old man to the covered passageway between the disconnected cabins, "is it true that you have two wives?" Her tone was neither stern nor accusatory. The Creek had heard that question before, from scandalized missionaries and perplexed registry clerks when he went to Muscogee to enroll himself and his family in one of the many "final" records ordered to be made by the government preparatory to dividing the Creek lands among the individual citizens.

For answer, Harjo called, first into the cabin that was used as a kitchen and then, in a loud, clear voice, toward the small field, where Miss Evans saw a flock of half-grown turkeys running about in the corn stubble. From the kitchen emerged a tall, thin Indian woman of fifty-five, with a red handkerchief bound severely over her head. She spoke to Miss Evans and sat down in the passageway. Presently, a clear, sweet voice was heard in the field; a stout, handsome woman, about the same age as the other, climbed the rain fence and came up to the house. She, also, greeted Miss Evans briefly. Then she carried a tin basin to the well nearby, where she filled it to the brim. Setting it down on the horse block, she rolled back her sleeves, tucked in the collar of her gray blouse, and plunged her face in the water. In a minute she came out of the kitchen freshened and smiling. 'Liza Harjo had been pulling dried bean stalks at one end of the field, and it was dirty work. At last old Harjo turned to Miss Evans and said, "These two my wife—this one 'Liza, this one Jennie."

It was done with simple dignity. Miss Evans bowed and stammered. Three pairs of eyes were turned upon her in patient, courteous inquiry.

It was hard to state the case. The old man was so evidently proud of his women, and so flattered by Miss Evans' interest in them, that he would find it hard to understand. Still, it had to be done, and Miss Evans took the plunge.

"Harjo, you want to come into our church?" The old man's face lighted.

"Oh, yes, I would come to Jesus, please, my friend."

"Do you know, Harjo, that the Lord commanded that one man should mate with but one woman?" The question was stated again in simpler terms, and the Indian replied, "Me know that now, my friend. Long time ago"—Harjo plainly meant the whole period previous to his conversion—"me did not know. The Lord Jesus did not speak to me in that time and so I was blind. I do what blind man do."

"Harjo, you must have only one wife when you come into our church. Can't you give up one of these women?" Miss Evans glanced at the two, sitting by with smiles of polite interest on their faces, understanding nothing. They had not shared Harjo's enthusiasm either for the white man's God or his language.

"Give up my wife?" A sly smile stole over his face. He leaned closer to Miss Evans. "You tell me, my friend, which one I give up." He glanced from 'Liza to Jennie as if to weigh their attractions, and the two rewarded him with their pleasantest smiles. "You tell me which one," he urged.

"Why, Harjo, how can I tell you!" Miss Evans had little sense of humor; she had taken the old man seriously.

"Then," Harjo sighed, continuing the comedy, for surely the missionary was jesting with him, "'Liza and Jennie must say." He talked to the Indian women for a time, and they laughed heartily. 'Liza, pointing to the other, shook her head. At length Harjo explained, "My friend, they cannot say. Jennie, she would run a race to see which one stay, but 'Liza, she say no, she is fat and cannot run."

Miss Evans comprehended at last. She flushed angrily, and protested, "Harjo, you are making a mock of a sacred subject; I cannot allow you to talk like this."

"But did you not speak in fun, my friend?" Harjo queried, sobering. "Surely you have just said what your friend, the white woman at the mission [he meant Mrs. Rowell] would say, and you do not mean what you say."

"Yes, Harjo, I mean it. It is true that Mrs. Rowell raised the point first, but I agree with her. The church cannot be defiled by receiving a bigamist into its membership." Harjo saw that the young woman was serious, distressingly serious. He was silent for a long time, but at last he raised his head and spoke quietly, "It is not good to talk like that if it is not in fun."

He rose and went to the stable. As he led Miss Evans' horse up to the block it was champing a mouthful of corn, the last of a generous portion that Harjo had put before it. The Indian held the bridle and waited for Miss Evans to mount. She was embarrassed, humiliated, angry. It was absurd to be dismissed in this way by—"by an ignorant old bigamist!" Then the humor of it burst upon her, and its human aspect. In her anxiety concerning the spiritual welfare of the sinner Harjo, she had insulted the man Harjo. She began to understand why Mrs. Rowell had said that the old Indians were hopeless.

"Harjo," she begged, coming out of the passageway, "please forgive me. I do not want you to give up one of your wives. Just tell me why you took them."

"I will tell you that, my friend." The old Creek looped the reins over his arm and sat down on the block. "For thirty years Jennie has lived with me as my wife. She is of the Bear people, and she came to me when I was thirty-five and she was twenty-five. She could not come before, for her mother was old, very old, and Jennie, she stay with her and feed her.

"So, when I was thirty years old I took 'Liza for my woman. She is of the Crow people. She help me make this little farm here when there was no farm for many miles around.

"Well, five years 'Liza and me, we live here and work hard. But there was no child. Then the old mother of Jennie she died, and Jennie got no family left in this part of the country. So 'Liza say to me, 'Why don't you take Jennie in here?' I say, 'You don't care?' and she say, 'No, maybe we have children here then.' But we have no children—never have children. We do not like that, but God He would not let it be. So, we have lived here thirty years very happy. Only just now you make me sad."

"Harjo," cried Miss Evans, "forget what I said. Forget that you wanted to join the church." For a young mission worker with a single purpose always before her, Miss Evans was saying a strange thing. Yet she couldn't help saying it; all of her zeal seemed to have been dissipated by a simple statement of the old man.

"I cannot forget to love Jesus, and I want to be saved." Old Harjo spoke with solemn earnestness. The situation was distracting. On one side stood a convert eager for the protection of the church, asking only that he be allowed to fulfill the obligations of humanity and on the other stood the church, represented by Mrs. Rowell, that set an impossible condition on receiving old Harjo to itself. Miss Evans wanted to cry; prayer, she felt, would be entirely inadequate as a means of expression.

"Oh! Harjo," she cried out, "I don't know what to do. I must think it over and talk with Mrs. Rowell again."

But Mrs. Rowell could suggest no way out; Miss Evans' talk with her only gave the older woman another opportunity to preach the folly of wasting time on the old and "unreasonable" Indians. Certainly the church could not listen even to a hint of a compromise in this case. If Harjo wanted to be saved, there was one way and only one—unless—

"Is either of the two women old? I mean, so old that she is—an—"

"Not at all," answered Miss Evans. "They're both strong and—yes, happy. I think they will outlive Harjo."

"Can't you appeal to one of the women to go away? I dare say we could provide for her." Miss Evans, incongruously, remembered Jennie's jesting proposal to race for the right to stay with Harjo. What could the mission provide as a substitute for the little home that 'Liza had helped to create there in the edge of the woods? What other home would satisfy Jennie?

"Mrs. Rowell, are you sure that we ought to try to take one of Harjo's women from him? I'm not sure that it would in the least advance morality amongst the tribe, but I'm certain that it would make three gentle people unhappy for the rest of their lives."

"You may be right, Miss Evans." Mrs. Rowell was not seeking to create unhappiness, for enough of it inevitably came to be pictured in the little mission building. "You may be right," she repeated, "but it is a grievous misfortune that old Harjo should wish to unite with the church."

No one was more regular in his attendance at the mission meetings than old Harjo. Sitting well forward, he was always in plain view of Miss Evans at the organ. Before the service began, and after it was over, the old man greeted the young woman. There was never a spoken question, but in the Creek's eyes was always a mute inquiry.

Once Miss Evans ventured to write to her old pastor in New York, and explain her trouble. This was what he wrote in reply: "I am surprised that you are troubled, for I should have expected you to rejoice, as I do, over this new and wonderful evidence of the Lord's reforming power. Though the church cannot receive the old man so long as he is confessedly a bigamist and violator of his country's just laws, you should be greatly strengthened in your work through bringing him to desire salvation."

"Oh! it's easy to talk when you're free from responsibility!" cried out Miss Evans. "But I woke him up to a desire for this water of salvation that he cannot take. I have seen Harjo's home, and I know how cruel and useless it would be to urge him to give up what he loves—for he does love those two women who have spent half their lives and more with him. What, what can be done?"

Month after month, as old Harjo continued to occupy his seat in the mission meetings, with that mute appeal in his eyes and a persistent light of hope on his face, Miss Evans repeated the question, "What can be done?" If she was sometimes tempted to say to the old man, "Stop worrying about your soul; you'll get to Heaven as surely as any of us," there was always Mrs. Rowell to remind her that she was not a Mormon missionary. She could not run away from her perplexity. If she should secure a transfer to another station, she felt that Harjo would give up coming to the meetings, and in his despair become a positive influence for evil amongst his people. Mrs. Rowell would not waste her energy on an obstinate old man. No, Harjo was her creation, her impossible convert, and throughout the years, until death—the great solvent which is not always a solvent—came to one of them, would continue to haunt her.

And meanwhile, what?

CHARLES A. EASTMAN (OHIYESA)

The Singing Spirit

"HO MY STEED, WE MUST CLIMB ONE MORE HILL! MY REPUTATION
depends upon my report!"

Anookasan addressed his pony as if he were a human companion,
urged on like himself by human need and human ambition. And yet in his
heart he had very little hope of sighting any buffalo in that region at just
that time of the year.

The Yankton Sioux were ordinarily the most farsighted of their people
in selecting a winter camp, but this year the late fall had caught them rather
far east of the Missouri bottoms, their favorite camping ground. The upper
Jim River, called by the Sioux the River of Gray Woods, was usually bare of
large game at that season. Their store of jerked buffalo meat did not hold out
as they had hoped, and by March it became an urgent necessity to send out
scouts for buffalo.

The old men at the tiyo tipi (council lodge) held a long council. It was
decided to select ten of their bravest and hardiest young men to explore the
country within three days' journey of their camp.

"Anookasan, uyeyo-o-o, woo, woo!" Thus the ten men were summoned to the council lodge early in the evening to receive their commission. Anookasan was the first called and first to cross the circle of the tipis. A young man of some thirty years, of the original Native type, his massive form was wrapped in a fine buffalo robe with the hair inside. He wore a stately eagle feather in his scalp-lock, but no paint about his face.

As he entered the lodge all the inmates greeted him with marked respect, and he was given the place of honor. When all were seated the great drum was struck and a song sung by four deep-chested men. This was the prelude to a peculiar ceremony.

A large red pipe, which had been filled and laid carefully upon the central hearth, was now taken up by an old man, whose face was painted red. First he held it to the ground with the words: "Great Mother, partake of this!" Then he held it toward the sky, saying: "Great Father, smoke this!" Finally he lighted it, took four puffs, pointing it to the four corners of the earth in turn, and lastly presented it to Anookasan. This was the oath of office, administered by the chief of the council lodge. The other nine were similarly commissioned, and all accepted the appointment.

It was no light task that was thus religiously enjoined upon these ten men. It meant at the least several days and nights of wandering in search of signs of the wily buffalo. It was a public duty, and a personal one as well; one that must involve untold hardship; and if overtaken by storm the messengers were in peril of death!

Anookasan returned to his tipi with some misgiving. His old charger, which had so often carried him to victory, was not so strong as he had been in his prime. As his master approached the lodge the old horse welcomed him with a gentle whinny. He was always tethered near by, ready for any emergency.

"Ah, Wakan! We are once more called upon to do duty! We shall set out before daybreak."

As he spoke, he pushed nearer a few strips of the poplar bark, which was oats to the Indian pony of the olden time.

Anookasan had his extra pair of buffalo-skin moccasins with the hair inside, and his scanty provisions of dried meat neatly done up in a small packet and fastened to his saddle. With his companions he started northward, up the River of the Gray Woods, five on the east side and a like number on the west.

The party had separated each morning, so as to cover as much ground as possible, having agreed to return at night to the river. It was now the third day; their food was all but gone, their steeds much worn, and the signs seemed to indicate a storm. Yet the hunger of their friends and their own pride impelled them to persist, for out of many young men they had been chosen, therefore they must prove themselves equal to the occasion.

The sun, now well toward the western horizon, cast over snow-covered plains a purplish light. No living creature was in sight and the quest seemed hopeless, but Anookasan was not one to accept defeat.

"There may be an outlook from yonder hill which will turn failure into success," he thought, as he dug his heels into the sides of his faithful nag. At the same time he started a "Strong Heart" song to keep his courage up!

At the summit of the ascent he paused and gazed steadily before him. At the foot of the next coteau he beheld a strip of black. He strained his eyes to look, for the sun had already set behind the hilltops. It was a great herd of buffalo, he thought, which was grazing on the foothills.

"Hi, hi, uncheedah! Hi, hi, tunkasheedah!" he was about to exclaim in gratitude, when, looking more closely, he discovered his mistake. The dark patch was only timber.

His horse could not carry him any farther, so he got off and ran behind him toward the river. At dusk he hailed his companions.

"Ho, what success?" one cried.

"Not a sign of even a lone bull," replied another.

"Yet I saw a gray wolf going north this evening. His direction is propitious," remarked Anookasan, as he led the others down the slope and into the heavy timber. The river just here made a sharp turn, forming a densely wooded semicircle, in the shelter of a high bluff.

The braves were all downhearted because of their ill-luck, and only the sanguine spirit of Anookasan kept them from utter discouragement. Their slight repast had been taken and each man had provided himself with abundance of dry grass and twigs for a bed. They had built a temporary wigwam of the same material, in the center of which there was a generous fire. Each man stretched himself out upon his robe in the glow of it. Anookasan filled the red pipe, and, having lighted it, he took one or two hasty puffs and held it up to the moon, which was scarcely visible behind the cold clouds.

"Great Mother, partake of this smoke! May I eat meat tomorrow!" he exclaimed with solemnity. Having uttered this prayer, he handed the pipe to the man nearest him.

For a time they all smoked in silence, then came a distant call.

"Ah, it is Shunkmanito, the wolf! There is something cheering in his voice tonight," declared Anookasan. "Yes, I am sure he is telling us not to be discouraged. You know that the wolf is one of our best friends in trouble. Many a one has been guided back to his home by him in a blizzard, or led to game when in desperate need. My friends, let us not turn back in the morning; let us go north one more day!"

No one answered immediately, and again silence reigned, while one by one they pulled the reluctant whiffs of smoke through the long stem of the calumet.

"What is that?" said one of the men, and all listened intently to catch the delicate sound. They were familiar with all the noises of the night and voices of the forest, but this was not like any of them.

"It sounds like the song of a mosquito, and one might forget while he listens that this is not midsummer," said one.

"I hear also the medicine man's single drumbeat," suggested another.

"There is a tradition," remarked Anookasan, "that many years ago a party of hunters went up the river on a scout like this of ours. They never returned. Afterward, in the summer, their bones were found near the home of a strange creature, said to be a little man, but he had hair all over him. The Isantees call him Chanotedah. Our old men give him the name Oglugechana. This singular being is said to be no larger than a newborn babe. He speaks an unknown tongue.

"The home of Oglugechana is usually a hollow stump, around which all of the nearest trees are felled by lightning. There is an open spot in the deep woods wherever he dwells. His weapons are the plumes of various birds. Great numbers of these variegated feathers are to be found in the deserted lodge of the little man.

"It is told by the old men that Oglugechana has a weird music by which he sometimes bewitches lone travelers. He leads them hither and thither about his place until they have lost their senses. Then he speaks to them. He may make of them great war prophets or medicine men, but his commands are hard to fulfill. If anyone sees him and comes away before he is bewildered, the man dies as soon as he smells the campfire, or when he enters his home his nearest relative dies suddenly."

The warrior who related this legend assumed the air of one who narrates authentic history, and his listeners appeared to be seriously impressed. What we call the supernatural was as real to them as any part of their lives.

"This thing does not stop to breathe at all. His music seems to go on endlessly," said one, with considerable uneasiness.

"It comes from the heavy timber north of us, under the high cliff," reported a warrior who had stepped outside of the rude temporary structure to inform himself more clearly of the direction of the sound.

"Anookasan, you are our leader—tell us what we should do! We will follow you. I believe we ought to leave this spot immediately. This is perhaps the spirit of some dead enemy," suggested another. Meanwhile, the red pipe was refilled and sent around the circle to calm their disturbed spirits.

When the calumet returned at last to the one addressed, he took it in a preoccupied manner, and spoke between labored pulls on the stem.

"I am just like yourselves—nothing more than flesh—with a spirit that is as ready to leave me as water to run from a punctured water bag! When we think thus, we are awake. Let us rather think upon the brave deeds of our ancestors! This singing spirit has a gentle voice; I am ready to follow and learn if it be an enemy or no. Let us all be found together next summer if need be!"

"Ho, ho, ho!" was the full-throated response.

"All put on your war paint," suggested Anookasan. "Have your knives and arrows ready!"

They did so, and all stole silently through the black forest in the direction of the mysterious sound. Clearer and clearer it came through the frosty air, but it was a foreign sound to the savage ear. Now it seemed to them almost like a distant waterfall, then it recalled the low hum of summer insects and the drowsy drone of the bumblebee. Thump, thump, thump! was the regular accompaniment.

Nearer and nearer to the cliff they came, deeper into the wild heart of the woods. At last out of the gray, formless night a dark shape appeared! It looked to them like a huge buffalo bull standing motionless in the forest, and from his throat there apparently proceeded the thump of the medicine drum, and the song of the beguiling spirit!

All of a sudden a spark went up into the air. As they continued to approach, there became visible a deep glow about the middle of the dark object. Whatever it was, they had never heard of anything like it in all their lives!

Anookasan was a little in advance of his companions, and it was he who finally discovered a wall of logs laid one upon another. Halfway up there seemed to be stretched a parfleche (rawhide), from which a dim light emanated. He still thought of Oglugechana, who dwells within a hollow tree, and determined to surprise and if possible to overpower this wonder-working old man.

All now took their knives in their hands and advanced with their leader to the attack upon the log hut. "Wa-wa-wa-wa, woo, woo!" they cried. Zip, zip! went the parfleche door and window, and they all rushed in!

There sat a man upon a roughly hewn stool. He was attired in wolf-skins and wore a foxskin cap upon his head. The larger portion of his face was clothed with natural fur. A rudely made cedar fiddle was tucked under his furred chin. Supporting it with his left hand, he sawed it vigorously with a bow that was not unlike an Indian boy's miniature weapon, while his moccasined left foot came down upon the sod floor in time with the music. When the shrill war whoop came, and the door and window were cut in strips by the knives of the Indians, he did not even cease playing, but instinctively he closed his eyes, so as not to behold the horror of his own end.

It was long ago, upon the rolling prairie south of the Devil's Lake, that a motley body of hunters gathered near a mighty herd of the bison, in the Moon of Falling Leaves. These were the first generation of the Canadian mixed-bloods, who sprang up in such numbers as to form almost a new people. These semi-wild Americans soon became a necessity to the Hudson Bay Company, as they were the greatest hunters of bison, and made more use of this wonderful animal than even their aboriginal ancestors.

A curious race of people this, in their makeup and their customs! Their shaggy black hair was allowed to grow long, reaching to their broad shoulders, then cut off abruptly, making their heads look like a thatched house. Their dark faces were in most cases well covered with hair, their teeth large and white, and their eyes usually liquid black, although occasionally one had a tiger-brown or cold-gray eye. Their costume was a buckskin shirt with abundance of fringes, buckskin pantaloons with short leggings, a gay sash, and a cap of fox fur. Their arms consisted of flintlock guns, hatchets, and butcher knives. Their ponies were small but as hardy as themselves.

As these men gathered in the neighborhood of an immense herd of buffalo, they busied themselves in adjusting the girths of their beautifully beaded pillowlike saddles. Among them there were exceptional riders and hunters. It was said that few could equal Antoine Michaud in feats of riding into and through the herd. There he stood, all alone, the observed of many others. It was his habit to give several Indian yells when the onset began, so as to ensure a successful hunt.

In this instance, Antoine gave his usual whoops, and when they had almost reached the herd, he lifted his flintlock over his head and plunged into the black moving mass. With a sound like the distant rumbling of thunder, those tens of thousands of buffalo hooves were pounding the earth in retreat. Thus Antoine disappeared!

His wild steed dashed into the midst of the vast herd. Fortunately for him, the animals kept clear of him; but alas!, the gap through which he had entered instantly closed again.

He yelled frantically to secure an outlet, but without effect. He had tied a red bandanna around his head to keep the hair off his face, and he now took this off and swung it crazily about him to scatter the buffalo, but it availed him nothing.

With such a mighty herd in flight, the speed could not be great; therefore the "Bois Brule" settled himself to the situation, allowing his pony to canter along slowly to save his strength. It required much tact and presence of mind to keep an open space, for the few paces of obstruction behind had gradually grown into a mile.

The mighty host moved continually southward, walking and running alternately. As the sun neared the western horizon, it fired the sky above them, and all the distant hills and prairies were in the glow of it, but immediately about them was a thick cloud of dust, and the ground appeared like a fire-swept plain.

Suddenly Antoine was aware of a tremendous push from behind. The animals smelled the cool water of a spring which formed a large bog in the midst of the plain. This solitary pond or marsh was a watering place for the wild animals. All pushed and edged toward it; it was impossible for anyone to withstand the combined strength of so many.

Antoine and his steed were in imminent danger of being pushed into the mire and trampled upon, but a mere chance brought them upon solid ground. As they were crowded across the marsh, his pony drank heartily, and he, for the first time, let go his bridle, put his two palms together for a dipper, and drank greedily of the bitter water. He had not eaten since early morning, so he now pulled up some bulrushes and ate of the tender bulbs, while the pony grazed as best he could on the tops of the tall grass.

It was now dark. The night was well-nigh intolerable for Antoine. The buffalo were about him in countless numbers, regarding him with vicious glances. It was only by reason of the natural offensiveness of man that they gave him any space. The bellowing of the bulls became general, and there was a marked uneasiness on the part of the herd. This was a sign of approaching storm, therefore the unfortunate hunter had this additional cause for anxiety. Upon the western horizon were seen some flashes of lightning.

The cloud which had been a mere speck upon the horizon had now increased to large proportions. Suddenly the wind came, and lightning flashes became more frequent, showing the ungainly forms of the animals like strange monsters in the white light. The colossal herd was again in violent motion. It was a blind rush for shelter, and no heed was paid to buffalo wallows or even deep gulches. All was in the deepest of darkness. There seemed to be groaning in heaven and earth—millions of hooves and throats roaring in unison!

As a shipwrecked man clings to a mere fragment of wood, so Antoine, although almost exhausted with fatigue, still stuck to the back of his equally plucky pony. Death was imminent for them both. As the mad rush continued, every flash displayed heaps of bison in death struggle under the hooves of their companions.

From time to time Antoine crossed himself and whispered a prayer to the Virgin, and again he spoke to his horse after the fashion of an Indian:

"Be brave, be strong, my horse! If we survive this trial, you shall have great honor!"

The stampede continued until they reached the bottom lands, and, like a rushing stream, their course was turned aside by the steep bank of a creek or small river. Then they moved more slowly in wide sweeps or circles, until the storm ceased, and the exhausted hunter, still in his saddle, took some snatches of sleep.

When he awoke and looked about him again it was morning. The herd had entered the strip of timber which lay on both sides of the river, and it was here that Antoine conceived his first distinct hope of saving himself.

"Waw, waw, waw!" was the hoarse cry that came to his ears, apparently from a human being in distress. Antoine strained his eyes and craned his neck to see who it could be. Through an opening in the branches ahead he perceived a large grizzly bear, lying along an inclined limb and hugging it desperately to maintain his position. The herd had now thoroughly pervaded the timber, and the bear was likewise hemmed in. He had taken to his unaccustomed refuge after making a brave stand against several bulls, one of which lay dead near by, while he himself was bleeding from many wounds.

Antoine had been assiduously looking for a friendly tree, by means of which he hoped to effect his escape from captivity by the army of bison. His horse, by chance, made his way directly under the very box elder that was sustaining the bear and there was a convenient branch just within his reach. The

Bois Brule was not then in an aggressive mood, and he saw at a glance that the occupant of the tree would not interfere with him. They were, in fact, companions in distress. Antoine tried to give a war whoop as he sprang desperately from the pony's back and seized the cross limb with both his hands.

The hunter dangled in the air for a minute that to him seemed a year. Then he gathered up all the strength that was in him, and with one grand effort he pulled himself up on the limb.

If he had failed in this, he would have fallen to the ground under the hooves of the buffalo, and at their mercy.

After he had adjusted his seat as comfortably as he could, Antoine surveyed the situation. He had at least escaped from sudden and certain death. It grieved him that he had been forced to abandon his horse, and he had no idea how far he had come nor any means of returning to his friends, who had, no doubt, given him up for lost. His immediate needs were rest and food.

Accordingly he selected a fat cow and emptied into her sides one barrel of his gun, which had been slung across his chest. He went on shooting until he had killed many fat cows, greatly to the discomfiture of his neighbor, the bear, while the bison vainly struggled among themselves to keep the fatal spot clear.

By the middle of the afternoon the main body of the herd had passed, and Antoine was sure that his captivity had at last come to an end. Then he swung himself from his limb to the ground, and walked stiffly to the carcass of the nearest cow, which he dressed and prepared himself a meal. But first he took a piece of liver on a long pole to the bear!

Antoine finally decided to settle in the recesses of the heavy timber for the winter, as he was on foot and alone, and not able to travel any great distance. He jerked the meat of all the animals he had killed, and prepared their skins for bedding and clothing. The Bois Brule and Ami, as he called the bear, soon became necessary to one another. The former considered the bear very good company, and the latter had learned that man's business, after all, is not to kill every animal he meets. He had been fed and kindly treated, when helpless from his wounds, and this he could not forget.

Antoine was soon busy erecting a small log hut, while the other partner kept a sharp lookout, and, after his hurts were healed, often brought in some small game. The two had a perfect understanding without many words; at least, the speech was all upon one side! In his leisure moments Antoine had occupied himself with whittling out a rude fiddle of cedar-wood, strung with the guts of a wild cat that he had killed. Every evening that winter he would sit down after supper and play all the old familiar pieces, varied with improvisations of his own. At first, the music and the incessant pounding time with his foot annoyed the bear. At times, too, the Canadian would call out the figures for the dance. All this Ami became accustomed to in time, and even showed no small interest in the buzzing of the little cedar box. Not infrequently, he was out in the evening, and the human partner was left alone. It chanced, quite fortunately, that the bear was absent on the night that the red folk rudely invaded the lonely hut.

The calmness of the strange being had stayed their hands. They had never before seen a man of other race than their own!

"Is this Chanotedah? Is he man, or beast?" the warriors asked one another.

"Ho, wake up, koda!" exclaimed Anookasan. "Maybe he is of the porcupine tribe, ashamed to look at us!"

At this moment they spied the haunch of venison which swung from a cross-stick over a fine bed of coals, in front of the rude mud chimney.

"Ho, koda has something to eat! Sit down, sit down!" they shouted to one another.

Now Antoine opened his eyes for the first time upon his unlooked-for guests. They were a haggard and hungry-looking set. Anookasan extended his hand, and Antoine gave it a hearty shake. He set his fiddle against the wall and began to cut up the smoking venison into generous pieces and place it before them. All ate like famished men, while the firelight intensified the red paint upon their wild and warlike faces.

When he had satisfied his first hunger, Anookasan spoke in signs. "Friend, we have never before heard a song like that of your little cedar box! We had supposed it to be a spirit, or some harmful thing, hence our attack upon it. We never saw any people of your sort. What is your tribe?"

Antoine explained his plight in the same manner, and the two soon came to an understanding. The Canadian told the starving hunters of a buffalo herd a little way to the north, and one of their number was dispatched homeward with the news. In two days the entire band reached Antoine's place. The Bois Brule was treated with kindness and honor, and the tribe gave him a wife. Suffice it to say that Antoine lived and died among the Yanktons at a good old age; but Ami could not brook the invasion upon their hermit life. He was never seen after that first evening.

LORENZO BACA

San Lorenzo
Day in Laguna

THIS STORY COMES FROM MY HOME IN NEW MEXICO. THESE Pueblos celebrate something Catholic, somewhat, but also Pueblo. We mix everything to make it work. I think it happens in all religions, anyway. Even if you swear by certain commandments, there are some you break. I think Pueblo people are really adaptable that way. My name is Lorenzo, so my saint's name is San Lorenzo. My son is Lorenzo, Leenkun Lorenzo Shpee Ye Wash Chee. The tradition goes pretty far back to when the Pueblo did a lot of farming, but the custom, the tradition, is still celebrated. It's my understanding that in the beginning, at a time of harvest, you had whatever you were growing—a lot of corn, squash, beans, peaches. You had some left over, and you'd go to neighbors and give them some. Somehow, that was tied into this celebration of the saint day on August 10—San Lorenzo Day.

On that day, everyone in the village of Laguna would have "Grab Day." You prepare for it. Everyone knows what day it will be, and families contribute things to give away: fruit, soda pop, all kinds of things.

When the day arrives, people meet at the house early. A man, like a town crier, announces through the whole village, "At the Atchees' they'll be throwin' at four o'clock, and at the Romeros', they'll be throwin' at five." It's very exciting—both when you throw, and when you grab. It's a fun event.

Well, for my son, his grandfather gives a speech and so we all go on top of the roof of the house because it's easier to throw, and the crier has already been out and announced. We take boxes of stuff, including water and water balloons, and put them all around the top of the roof. When it's close to the time, the family members start climbing the ladder to get to the roof—everyone, the grandmother, the fat ladies, everyone. Then the grandfather gives a speech and people start coming and they're all around. The grandfather starts his speech, thanking the people for being there and sharing in the prosperity. It's a celebration of ours for the prosperous year, good health, and so on, because we've been so lucky to have all this that we want to share it.

The grandfather introduces me by my Laguna Pueblo name. He introduces my son by his Laguna name. Grandfather is the first to throw something. But before that, he has a container of water, because the celebration has always begun and ended with water, which is very important to us in the Southwest. It's a blessing, a blessing of the people with water, very precious, but also a lot of fun, because people get wet. That's what the water balloons are for, and we have big jugs of water, so after the initial water blessing, it's just fun.

The grandfather throws the water out, and then my son throws some Crackerjacks, and then we all start throwing—just pitching in all directions—everything that we have. We throw dish rags, dish towels wrapped up, a beach ball, which is fun because people are jumping and trying to grab it, and it's bouncing all around.

And it's interesting that when people are catching or grabbing, you establish a little place around you, and you just stay there, and it comes to you, and people will call your name, and if you see someone in the crowd who's a Lorenzo or a Larry, then sometimes you'll select them out and say you have something special for them, or one of the grandmas. Or you'll have set aside a little basket special for them.

Well, one time I threw—I was just throwing, and my ring slipped off my finger and I saw it fly out into the crowd. I noticed it was gone, and I yelled out, "My ring!" And I don't know if this would happen any other place, but a man held it up and threw it back to me. I caught it and stuck it in my pocket.

In the excitement, you want everyone to share, so you make sure that everyone gets something. This goes on for ten minutes or so, and then it ends, and water is thrown, and you thank the people for coming.

Then we get down and see what we got. Then someone says, "Well, hurry up. Get your bags, the Romeros are going to throw." Then we go to the Romeros' house—the medicine man—and the same happens. You just dump things in your shirt, so you come walking out like a fat guy.

This is fun because Mr. Romero gives a speech and then has fry bread in plastic. When he threw it, the wind caught it and the plastic hooked up on the TV antenna, and everyone started cracking up. It was fun. Then they throw something else that is flat, and one of the women throws it, and it takes off like a Frisbee and lands behind the house. And then this tall guy, they say he's Laguna; maybe his mom is Cheyenne or something—see, we're not very tall—this real tall young guy, about six feet tall, came, and when the stuff starts flying toward us, he just reaches up and grabs it. The rest of us are jumping in the air, but he grabs the stuff. That's part of the fun. We laugh while he gets what he reaches for.

We go back to the house and have all kinds of stuff, taking a break to eat, and then heading out where someone else is throwing stuff. When we get there, people are still bringing stuff onto the roof. I notice there are some tourists standing back—two tall black men and two white girls—their girl-friends, I guess. And then things start to be thrown and we are all jumping and grabbing. I take a nice big jump and get myself a roll of paper towels, put it down, and get this and that. I notice the girls start moving up, crowding us, our space. They keep moving up, and of course the men move with them. And the girls get into it. It is exciting. But I see the difference. Pueblos are more reserved, I guess. But these girls just scream and the guys announce, "Man, did you see that?" You know, "Did you see what they threw over there? Wow, did you see that?" I mean, they're loud. People just look at them, tourists.

Then they start throwing cans of soda pop. And there are a lot of them, so I am catching and dodging, and then I see a can of soda go by, and I hear it, *pow!* I think it hit the ground, I'm busy catching my stuff. Then my friend says, "Give me those towels." So I watch the cans to catch them, and ask "What?" She says, "Over there." I look at one of the tall guys, who has a fancy haircut like they do in the cities, we knew he wasn't from around here, tourist. His head is shaved in lines and geometric designs. She rushes over to him, the one holding his head. He is full of blood, so she gives him some paper towels to hold on his head. We catch more stuff. This is going on over there.

Then they call Emily. She's a nurse. That is her job at the hospital. She examines his head and says he needs five stitches. I watch and grab. My friend gives him some more paper towels. He has them on his head. We can't help but laugh. They group together. The same people move back and start heading back to find their car. Everyone looks at each other, wonders about this poor guy holding bloody paper towels to his head. It is all quiet as we watch. Someone says, "It must have been his first time." Everybody laughs. It's his first time. Tourist. He is not Laguna, doesn't know about flying cans and such on San Lorenzo Day.

D. RENVILLE

Siobhan La Rue in Color

SIOBHAN LA RUE HAS CALLED ME THREE TIMES NOW, AND though I've listened to her messages scores of times, I've not returned her calls. I can't even stay in the same room in which they're playing: They are, for the most part, a soundtrack to a blank TV screen in my dead grandparents' living room. Every day the messages echo a bit more severely, as every day the house they sound in becomes emptier. For the past month, I've been removing my grandparents' belongings, and storing them in the garage of the Old House, up on the hill. The excess things I've been burning, and so I've lately been walking around smelling like a fire.

I've also been filling in cracks in the walls and re-weatherproofing the windows; for the first time in my life, I'm leaving my grandparents' house better than I found it. Each time I finish a crack or a window, I imagine the house to be that much more airtight. I find this concept very appealing these days, and often I've glared out into the stormy flatland I've exiled myself to, waiting for the world to fill up with water to test my handiwork.

I've done all this largely on my own, though this last weekend my cousin Caitlin arrived with a case of beer and a pair of smiley face buttons and pulled me temporarily out of my grief-driven asceticism. By midnight, we'd laid ourselves out on the kitchen floor and were trading stories of our kunsi and tunkansina, and by two, I was addled enough to play Siobhan La Rue's messages for Caitlin. She ambled out of the back room afterwards, plopped down in front of me, and said: "Why don't you just call her?"

Yes, I thought. Yes, well, it's like this . . .

———————◆———————

Shortly before I drove through fire to reach what turned out to be my grandparents' deathbeds, I called Siobhan La Rue from Roundup, Montana. It was her birthday, and she was depressed because from now on, more of her cells would be dying than reproducing.

"The tortoise and the hare is being played out inside me at a cellular level," she said. "The tortoise is now winning."

"Well, happy birthday, anyway," I said. "It's your silver anniversary as a person, you know. A quarter of a century on earth."

"When you coming back?"

"As soon as possible," I said, believing it.

"Sure," said Siobhan La Rue, who didn't.

The next night my grandparents died within an hour of each other in a hospital in Great Falls. My grandfather died while I was in a downstairs restroom, shaving two days' driving worth of fuzz off my face, wanting, as always, to impress him. I arrived in his room to the cacophony of Caitlin's and my Aunt Renata's grief. A bearded doctor, hands frozen in the air, looking both ineffectual and false, stared at me from beside my grandfather's bed. My grandfather lay with his head cocked towards me, eyes closed, unimpressed.

Later, while I sat in a waiting room dialing the number of relatives, Caitlin's wail came through the door from down the hall.

"Kunsi's dead," I said into the phone.

"Oh, Tim," my Uncle Simon said from South Dakota.

I put down the phone and cursed myself for not being there a second time.

◆

It's never been clear how my grandparents' car came to rest in a ravine a few miles outside of Great Falls, Montana; they had traveled there from South Dakota to visit relatives. (Though my grandparents were Assiniboines from Montana, they had moved to South Dakota to be next to my parents when I was born. My parents were there because my mother was Dakota from the Lake Traverse Reservation and couldn't bear to live away from her family for very long.) Their car had rolled several times, but my grandfather had not braked before leaving the road, which led some at their wake, held in a gym at their home reservation, Fort Belknap, to speculate that it hadn't been an accident. Kunsi was dying of pancreatic cancer, after all, and who could imagine them not together? I rejected this when I heard it, and angrily swept out of the wake. I stood in bitter October cold, and blew smoke at the full moon.

The next morning, a team of horses pulled a wagon carrying my grandparents' bodies away from the gym. A pickup trailed behind, a drum group in the bed. Somewhere up front, Caitlin was among those leading us on horseback to a small cemetery on a rise.

I was sitting in the backseat of a station wagon, holding my three-year-old niece Lisa, who was pressing her face into my shoulder. As I patted her back and sang softly to her, "Ah, boo," I wondered what she would remember of all this.

My parents had died in 1977 in South Dakota under similar circumstances: Their car, too, had been found in a ravine, and officially, their deaths were listed as accidents. Sometime later, my Aunt Renata, who was to take in my twelve-year-old self, largely against my kunsi's wishes, obtained through the Freedom of Information Act a copy of my parents' autopsies. In addition to the injuries incurred when the car had plunged into the ravine, my mother and father each had a bullet in the back of their heads.

Their funeral had been a loud, crowded business: I remember scores of men and women, some familiar and some strange, many dressed in khaki green jackets and jeans and wearing bandannas and black armbands, the men singing and the women trilling. I remember Aunt Renata lopping off most of her hair over my parents' graves. And I remember that when we returned to visit, red, blue, yellow, and white flags flew at all corners of the mounds.

"Ah, boo," I sang to my niece.

Later, as I stood above my grandparents' graves with a shovelful of dirt, I glanced up and saw my niece watching me, troubled by the sight. I threw the dirt into my grandfather's grave and then handed the shovel to one of my cousins. Lisa's eyes never left me. She will remember this, I thought. And later, when Lisa turned away from me at the feed, I thought, She is remembering *now.*

———◆———

When I finally made it back to Berkeley, I found Siobhan La Rue sleeping in my bed. I sat at my writing table and watched her for the better part of an hour, trying to imagine myself back into the world where we had both lived. I ran through my friends' names—Ollie, Patti, Lyle, Brett—hoping they would fix me in place, but after a while I stopped, and wandered into the kitchen. I checked the buzzing refrigerator and found a stray beer. I settled into a creaky metal chair and drank it at our dining table with the worn Formica floral pattern. I sat there quietly, next to an ashtray badly in need of emptying. After a few moments, my roommate Stefan surprised me, emerging out of the room he had so seldom occupied in the past six months.

"Tim," he said, smiling a groggy smile. "You're back."

He further surprised me by giving me an affectionate hug.

Eyeing my beer, he said, "Want some celebratory scotch? Couldn't hurt . . ."

"Well . . ."

"Might help."

"Sure."

He returned from his room with the scotch and some pink metallic tumblers. . . . Then he was playing the guitar I hadn't seen for some time, and we were singing, badly for my part. . . . And then Siobhan La Rue appeared, her light blonde hair, shot through with black streaks, no longer bound tightly against her head, but loose at her shoulders. I spoke her entire name, as I usually do, because it has always sounded like some sort of magic incantation coming out of my mouth.

"Why didn't you wake me up?" she said, voice hoarse from sleep. She blinked her deep brown saucer eyes rapidly a few times, trying to squeeze the weariness out of them.

"I was giving peace a chance," I said.

She smiled, and sat next to me.

"Can I kiss you?" she asked.

I nodded. And through her mouth passed into mine the world we had both shared, and by dawn, I was already denying I had lived in any other world.

———◆———

After we left Roundup on the way to the hospital in Great Falls to see our stricken grandparents, Caitlin and I drove up towards Grassrange on Hwy 87, a fairly lonely stretch of road that I've never actually seen during the day. I've had to imagine the dark terrain, and that particular night I was imagining endless nuclear warheads lurking just off the road: I had recently heard that were a nuclear war to break out, Montana would be one of the worst hit, owing to the scores of missile silos dotting the countryside. I kept seeing in the shadows strange lights and the outlines of chain-link fences and the occasional glint of surveillance cameras, all far more frightening and starkly treacherous than any living things that might bound out in front of me.

Caitlin saw the dark red stain on the horizon first, but she kept it to herself. I did much the same, but when it became clear that we were both seeing the same thing, I stopped the car.

"What the hell is that?" we both said together.

I shut off the lights in the car to be sure that it wasn't some sort of reflection on the windshield. That established, we began to speculate.

"It's a fire," I said. "It's reflecting on the smoke."

Caitlin nodded. "Maybe a city, too. You know, the lights."

But as we drove on and the red stain loomed larger, we began to abandon our more rational theories.

"What if it's a UFO?" Caitlin said, perhaps inevitably.

"That big?"

"Maybe it's the mothership."

"Maybe it's a cici."*

"Don't say that."

"Maybe Hell's opened up and we're driving right into it," I said.

She chastised me in Assiniboine, but we were both spooked and felt a creeping dread that grew stronger the closer we came to the dark red stain. We fell into silence, contemplating forthcoming communions with aliens or scary monsters or the Devil himself; the car hummed through a darkness made corporeal by our fears.

We drove into the smoke as the road began to curve toward Grassrange. It was everywhere, like a gray veil pulled over the landscape. Once in town, we pulled into a gas station, filled my car up and asked where the smoke was coming from. The cashier told us there were wildfires all over the state, but none closer than Lewistown, still thirty miles away. We would have to pass through Lewistown.

The smoke got worse the nearer we got to Lewistown, and we came into the fierce winds that were fanning the wildfires. The road began to narrow as we drove into a mountain range, and I fought the steering wheel, trying to keep us on the road. We saw the first flames a few miles outside of town, leaping above the peaks of the mountains, clawing at the sky. We passed a mountain bright with fire, the flames spinning down its side, unchecked. Finally, the road lowered and the mountains folded over the fires and we were in Lewistown.

We called Great Falls from outside a convenience store, and Aunt Renata told us to stay put: Our grandparents were stabilized, and there

* a being often invoked by parents to scare their children into obedience

would be no point in driving straight through, particularly with the winds blowing the way they were. Come in the morning, she said.

We drove up and down Main Street and finally found a motel room, apparently the last one left in town. Lewistown was filled with evacuees fleeing the fires. The room was oddly placed in back of the motel, the only one like that, and the motel, used to not having it rented, had put up a NO VACANCY sign. We found out about it accidentally, having gone into the motel office to ask how far it was to the next town.

It was an old room, the motel itself having been built back in the fifties, and looking like it. I took to the room immediately, and I described it enthusiastically on the phone to Siobhan La Rue, who had, that day, moved into the house I lived in back in Berkeley.

Caitlin sat, amused, watching me from the bed next to mine. When I was off the phone, she asked me if I had ever dated an Indian woman.

I shook my head: "Not as far as I know."

"You know, I'm pretty sure Auntie told kunsi your girlfriend is Indian."

"She did," I said, considering this. "Well, Siobhan La Rue isn't Indian."

"No Indian princess grandmothers in her family tree?"

I shook my head again. "No. No Cherokee chiefs as far as I know, either."

Caitlin sipped at her beer, thinking of what to say next.

"Well, I think you should date an Indian once. Just to see what it's like."

"You mean, just so I can say?"

"Something like that."

I turned the radio on and a country song came blaring on too loud, though it was soon interrupted by the disc jockey, telling the general populace the latest about the fires, telling them not to panic, that if the winds were to change and the fires change direction, seventy-five firemen gathered in the local high school gym were prepared to respond, and things were under control. Even so, as the night wore on, he endlessly cut into the middle of songs to send out the same message of non-urgency.

"I think I need a beer," Caitlin announced after a time.

There was no discussion: We pulled on our jackets and tramped outside, in search of a store.

As we ambled down Main Street, our eyes drifted up to the mountain that stood above Lewistown: It was dark with shadow, its peak outlined by the dull, pulsing glow of the fires somewhere behind it. My eyes were already drifting away again when a bright yellow flash exploded off the mountain.

"Holy!" Caitlin shouted, and out of what she later termed "some weird maternal impulse," she threw a protective arm in front of me, which hit me across the chest and effectively stopped me in my tracks.

"What the hell is it?" I said.

The flash meanwhile grew more intense and reached higher into the sky, dispelling the darkness there, as if the sun was erupting out of the mountain and was now rising over Lewistown.

I was waiting for the inevitable report, but none was forthcoming, and then, as I was thinking of turning and running, the flash died out, and the mountain fell into a even deeper darkness, the glow of the fires behind it gone.

I turned to Caitlin, who was already looking at me; the outline of the mountain was bouncing around in our eyeballs, sticking and unsticking to our own images.

"What the hell was that?" she said. "You saw that, right?"

We quickly glanced at the street around us: The lights in town were blinking normally; no electromagnetic pulse had passed through Lewistown. Traffic puttered by calmly, and no one we could see was standing at their windows or in their doors staring up at the mountain in disbelief. We were apparently the only ones who had seen it.

We hurried to the nearest store and got our beer and made tracks back to our motel room.

Later, while we sat in our beds, the smell of smoke came drifting into our room, accompanied by hollow-sounding voices. The voices didn't sound close at all, and it was hard to pinpoint where they were coming from. The smell of smoke got stronger, and I thought of those seventy-five firemen, lounging in a gym somewhere in town.

Caitlin, sitting on the floor at the edge of her bed, said, finally, "Cicis."

We spent most of the night drinking our beer and listening to the radio, to music interrupted by nerve-wracking assurances that everything was fine, the both of us waiting to be scuttled out of our room at any moment by firemen with grim smiles, fresh from a gym, smelling of floor polish and dried sweat.

❖

I told Siobhan La Rue about the mountain we'd seen above Lewistown, and how a cousin at Fort Belknap told us it was probably phosphorus being dropped on the fire, but that the explanation hadn't made it any less creepy.

We spent most of the first week I was back in the house in Berkeley trying to talk, about anything, but never any one thing. I tried to tell her that I felt like I was being chased, or that maybe I had been infected by something, a fever, amnesia, when I was out in Montana.

When she would go to work in the mornings, I would stumble around the rooms, carelessly invading the privacy of my roommates. I would rummage through their possessions, as if investigating the mysteries of their lives. I would handle their possessions with my eyes closed, appealing to sense memory in my attempt to ground myself once again in their world. I would lie down on Stefan's or Siobhan La Rue's bed, trying to blink out the flames that kept leaping up behind my eyes. Siobhan La Rue would come back in the late afternoon to find me sitting on the covered porch, and she told me later that, coming upon me like that, she always thought I had locked myself out.

"Are you Indian at all?" I asked Siobhan La Rue late one night.

Stefan's James Brown CD was blaring in the other room, but I was perfectly clear.

"I knew you were going to ask me that," she said.

"How come?"

"The way you look at me. I didn't get a haircut, I didn't gain or lose weight, I haven't changed the way I dress. No corrective surgery. Why?"

"What?"

"Why do you ask?"

"Aunt Renata told them you were," I said. "I was just wondering where she got that."

"She told your grandmother that I was Indian?"

"Kunsi wanted me to have only Indian girlfriends . . . Assiniboine girl-friends, especially."

Siobhan La Rue was staring at me.

"Listen," I said, "she wasn't a racist or anything. It was just that . . . our tribal population isn't what it used to be." I smiled. "I'm supposed to help repopulate the race."

Siobhan La Rue smiled now, too.

"And you can't do it with a white girl."

"I didn't say that—I just can't repopulate the race with a white girl."

She jumped up and tackled me in my chair.

"Ambush!" she shouted.

Later, when the night was darker and we were more evenly covered with shadows, she said:

"What tribe? Assiniboine?"

"I'm not sure. . . . Caitlin didn't say. Maybe Assiniboine—that would've made her happy."

"It'd make you happy."

"Yes," I said. "It would. My parents are dead. I have no brothers or sisters. If I married a white woman, it would be the beginning of the end of my mother's line. If we married, our child would be more white than Indian, because I'm not a full-blood. It didn't bother me before, if that's what you're wondering. I'm not sure why it's bothering me now. I don't know—I'm thinking differently these days, like I've been possessed or something."

I tapped my fingers on the carpet like I was tapping ash.

"I know all this talk isn't some sign of maturity," I said. "The only sign of maturity I've managed to show so far is that I've gotten fatter. I mean, really, what's so great about my DNA?"

"I don't think it's your DNA you're worried about."

"Well, don't be so understanding."

"I'm not. . . . At least I know your intentions regarding me are honorable."

I turned to her, dismayed: "I'm being stupid about this, aren't I?"

"No, no," Siobhan La Rue said. "Just confused. I know a thing or two about that."

We left it at that.

I left two months later.

My grandparents' probate came up, and I went to Montana to settle their affairs. I ended up inheriting their house and property in South Dakota, where they had lived out the last years of their lives, having remained even after my parents' deaths. After the probate business was over, I traveled to South Dakota, and stayed.

I'm not sure why I didn't return the first call. I just remember being vaguely angry that she had called, and perhaps in a juvenile way, I was punishing her for pushing me into a decision. The second call, I was standing above the answering machine with my hand on the phone. I had a funny feeling she knew I was there, because she paused after she said "Call me," as if she were giving me a chance to pick up. I don't know that if she had just waited a few more moments, I would've picked up the phone, said her name, and let that world—hers, ours—come into this one. I don't know. I know that when she finally hung up, I was disappointed, but also relieved, as if we had finally come to some sort of a decision.

When Caitlin rescued me, at least for the weekend, I told her about my newly colorized emotions, but underneath the automatic sympathy relatives have for other relatives' plights, I could detect a note of approval.

"Do you love her?" she asked towards the end of the night.

"Yes," I said, though I said it like I was just remembering it, like something drawn out of me in a hypnotic state.

"Then," she began, "then you should act like it." But she added: "I guess."

Caitlin left a few cigarettes behind when she left, and so now I've taken up smoking, if in a half-assed way. I smoke half a cigarette, get overwhelmed by the head rush, and toss away the butt. I always think I want a smoke, but I never really do; even so, I've been carrying a pack, my razor in a case just in case of depression.

I'm smoking now, off the back porch. The phone is ringing behind me.

I can see Siobhan La Rue sitting at the end of my bed, with the phone cradled between her chin and neck, maybe lighting up a cigarette herself.

She doesn't really expect me to answer right away. . . . She's giving me time to think about it.

I blow smoke at the blank sky. The moon and the stars have dropped out of this particular night, and I am left with darkness. I tap out ash, and from the corner of my eye, it looks like the ash is falling directly out of me.

She is talking now—I can hear her behind me.

I close my eyes and I can see Siobhan La Rue's voice coming through the openings in my grandparents' house, through the cracks and the places I haven't yet sealed up. Her voice is spilling through these openings, cascading down the walls like blue sheets of rain.

"Call me," she says now, and she waits. I can hear her. She is waiting. We wait.

ANNA LEE WALTERS

Bicenti

THINGS WEREN'T RIGHT.

Maya sat on the mattress and sank into its springs and lumps. She
contemplated the squareness of the small room, sharpened by the afternoon shadows strewn across the floor. The angular walls, the floor and
ceiling tiles cut impotently into infinite space and time, but the fragile
structure confined her there indefinitely. She stared out the rectangular
window to an identical house across the street, and closed her eyes
tightly.

"I have this feeling that something is wrong," Maya said sheepishly
to Wilma, when Wilma entered the room. Wilma was round and her circular shadow broke up the box space in the sparsely furnished room as
Wilma gestured and moved around.

"Oh? What's the matter?" Wilma asked with concern. Her eyebrows
lifted in a question.

Maya's oval brown face cracked slowly into a crooked smile. She asked,
"Did you ever look at this room, Wilma? The squareness of our little
worlds? The insignificant walls? Have you ever wondered if there were a
futility and senselessness in these structures? Why are we so infatuated with

squares? Are these squares in the real world?" Maya giggled at herself and pointed out the window with her last question.

As Wilma sipped her coffee noisily, she studied Maya's face. It wore a nervous frown that was there one minute and gone the next. "You didn't come here to ask me about this room," Wilma said matter-of-factly. "You didn't drive all the way from Albuquerque to Santa Fe, to question me about this room. Huh-uh."

Maya put down her own mug of coffee and looked into the eyes of her old friend intently for a few seconds, making a decision to tell Wilma everything. She dropped her voice to barely a whisper. Wilma had to lean toward Maya to catch the words Maya let go. The words visibly hung in the air between the two women for seconds.

Maya said, "Things have been happening to me lately. I've lost some things. Well . . . actually they were taken, you know, uh . . . stolen." Maya watched Wilma's response. Wilma's face was blank. Maya continued, "Then, there have been accidents on the highway, traffic accidents, all occurring within seconds from me. Too close!"

Wilma was sipping coffee. Her shadow slipped under her and stayed a step ahead of her as she glided to a chair, one of three pieces of furniture in the room. Maya bent and leaned even closer to Wilma. The wooden chair holding Maya's weight made a little sound. Planes of light and shadow played over Maya's face as she asked Wilma, "Do you know what I am talking about?" The frown was laying over Maya's face again.

Wilma nodded her head decisively. "Yes . . . , oh sure. I was just thinking about things you can do about it. First, tell me about the items you've lost. Did you get anything back? Returned to you?"

Maya leaned forward and held her oval face in her long fingers. Her pointed elbows were on her knees. "Well, first two blankets disappeared. That pretty purple one with the tan and black stripes. Then I missed a red one with green fringes, both taken from the place I am now staying, in Albuquerque."

"Go on," Wilma encouraged. Maya looked thoughtful and far away. Maya's round figure stood before the rectangular window. Clouds floated on her shoulders and through her black hair.

"A purse was taken next. Everything in it," Maya said. She waved her purse away with a soft bare arm. A streak of sunlight radiated under her arm.

"And the accidents?" Wilma prodded.

"Always to other people, just ahead, or just behind me, a split second from me. As far as you are to me. It's happened three times now, people died each time." Maya poured the remaining coffee into her mouth and sat back on the chair.

The room became quiet. The sunlight on the floor crawled from Wilma's feet to Maya's, halfway across the room. Maya's face went through a variety of expressions in this silence, while Wilma's face stayed blank, noncommittal.

Then Wilma soothed Maya's prolonged frown. "Stay here tonight, you can—can't you? We'll talk and think this thing through. Okay?"

Maya nodded her head, though she did not speak. She went again to the window, staring beyond the house across the street, into infinite space and time.

"If we can't come up with any answers or solutions, then you go to Bicenti. You ought to anyway, to find out about your missing things. He will locate them for you. Okay?" Wilma asked while Maya nodded her head again. Their shadows had stretched longer by then, and the planes of the room were elongated, distorted by the hour at hand.

—◆◆◆◆—

The Sangre de Cristo Mountains loomed in the east, soft and rolling cones, under a melting orange and purple sky. This evening was cool, a gentle wind from the south played on the two women.

Maya and Wilma sat on the porch. Wilma hummed a tribal song as the two watched the mountains, and the sky and clouds dissolve into darkness.

Maya said, "Wilma, you've been listening to my problems all day. I didn't even ask you about the vandalism you have been experiencing out here. What's happening?"

Wilma answered, "Well, we are about ten miles from town. I guess distance may have something to do with it. But things have been quiet lately.

If you don't count the weird incident that happened next door." She raised a finger and indicated her nearest neighbor's house. Then she continued, "It happened about a month ago. And Maya, you can't really call it vandalism. All that can be said about it is that it was *very strange*. Bizarre might be the word to describe it. That reminds me, Maya, you ought to park your car up here by the house."

"Well anyway," she went back to her story, "this lady and her husband next door, they're Spanish people . . . One evening they came home and parked their car out in the parking lot in front of their house. See? The next morning, *the car was upside down*. It was pretty strange. No one heard a sound during the night. But sure enough, the next morning there was this car sitting in the exact spot where it had been parked the evening before, but it was upside down!"

Maya laughed, "I guess so! I hope things like that don't happen too often. Are you afraid living out here by yourself?"

"Not at all," Wilma chuckled. "I usually enjoy it. I can't stand the thought of living cooped up in town. The houses are so close together. We're close here too—but it's different. Besides Raoul is here more often than not. You haven't met him but you'll like him, Maya, when you do meet him. He's mostly Spanish, but he's part Indian too."

"Is everyone here Spanish?" Maya wanted to know.

"Mixed, but mostly Spanish. There's a Taos family on the other side, an old Comanche woman down this street, and then there are *Dine*—Navajos." She laughed. "The rest are *Bilagaana* or *Nakai*." As an afterthought, Wilma said, "Indians are everywhere, no matter where you go."

Maya smiled. "It's a nice, peaceful community," she said. "Too bad about the vandalism. As often as I've been here, I would never have known the problem exists out here—if you hadn't told me."

The two women sat there for a while longer until Wilma asked Maya if she were tired. Maya admitted that she was, stress had taken its toll. Before they retired, Wilma said, "Maya, why don't you move your car up here, beside the porch?"

Maya said, "Nothing's ever happened before. I'm sure that it will be okay. I'll just leave it where it is."

Maya stretched out on top of a sleeping bag in the middle of Wilma's square floor. Her eyelids soon twitched in a deep sleep.

Wilma stood over her friend for a long time that night, thinking of the words Maya had dropped in the next room. A frown creased Wilma's forehead now that Maya couldn't see. Wilma went to the only window in this room to close the drapes. She raised the window several inches to allow a breeze to circulate. She saw Maya's car sitting under a streetlamp that emitted a yellow circle of light around the car.

About midnight, Maya woke. Her eyes stared into the blackness of the square room. She was fully conscious. Her thoughts went immediately to her car. "They're doing something to it," she whispered. She rose, went to the window and looked out. The car sat safely under the high beam of the streetlamp. Maya breathed a sign of relief. She sat in the rocking chair beside the window and kept a vigil over her car for a few minutes. Then, satisfied that for the moment it was safe, she lay back inside the sleeping bag. The breeze was stronger, billowing the drapes.

———◆———

At 5:30 the next morning, the alarm clock buzzed.

The Sangre de Cristo Mountains were a faint shape outside Wilma's house. A white line curved around the horizon of the mountains, sun streaks spread fan-like at one end of the range.

Wilma got out of bed and stopped the buzzing alarm. The house was all dark. She walked from her room to the one where Maya slept. She pulled the cord at the window. The drapes, like stage curtains, parted on the glowing horizon. A cold wave slid into the room. The window was still open. Outside in the parking lot, the streetlamps were dark. Wilma could see the faint blue mountains in the east, the silhouette of night in the west engulfed nearby houses.

Wilma went to the kitchen to put coffee in the percolator. She turned on the radio. Its dials were fluorescent when Wilma flipped off the light switch.

Then she went into the bedroom, stripped off her clothes, and went naked into the bathroom. In a few minutes, the shower could be heard.

Maya woke to a country and western singer moaning on the radio and the shower beating into the bathtub. She lay there a moment with her eyes closed listening to the music drift into the room. The odor of perking coffee followed the music.

When Wilma entered the room in a long white terry-cloth robe, Maya asked, "What time is it? I have to be in Albuquerque by eight. I have one of those awful early classes today."

"It's about five forty-five," Wilma answered, drying her long hair with a red towel. "I set the alarm a half hour early, so we can visit a little longer. I have to go to work too. I hope you don't mind my getting you up so early."

"Oh no, I'm glad you did," Maya said. She sat on the sleeping bag and added, "Wilma, thanks for everything. I feel much better, refreshed and in a clean frame of mind. I'll go to Bicenti this weekend."

"Good, I'm glad that's settled," Wilma answered, shaking out her long wet hair that had fallen to her waist. She said, "Maya, I think the coffee's ready. You want some?"

But Maya held up a hand and said, "I'll jump in the shower first." She gathered her clothes and carried a small suitcase into the bathroom. The light in there escaped from under the closed door. The rest of the house was dark.

Wilma went to lower the open window in the room. Her wet hair had chilled her. While she was pulling the window down, she looked toward Maya's car. It was assuming a vague shape in the dawn. Wilma paused momentarily, straining her eyes at the car. "Hmm," she said and went into the kitchen.

She poured a cup of coffee and looked at the radio when the female announcer came on and said in a seductive voice, "Good morning, sleepyhead. It's six A.M."

Not too long after, Maya padded into the room. Her hair was wrapped in a towel turban-style. She wore blue jeans and a turquoise blouse. Her toes stuck out of her house shoes. She poured herself a cup of coffee and took a taste. That's when Wilma said, "Maya, it looks like there is something on your car."

"Oh?" was Maya's response. Her feet padded to the open window. The sun had not risen yet, but the mountains were purple and the sky above them was a delicate pink. Daylight was spreading tentatively toward Wilma's community. The community buildings, however, were still square silhouettes against the fingers of down. "It's a beautiful morning," was Maya's first observation. Then her eyes went to the car.

There *was* something on it, but she was nearsighted and without her glasses. She said, "Yes, Wilma, there does seem to be something on it. But I can't make it out that well." Her words made her remember the vigil at midnight.

Wilma stood at Maya's side. She said, "Let's go see. Maybe they punctured the tires, or something like that."

The two women walked out of the house. Maya carried her mug of coffee. They stood on the porch. Wilma pointed to her flower bed. The flowers were uncurling. They walked past the marigolds and down to the parking lot. None of the other houses were lit, not even the apartment complex at the end of the block. The local streets were empty of early morning traffic. "That's strange," Maya said. "There doesn't seem to be anyone stirring but us."

Wilma looked up and down the streets, her damp hair clung to her shoulders. "Yes, that's right, isn't it?" she agreed with Maya. The domed sky was turning a pale blue. Clouds skirted the mountaintops.

Maya's car pointed north. As she walked toward it, she noted that the windows were unbroken, the tires inflated. The car appeared to be unharmed, at least on one side. But what was that on top of it? A black shadow lay on the roof of the car. It stretched the entire length of the roof. Maya and Wilma stopped about ten feet from the car. Their eyes locked briefly. Then both women had the same thought, they gazed at the houses around them. The houses were mute and lifeless forms. Wilma pulled her wet hair over her right shoulder and looked southwest. The Sandia Mountains were now distinguishable in the dawn. A crescent moon glittered on Sandia Peak. A few cars on Interstate 40 still had their lights on. These lights zipped east and west without a sound.

"Strange," commented Wilma. Maya took a shaky step closer to the shadow on her car. Wilma followed. And when Maya stopped just at the left headlight, Wilma did too.

"What in the world?" Wilma asked in a breathy and perplexed voice.

Maya was frozen for a second, desperately sorting images that flashed before her eyes. She saw herself standing in front of the car, moving like an actress in a bizarre play, detached from herself but nevertheless affected. The only thing she could say was, "What?" and again, "What . . . ?"

The thing on the car grew into a foreboding shape in the morning light. A large dog was draped over the roof of the car. The outline of its head was clearly discernible.

"What?" Maya repeated. "How . . . ?" She didn't finish the question.

The animal did not move. Maya half expected it to pounce on her or off the car. Again Maya's eyes zeroed in on the houses. Not a curtain in any window fluttered. She noted that Wilma too was studying the houses. When the dog did not move. Maya put her coffee mug on the hood of the car and took another step.

It was then that she saw the spray of blood covering the front window, on the passenger side. It had dripped down the side windows on the other side of the car. Dried pools of red stained the cement.

The jaws of the dog hung open and it looked as if this was from where the blood has gushed until the animal was thoroughly drained.

Maya tried to make sense of the scene. She went through a flood of emotion; anger, compassion for the dead animal, and resolution not to submit to fear.

"Let's go inside," she told Wilma. Wilma nodded, grabbed the mug she had placed on the hood, and involuntarily shivered.

Inside the house, Maya grabbed Wilma by the shoulders and asked, "What's happening?"

Wilma's eyes were round and her mouth was round too as she said, "Oh, Maya, I don't know. It's like that incident with the car. Weird as hell. What shall we do?"

"I don't know," Maya said. "Let me think." She kicked off her house shoes and slipped on leather sandals. While she did this, Wilma threw on the clothes she wore the day before.

"We have to get rid of it," Maya said. "Someone gave that thing to me. I don't want it and I refuse it. I'm taking it back to wherever it came from . . . "

"We'll have to clean the car," Wilma said. She ran to get a plastic jar of dish detergent, and she filled a Tupperware bowl with warm water.

"I don't get it," Maya said, looking out the window once more. "Where is everyone? There used to be early morning traffic here, I remember that!"

"Don't try to figure it out now, Maya. Let's act, move, do something!" Wilma said. "This absence of the neighbors—maybe we can use it to our advantage."

"Yeah, okay." Maya nodded her head. She took a roll of paper towels Wilma handed to her.

Again, they ventured out. The sky was opaque, the sun had not yet climbed the lowest mountains. Not one car passed on this street, or down the side streets.

Maya and Wilma acted quickly and in coordination. The two women lifted the dead animal off the roof of the car. Its body was stiff and heavy. It must have weighed a good seventy pounds. They laid the rigid body just off the walkway in front of Maya's car. Again anger filled Maya as she poured soapy water on the dried blood. Wilma scrubbed the front of the car while Maya did the side, wiping the car clean and dry with paper towels. It took a few minutes. Wilma went back inside the house. Maya stayed to empty the remaining water on the pools of blood on the cement. The soapy water colored a pink tint and ran in rivulets down the street.

Then Maya noticed something she hadn't seen before. A trail of blood led to her car from across the street. She followed it and came upon another pool of blood just in front of the house opposite Wilma's house. From there the trail went down the block. Maya stood in front of that house for a moment. Then she quickly walked to the place where she and Wilma had carefully laid the animal, a few feet from the car.

She picked up the stiffened body by its front and back legs, and she carried it across the street, struggling with her burden and panting when she was done. She left the dog in the pool of dried blood there, stood defiantly and challengingly in front of that house. There were no signs of life in the neighborhood yet. She scooped up a handful of dirt from that yard and carried it to her car where she scattered it over the drying pools of water and blood. She rubbed the dirt over the cement viciously with her sandals. The blood darkened to brown spots.

"Now," Maya whispered, "we'll see what happens."

At that moment a light came on in a house on a corner. She heard a door slam somewhere. A quick look inside her car reassured her that nothing more had been done to it. The tires were in good shape. She retraced her steps to Wilma's house. Wilma met her at the door. Wilma's wet hair was tied with a rubber band and she wore a sweater.

"What now?" Wilma wanted to know.

"We wait and see what happens," Maya said. "No matter what does happen though, we don't know anything about that dog, okay?"

"It's the best way," Wilma said.

Maya unwrapped the towel around her head. "What time is it?" she asked.

"It's about six-forty," Wilma said. "You should leave before seven if you want to make that class."

Maya asked, "Will you be all right?"

Wilma went into the kitchen, searching for the coffee cup she'd put down someplace earlier. As she poured a hot cupful of coffee, she answered, "I'll go to work. No, maybe I won't. I have time I need to use for my leave anyway. But, I'll be all right."

Footsteps were coming down the sidewalk outside. Wilma came out of the kitchen and looked questioningly at Maya. The steps ended on her front porch. Someone pounded on the door.

Wilma opened it. Maya sat in the living room and listened. "What did you do with the dog?" a female voice asked in a huff.

Maya heard Wilma ask innocently, "What dog?"

The woman repeated the question. Wilma asked again, "What dog? What are you talking about?"

To this, the woman shrieked, "You're going to pay! Killers!"

Wilma then said, "Look, lady, calm down. If I can help you in some way . . ."

But the woman interrupted the offer of help, threatening Wilma with curses and vile names. Maya heard Wilma close the door.

Wilma returned to Maya. She looked calm, but Maya saw her hands shaking. "Did she frighten you? Who was she?" Maya asked.

"I don't know," Wilma said, "but it wasn't the woman who scared me. It was the man."

"The man?" Maya asked in surprise.

"Yes," Wilma said. "There was a man with her, standing behind her the whole time. He stood there in silence and made obscene gestures at me. His gyrations were so unnatural, not humanly possible. It scared the hell out of me!"

"You didn't show it, did you?" Maya asked in alarm. "Fear won't help us, Wilma."

"No, I don't think it showed. I was just so startled. But it was the damndest thing!" Wilma gulped her coffee. Maya put an arm around her friend. "Are you okay?" Maya asked. Wilma shuddered, but managed a smile.

"Listen, I'm going to have to leave. I hate to just walk away like this, I don't understand any of this," Maya said.

"It may be that walking away is the only way to respond," Wilma said, pursing her lips. "But I am convinced that you need to see Bicenti, now more than ever."

Maya nodded in complete agreement.

Footsteps were at the door again. Wilma looked at Maya and went to the door. "Killers!" the woman was screaming. "The state police are coming after you." Maya saw her lift a pudgy finger and stick it in Wilma's face. The woman was clownish in appearance, her face painted in brilliant hues. Maya stood behind Wilma.

There *was* a man with the woman. He was dark, possibly Hispanic or Indian. He bobbed up and down, as if there were springs in his legs and feet. He waved his arms imitating a grounded bird, and he contorted his face into grotesque masks that changed and flitted away as quickly as they settled over his features. Then his hands went to the crotch of his pants and he mimed an unearthly performance, contorting his body beyond the bounds of human ability. The woman with him blocking the doorway was unconcerned with his antics, she continued to shout obscenities at Wilma. They poured out in a torrent of stinging words.

Then Maya said to the woman, slowly and very clearly, "I don't know what's happening, or who you are—but you are not welcome here, and neither is anything that you bring with you." The words hung in the doorway for seconds.

The woman's eyes blinked surprise at Maya's words. For a moment, the woman's own stream of words stopped. She balanced her bulky weight on one foot. Her painted face became a frozen mask. The dark man behind the woman ceased his gyrations for a split second fracturing time and space after Maya spoke. He poised himself in the interlude, unnaturally immobile. The feat was startling. Maya was elated, felt a jab of tiny victory that her words had somehow paused his weird pantomime.

"Close the door," Maya said in Wilma's ear. Wilma pushed the door shut on the two figures. Outside, the woman again started her harangue, and then the din subsided. There were no sounds of departing footsteps. Only abrupt silence.

Wilma went to the window to observe the walkways and parking lot. "Nothing," she said in a low voice to Maya. "Nothing."

They gathered up Maya's things and prepared to go to Maya's car. Maya took out her keys from her pants pocket. They were ready to face whatever waited outside.

Before Maya opened the door, she said to Wilma, "Wait until I see if the car is going to start. Don't leave me until I know for sure. Then I'll wait until you're back inside before I drive away."

The streets were silent. None of the occupants of the dozen houses around them were visible. Wilma and Maya were completely alone. The orange rim of the sun was spreading up behind the mountains then.

"I'm sorry to have to leave like this," Wilma said. "But don't worry about me. I'll let Raoul take me to someone like Bicenti and learn something about this mess. I'll be all right. Now you just promise me that you'll see Bicenti as soon as possible. Promise."

Maya nodded and looked back toward Wilma's house. That dark man who had been on Wilma's porch a few minutes earlier now stood on the walk. Maya's head went up sharply and she sucked in a deep breath. Wilma turned to see what had affected Maya this way. The man seemed suspended there on a background of cumulus clouds. He was detached from the earth and everything that Wilma and Maya knew. He began to bob, spring up and down, a jumping-jack. Again, his hands went to his pants crotch and Maya turned away. So did Wilma.

"Is it possible that I am cracking up?" Maya asked Wilma.

Wilma smiled a caring and trusting smile. "If you are, I am too," she told Maya. "Look, Maya—don't mention this, *what's happened here,* to anyone. You know what I mean, other than the likes of Bicenti. Few people understand, have seen beyond . . ."

Maya looked again to where the dark man had been. He'd disappeared into Santa Fe's thin air. "Yeah," Maya said, "I know. I agree. Our people understand . . . this kind of fracture of space and time . . . But like you say, there's only a few who do. Don't worry, I won't say anything. Now you go inside as soon as the car starts." She unlocked the car, took her glasses from the glove compartment, and put the key in the ignition. The car started smoothly.

"Okay," Maya said to Wilma, "go on. I'll wait until you get inside." Wilma reached inside the car and hugged Maya, then she turned and retreated to the house.

Maya backed out of the parking lot slowly, noting that the curtains in a few houses were moving. She turned on the radio and set the dial on the Santa Fe station. The woman's voice had not abandoned the seductive tone. And it was now 7:05.

———◆———

Wilma waited alone in her house all day, expecting something to happen but nothing did. About mid-morning, the neighbors showed some signs of life and activity. Cars cruised the streets.

Maya drove directly to Albuquerque, negotiating the tricky freeway traffic in time to make her 8:15 class at the university. But her mind played a reel of events that had happened to her recently; broken images of the dawning hours returned to her. By then, she was doubting her senses, asking herself if any of it had happened. In a university parking lot, she climbed out of her car, ambivalent about what she should do. She gathered her books from the car trunk and slammed it down hard. Then she went to put a quarter into the meter. Splotches of dried red blood on the car caught her eye. Suddenly her doubts vanished, her mind cleared. She set her jaw in determination, and she climbed back in the car. Bicenti was in Arizona, six hours away.

It was nearly four when Maya arrived home. Her family met her at the front door. "What's wrong, Mom?" one of her children asked. "You're not supposed to be home yet. Are you cutting class?" The boy laughed and then he noticed Maya's strained face. He asked, "Are you all right?"

"No," Maya answered. "Let's talk."

———— • ————

In Santa Fe, Raoul knocked on Wilma's door. Wilma let him in. He hugged her, his white even teeth showing in a wide smile. "How's my girl today?" he asked.

Wilma answered him, "Raoul, how would you like to take me for a long ride today?"

"How long?" Raoul questioned.

"To Cañoncito, thirty miles from Albuquerque," Wilma told him. "I'll make it worth your while," she said with a wink.

"Okay by me, but why are we going to Cañoncito?" Raoul inquired.

"I have to see a man there," Wilma said.

Raoul smiled and teased, "Won't I do?"

Wilma laughed, "Afraid not, lover boy. The man we're going to see finds things, tells you what's wrong. Know what I mean?"

Raoul nodded. He understood.

———— • ————

At dusk, Maya and her man were riding down a treacherous road that wound through sagebrush and piñon trees. The Chuska Mountains were dark green behind them and Black Mesa was ahead of them some forty miles distant. A cribbed log *hogan* and a house were in sight at the end of the road. Sheep were penned in a nearby corral, and their bleating sailed through the evening's space and time.

Maya's man went into the house and not long after came to get Maya, waiting in the pickup truck. "Bicenti is in the hogan," he said. He opened the truck door. Maya followed him inside the dark hogan.

Maya's man greeted Bicenti who sat on a sheepskin that covered the earthen ground. They touched each other's hands, then Maya touched Bicenti's hand, and took a place on the sheepskin beside him. Through the smoke hole, Maya watched the pink sky fade. In time Maya told him everything. *Things weren't right,* she said intermittently while he sat and listened, not surprised at anything she said.

They left Bicenti's hogan over an hour later. The eastern sky was sprinkled with early stars and the world appeared as it should be. Bicenti would come to Maya's house the next night. He would quietly tell all. Then he would bind the tiniest fracture in infinite space and time. Then, he would go silently away, until the next time.

CARTER REVARD

Never Quite a Hollywood Star

IF YOUR SCALP ITCHES, IT MAY BE BECAUSE I AM TEMPORARILY
controlling your mind. So don't try a dandruff shampoo unless you have
already looked out the window for the Indian attack; we are hiding behind
the trees and shrubs on your lawn. I myself am from the stars; and my
Omaha friend Cliff works at the Army Arsenal here, where we have all the
needed guns and grenades. But seriously, folks, these words popping out on
the page as you read are pouring out of the constellation you call the Big
Dipper. Like neutrinos they pass through everything until they just happen
to get the right brain to interface: then they break into the word-hoards, put
on English, and come marching out all together, clause left, clause right,
wherever England was pink on the globe, and while you watch them take
cover behind a yew hedge you can uncover the plot we are involved in. Their

strength is your weakness—leaving a story unfinished is as hard as stopping in the middle of other acts to which our appetites drive us. Not to be obscene, I leave you to imagine that, but it may be said that thirst for water or love is not stronger than need to finish a story or remembering that can make you sure you are still you. I have used this story-sense to log into your mind, or as Cherokees say I am walking in your soul, my friend. Unless we *are* friends, of course, this is an Indian attack, and you will be trying to kill me, our story, if you don't trust me. But its corpse will nag: not truly American till you've been in an Indian attack, it says. So, shall we begin?

The story. Oh lord, I forgot to mention. It's aimed at you, but its words pass through you to others, one of whom you need to know is William F. Buckley Junior, a former Yalie. (I see you there, Billy Boy, on your Firing Line in the back of this reader's mind where I've set you. He doesn't really want you there like a ghost on his dark TV tube which he's trying to tune to Indian affairs. Go ahead, though, try to convince him that I am Sandinista. He of course will get very frustrated if I keep talking over his head to you, so please, sweet William, keep quiet for the moment and let my story begin.)

It begins in starlight: very dark, but in the clear night air of early spring stars are brilliant, even through branches thick with new buds here on the creekbank where the doe is poised, wanting to bend her head and drink but looking carefully round first. Now she plants her front hooves wider, bends the neck slowly, dips her muzzle slightly, jerks the head up and turns ears back, sniffs. She hears a rustle, flinches to leap but can't decide which way, hears the bow *thonk* and gathering to jump is hit by the arrow behind her left shoulder, her head flies up, she springs, but a long-tailed shape flies through the air from the sycamore on her right and behind her, lands on her back with a grating snarling cry and fastens long teeth into her neck. She bucks, struggles, the mountain lion throws her off her feet and fastens teeth in her throat, throttles, growls, shakes her, has her pinned and subsiding. Again the bow *thonks*, an arrow strikes and pierces his chest entirely; he leaps free of the doe, turns and strikes and snaps at the arrow's feathered end, rolls on his back and screams and snarls, kicks, is on his feet and leaps for the sycamore tree, falls short of the branch and claws upward on its trunk. A third arrow drives into his back, splits his heart; he snarls, falls, thrashes briefly. The doe, ten feet away, is moving feebly, her head rising and dropping, beating against the ground. Now she and the cat lie unmoving, death throes over. And now a man stands up where he was kneeling among tall dead weeds to the left of the deer-trail down to the creek. He watches, listens as carefully as the doe had done, looks into our camera, an arrow notched and ready, does not see or hear us in this blind of time. He waits, a minute, two, three, looks carefully up into the sycamore. At last he moves one moccasined foot to a leafless grassy place, then the other, but freezes at a noise, a splash. He kneels, lowers himself to prone position, sights across the creek: an otter's head, swimming downstream, had made the splash. The man stands up. He looks up through the branches at the Big Dipper, checking the time: a meteor flashes down and fills the dipper with light as it vanishes. He speaks quietly to deer and mountain lion, takes out his obsidian knife. We kill him. He turns into a myth as we pour our words over him and he disappears, then rises like mist, takes human form again and walks down off the stage to the back of your mind. He sits down there beside William Buckley, who looks distinctly uneasy but is trying to hide it.

As the story continues, snow has fallen and bitter strong winds have drifted it. A pickup truck is carrying two young Indian men and a white reporter out from the church at Wounded Knee, now occupied by militant American Indian Movement warriors and their supporters from Mohawk, Chippewa, Ponca, Apache, other peoples. In the pickup truck is a rifle. Our story does not tell what kind of rifle it is, because we do not want the two Indians arrested; it is therefore an *alleged* rifle. They are going to kill a steer, allegedly, so this reporter can file a better story, indubitably. They drive out into a field where whitefaced cattle are gathered around a feeding station; some are eating hay from mangers. The reporter and the Indians look the cattle over, decide on one. It looks worried as they keep staring at it, turns broadside to them, looks alert and poised to run. None of the three has ever slaughtered a steer, but the Indians were taught to kill humans in Viet Nam. There is a report of one of them as having shot the steer in the chest. The steer, we are told, bellows and trots away. Again, reportedly, the rifleman shoots it, this time from behind and to its right. The bullet is said to have ranged into its flank and stomach and lodged behind a rib, causing the steer to stagger but not fall. The reporter is, on oath, angry and guilty. The Indians, said one rumor, were embarrassed. The reporter has taken pictures which are not only not admissible, but not interesting. Now the steer is weakening, drops to its front knees—is that, the reporter wonders, really the right word?—and goes over on its side. It lies suffering, rolling its eyes, wheezing blood out its nostrils. The other cattle have run off a ways and stand with eyes blared, watching the three people talk and talk. Finally a rifle-carrying person appears to walk up, stand over the steer, and fire into its skull not far from its left ear; the steer convulses, twitches, lies dead. The three persons look up to a helicopter flop-flop-flopping overhead with someone named Billy taking pictures of them out one window. Then the three confer on how to get the carcass back and butcher it. None of them has ever skinned, gutted, cut up a dead animal. The reporter will not take photos of this; the feature will explain that these are not real Indians. The sur-rounding Airborne Division soldiers, the machine guns on the APC's or emplaced elsewhere, their tracer bullets that come into the church at night so brilliantly shining and kill an Indian lying next to its wall, are not real either. They are, the reporter explains, a public relations exercise. Some crows come down to investigate the steer's eyes, also blind. The crows tell a different story. It is kept in a blue cage made of western skies and cannot reach *The New York Times*. Here come the press trailers and vans full of equipment pulling out of Wounded Knee. Behind them shots break out but do not exist.

———◆———

Ah, now the circus is coming to town—a funny car full of clowns, elephants in single file holding each other's tail with their trunks and baggypantsing along; floats with trapeze artists and tumblers, the band with its great bass drum and trombones, and now at the end of a flatbed truck with real Indians on it, warbonnets and buckskin fringes, beads and scalplocks, look-ing out across the crowd to the Sierras. Their float moves slowly down the street towards a bar here in Maryville, California, a bar with a big Coors sign over it. Just as the Indian float comes opposite, the door to the bar opens and some patrons come out to see what the noise has been. A very tall man, six four, comes out. He has black straight hair, high cheekbones, gray-blue eyes. Right beside him is a short, brisk-stepping Indian woman. She runs to the curb, waves frantically at the Indians on the float.

"Hey, I'm Indian! I'm Ponca! I'm Indian too!" she yells. On the float suddenly the man in buckskin and warbonnet stands, looks, waves to her.

"Ponca Washtage!" he calls, loud enough for her to hear.

"Woody, look!" she cries. "Look, it's Sugar Brown, remember that great dancer—look, there's his boy! Hi, Elmer! Oh, for goodness' sake!"

"Come see us at the circus," Sugar Brown is saying as the float moves out of range. The tall blackhaired man and his Ponca wife are grinning, could not be happier.

———◆———

"I'll be damned, right here in Maryville, California," the tall man is saying, "what do you know. Jewel, let's get right over there."

You feeling more at ease, reader, now the story has taken us this far? That is, catching on to what I'm driving at, have you begun regaining control of your mind, know where the brakes are, accelerator and steering wheel in range again? I hope very much that this is so, but remember old Billy Buckley back there wants to be a backseat driver. He says even though all these Indian attacks have been most contemptible, you should be scared of them. One was merely expert savagery, another a savage fraud incepted by the media, the third an assault on your bleeding heart, reader, Billy says. He is afraid of active unAmericans and every time he pops out of your TV, sees Indians everywhere he looks, in Nicaragua, West Germany (green Indians there), in Yale, in Hollywood. Worst of all, they are spending his money uncontrollably even as they accuse him of starving them and taking their land, resources, rights away. It is, one thinks, just short of impossible not to be impressed by such paralogisticism.

———◆———

But please join me, nonetheless, in this old car speeding down a stretch of U.S. 60 between Panca City and Pawhuska, on the Osage Reservation. It is long after midnight, we are doing eighty and the asphalt road is dips and curves which our headlights shadow and highlight dizzily as we careen and thump over and round them. In the front seat are two Indian men. The man in the passenger seat is slumped down, may be asleep; the driver, like his passenger, is nodding. Now, though, he straightens, shakes his head, looks to his right and speaks loudly, asking for a cigarette. He gets no answer, and reaches over to shake the sleeper. "Hey. Elmer. Gimme a cigarette," he says. But Elmer does not wake, and the cigarettes are in his right shirt pocket. The driver tries to reach over across Elmer and fish them out. He has taken his eyes completely off the road, and as he leans he pulls the steering wheel right, the tires hit the soft grassy shoulder, the car lurches, the driver jerks round in panic, yanks the wheel back just as his right front wheel goes into the culvert and the car turns a twisting crunching somersault, lands in the ditch on its top and bounces onward, crashing over and over, windshield and windows shattered, driver thrown out and crushed under the rolling car as it makes a next-to-last headstand and tumble. The man on the passenger side, tossed like a rag dummy, is still inside as the car, one headlight impossibly shining, a taillight dully glowing, crumps once more and stands, tips, gently sags upside down on the barbed-wire fence at the top of the borrow-ditch. The front passenger door is open and Elmer hangs half out of it, head down, limp. He has been awake since the first screeching of tires but thinks in his numbness that it is a nightmare. He cannot move, or feel his body, but his open eyes see grass, prairie hay in clumps just above his head, and beyond it many twinkling lights. Then he finds he is looking at stars, but can't think why they are below him. The grass seems to be growing downward. Blacking out, he is thinking that he must be upside down. He hears himself breathing loudly. When he wakes up he is in a hospital and beside him sits a man he knows, who helped raise him, who in the Ponca way is his father-uncle, from whom he learned to be a great dancer. "Take it easy, Elmer," the man says. Elmer tries to sit up but nothing happens. "Gus, what's the matter?" he asks. "Johnny got killed," Gus says, "but they got you out. Doctors pulled you through." It does not take Elmer long to realize that he will not walk again, that he has very limited use of arms and hands, that one lung is ruined. He has been a circus acrobat, Hollywood stunt man, champion war-dancer on the powwow circuit. He will learn to use a wheelchair and be helped by others into and out of it.

Now through September drought and heat we are going to White Eagle for the Ponca Tribal Dances. You drive south out of Ponca City, through several miles of refinery stink: searing sulfur dioxide, rotten hydro-gen sulfide, a sweetish warmth from the orange flares, creating the power you drive with. Presently you drive between wheat and oat fields, pass a beer joint, then churches, come to a billboard announcing Ponca Powwow. You turn off right here, toward Salt Fork, wind around a little, turn off the asphalt after passing the Ponca Tribal Building and the medical clinic building. You can see trees and greenery down toward the river, and turn-ing down that way you see some canvas tents ahead, olive green or khaki or blue, cooking fires in front of them, people with kettles and pans. But first, explain to one of the young Ponca guards here that you are one of us, not them. They want you to pay. You say you are Aunt Jewel's nephew. Finally you give them five dollars, because what the hell. It ought to go to the drum when you dance, but it is after all a contribution. (You see, reader? I have made you for the occasion one of us. Just keep Mr. Buckley down in the backseat there and have him narrow his Yale Blue eyes sufficiently.)

First time you've come here without an older member of the family to avouch you; firs' time for many years you've been here; the young men don't recognize you. Now ease this big old Dodge Polara down the dirt road, the knoll and sharp right down-turn, and here under the walnut tree are Aunt Jewel and the family. Hey, here's cousin Buck, Carter and Linda, Craig and Stephanie, Kelly, Uncle Joe, the twins, after a while Mike and Casey and the kids, Julie, Wesley, Suzeta and Huggy-bear in the green van with Shongeh-ska's name on it, then Darlena and her man come down from the house. Now there is catfish Mike caught down by Fairfax being fried here, lots of everything to eat, fry bread, we feast. It is late afternoon, there has been gourd-dancing up at the arena already. Everybody sits around the fires in front of their tents, in the shade of trees along the winding dirt road that goes up toward the dance grounds, and Aunt Jewel's place here is not far

from where the creek-bottom's underbrush and tall weeds begin. Some of
the young men that will be wardancing are here to eat with Aunt Jewel.
They do not know you and for a while they look less than friendly. After
they listen to you talking with Aunt Jewel and Craig and Buck they relax a
little. Craig gets you into some dominoes with him and three of them. One
is heavy and muscular. Otoe, he says, looking as if that was not a good question. Craig introduces you to Elmer, who is sitting in his wheelchair near
the fire with a beer in his right hand. Craig takes out a cigarette and puts it
into Elmer's left hand, then when Elmer raises it hesitantly and puts it into
his mouth, Craig lights it. Elmer blows out a stream of smoke and looks at
you. He says it is good to be at the dances again. This is where he has always
camped for the dances; Uncle Gus and the McDonalds have made this
their place. He says, looking toward an open area between trees and creek,
that he used to ride his horses here, racing the other men's best horses. It is
darkening, and the dancers go back into their tents to put on fancy wardance gear. Presently we hear the bells, the jangling as they walk up toward
the arena. It is the first night of the wardance competitions that Uncle Gus
used to win for a long time, and that Elmer won. "Right here," he says,
looking away, "I first raced my pony when I was just a kid. I saw this place
when I was hanging there upside down from the car. I saw these trees and
a cooking fire. They were right in the drinking-cup part of the Big Dipper."

When it is quite dark we go up under the stars to the arena, where the
drum sounds and voices sing the wardance songs. Now Carter and Craig
push the wheelchair and Elmer in and along at the bottom of the bleachers, turn it so he has a front-and-center view of dancers and drum. We sit
just behind on the front row. There is a break now before the finals; water-
boys carry round to drum and dancers the buckets of cool water with their
longhandled enameled dippers. Now the finals begin, drummers play the
trickiest rhythms and fastest songs; the dancers must keep precise time,
stopping exactly wherever the drum may suddenly end, anticipating so
there is no slip, awkward pause, off-balance move. Only six are left dancing, and the crowd is happy; these are the best of the best. Then, as one
dancer does a spectacular spinning and fast-stamping bit, the crowd goes
Ooooooh, and I nod wisely. "He's really very good," I say. Elmer smiles, turns

partly toward me, says very quietly, "That's the people that just lost money on him; he missed a beat." I sit and watch and do not say anything more. When the last song ends, the dancers walk round the circle in the sun's direction, all coming by to talk and laugh with Elmer while they wait for the decision. He congratulates winners.

You can come into my study now. It's pretty badly messed up, paper and books all over, but it does have three big south windows looking directly into the upper branches of this sweetgum, and the winter sun comes streaming in through its branches. Hundreds of seedballs hang from its branches, brown and burry, like geodesic stars. I am here among the stars, it appears. See, down on the ground the snow has appeared overnight, and it is dazzling. Now a sudden flight of juncoes sweeps into the tree. Immediately one of them flashes down to the untouched snow, hops neatly across it. Soon it will be Valentine's Day, when birds choose their mates, and I will be teaching Chaucer's *Parlement of Foules* about their gearing down of love from star-motions to birdsong to class warfare as they make their social contracts. Now,

> *Here's a junco neatly*
> *hopping, print print print*
> *in the brilliant snow, now*
> *he draws his feet up*
> *into the white soft down*
> *of belly-feathers,*
> *spreads wings to catch reflected*
> *warmth off dazzle, fluffed like charcoal*
> *grey heatsink, "brooding*
> *in the snow," Shakespeare said–*
> *no, warming his toes and thinking*
> *which seedball in the tree,*
> *this sweetgum granary, he'll*
> *fly up and hang by while he*
> *feasts,*
> *below zero*
> *on a sunlit day, blue sky and*
> *feathers full of sun, his crop*
> *filled, his message*

cuneiformed on snow;
track me this far,
see me brooding on this
white death, then just
a blur where trackers say I
ended, but blue-eyed
weasel looks up
where I feast on the round
seedball under the round
undying sun,
already turning north toward
new leaves and flowers.

Now you can scratch your scalp if it itches; you see it's safe, we all are among the stars, grenades only seedballs, this Indian just professor. Still, if you stick a junco feather in your hat and call it macaroni, please be careful: it is a Federal offense unless you are licensed to take part in Indian ceremonies involving feathers. You see, we are different after all, we Indians; but friend, it's legal.

VICKIE L. SEARS

Everything Works Together

1. AH DA TO DAH

IT'S TRUE. THERE WILL BE NO APOLOGY. I HAVE ROMANTICIZED my father. It was hard not to. I knew him so well. I knew him so little. Everything about him is clouded by a bright patina.

My father is not so idealized that I cannot see his foibles. To exercise harmony and create a balance, I will tell you his faults. His shadow was a long-cast quietness of slow measured movements. When he came home, he'd kiss my mother and tousle my brother's hair. Then he would reach for me. Sometimes my time was shared by a bottle of beer. Sometimes he went to the yard to sing with his friends. It took him months to become angry, but once he was, there was either a voluminous eruption of anger or a silent walk away to reach for his bugle.

Most often, he took me on a walk. We'd talk about animals, the sky, water, or the lack of it—anything. However, if my mother seemed to need attention, he would simply put me to bed in a very short while and then go to talk with her. I never disturbed them, as it was her time. I believed I would feel his holding hand when it was my turn. There was an osmosis in learning from my father. He hardly spoke. He would pitch his head to the side and nod as a signal to follow him. While I could ask him about anything, I seldom got what I saw as an answer. I was four when I started to ask about spirituality. There was confusion. Mom was Roman Catholic and Dad a pantheist. One Saturday I asked, "Who's God?"

For a long time, my father stared at me; finally he said, "Everything works together."

My eyebrows rose, I wiggled my toes in the dust and the blue sky was luminous. I did not speak. It was, to my mind, a typical nonanswer. In the silence, my father looked all around the yard. Ah da to dah reached down to guide me toward a prickly pear cactus. "Look," said my father, pointing to the base of the plant. There was an ant nibbling at the moist meat. A mouse watched. Before the ant had drunk his full, a termite flew on to him. The termite quickly ate him. I turned my head away from the carnage, but my father cupped it, and returned my face toward the cactus just in time to see the mouse leap onto the termite. There was a crunch as the termite became the mouse's lunch, and then the mouse ran up the plant. Dad reached inside the prickly pear, carefully gouging out some meat. He gave each of us a drink; it was warm, but sweet.

"Later a hawk, coyote, or someone will eat the mouse."

He leaned into the sand and drew a circle, then took me to his lap to listen to the bugle song.

I looked from the birds drinking at the plant to my father. I knew something had happened. But who was "God"?

2. RACCOON

The first time I saw her, she hissed at me and bit me. I was shocked. She was nonplussed and ran to the other side of the creek. Her butt was a wibble wobble ball. Her back fur was a gray puff. She looked at me from the far side of the creek, as though I was in her territory. She loudly hissed at me. She stood on her back legs clawing the air with her front paws.

I thought raccoons were mean. She proved me right and wrong.

I lived on a farm where I picked apples. I was not allowed to eat them, and wouldn't, but I occasionally began to steal them for that raccoon.

We met when I was sitting against the log she had made her home. It was by the creek. Noises from my nestling back must have bothered her. She came out of her log to let me know that I was in the wrong place and bit me. Then she ran off. With my finger bleeding, I returned to settle on the log. It was a wonderful log, smelling of grubs, rotten wood, and a newly dug-out middle. It invited sleep. I did.

After a while, I heard rustling and clawing inside the log. I opened one eye. I felt fur along my cheek, but didn't dare move. A fetid breath filled the air. Then my face was covered with gray-brown hair. I moved enough to unbury my nose. The fur smelled of rancid peanuts, while still being sweet. She was pleasantly warm, but my movement brought a slight growl. Wishing the growl to become a soft burble like Henry's, I rolled an apple from my pocket into my hand. I laid perfectly still with the apple in my palm. In a few minutes I heard sniffing; the raccoon grunted, then shuffled to the far side of the log, away from me. I heard her sniffing as she pawed the ground, coming closer. Her fur was plastered to her body from her dip in the creek. She was beautiful. She tentatively reached for the apple. I stretched my arm for her to take a bite. The startled raccoon scuttled backward. I took a small bite of the apple and extended the newly exposed fruit again. She clawed it with her right foot, then smelled her nails. Suddenly she grabbed the apple, taking it to the creek. She dropped the treat into the water. She rolled it. She smoothed it with her hands as though it were dirty; around, around, around, it curled until she thought it was clean. She was meticulous before taking a bite. From that distance, she studied me, and then quickly ate all but the stem of the apple. Having eaten, she cautiously moved toward me. She waddled to sniff my hand. She stood and felt my sweater pockets. Her fingers were sharp, but gentle. Seeing that I had no food, she made a little throat trill. She lay down with her back snuggling against my body. We both slept.

The rattle of rocks awakened me, although the star brightness could have had I not been so sleepy. I startled awake, sitting up. The raccoon had gone. There were noises from what I saw were several rabbits running up a dry creek-bed. The raccoon was advancing toward them. I wanted to simply roll over, but I got up and started back toward the barn to cuddle with Henry.

When I arrived, Henry ran in circles with soft, happy squeaks in the hay bed. I flopped into the hay and he ran to my cheek to nestle into a sleep position.

The next afternoon, for the first time since being sent to the farm home, I took off my one piece of clothing, a dress, and washed it as the raccoon had washed her new apple. We slept together again. I was happy with the warmth of her fur.

I did not wash my dress every day. Sometimes I did my underwear.

After a few days of our intimacy, the raccoon, now called "Coonie," began to feel my fingers and toes. The only time I was offended by her explorations was when she pulled my lips apart to tickle my teeth. Her dried fingers stuck to my lips and felt as though they were ripping them. I growled. Coonie quit.

Generally, I liked her playing, but, unlike Henry, she did not bring or share her food finds, until one night she left a large, uneaten pile of fresh-water mussels.

3. DOLPHIN

At twenty-one I was invulnerable. I floated in early morning sun, my hands across my chest. Nothing could touch me; I was in the water. Until I heard the splash. I looked east toward the shoreline without my glasses. I could not see it. I panicked. Then I felt a bump along my side.

"Shit. A shark. Don't make a lot of noise. You'll be eaten for sure then. Roll over quietly onto your back and paddle softly."

I did that and was moving slowly toward a shore I believed I would never find. Then I felt the second bump. I swam a little faster, but I was a swimmer swum too far. When the third bump slid across me I put my hands out, fending off the beast. It was soft and warm. Sharks were supposed to be cold. They were creepy. But this . . . this was warm. I was puzzled.

"If I'm going to be eaten, let it be quick. I don't want one of those horrid, tearing death scenes."

Then I felt the water pool around me. There was a sucking, as a tide felt. The beast sprang up from the water, in a fine arch with a shrill whistle. Multicolored pyramids of water dripped from its body. It was silvery-gray, silky, and, I am sure, a woman. She twisted around. In and out of the water she came, bumping and nudging.

What was she doing? Her intent was obviously not to hurt. She was playing. She wove under my arms and between my legs, encircling my body with silliness. I made a hoop of my arms through which she could jump. I petted her head; I stroked her cheeks with the back of my fingers. There came a sound that seemed between a growl and a purr. We were both suspended in pleasure. I flattened my hands against her side. She guided herself along my hands. She quite seemed to know her wants. I gave her a hug, feeling the warmth of her body as she cuddled me.

For at least one-half hour we played. I felt no fear. We spun and twisted in the water until my feet tapped the sea floor. My legs were wrapped in dark green, wide bands of seakelp. I could stand! No! I wanted to stay a part of my friend. It was too soon to part. I sat in the tide flow. The dolphin swam back and forth, singing for a bit. Because of my own sadness I felt the song was a keening. When I no longer heard her, a sense of poverty overtook me. I had been blessed and had it taken away.

But in thirty-six years her softness has stayed.

SULEIMAN RUSSELL

How Old Man Coyote Lost His Manhood

IT IS A WELL-KNOWN FACT IN OUR MODERN AGE THAT THE Native trickster spirit Coyote can regularly get himself into trouble by trying to be what he isn't. It's almost as well known that he gets into as much trouble from trying to get something for nothing. But sister, I gotta tell you, I didn't realize how much more trouble he could get into by trying to do both.

Let me start this story by telling you how I came to learn it. The rest should flow from there. Y'see, I've spent most of my adult life as a trucker hauling things from one coast to another. There's this one truck stop that I visit religiously, called Mabel's, just outside of Phoenix. One night not so long ago, I picked up a hitchhiker about twenty miles outside of Phoenix, and I took him as far as Mabel's. He was a scraggly, longhaired guy named

Joe, either Italian or part Native (I can never honestly tell the difference), about twenty years of age, with a mild tenor voice and an inviting smile.

While I was driving we made idle chatter, and I found out that he was one of those crystal-waving spiritualists who went from mesa to mesa chasing UFOs. The conversation was interesting enough, even considering his fixation about ancient kachina masks actually being representations of alien space suits garbled in the retelling. When we got to Mabel's, he asked if I could spare the price of a meal, as he hadn't eaten for about a day and a half.

As were enjoying a couple of Ted's famous greaseburgers, a pair of stunningly beautiful women walked in. Before I could do more than smile appreciatively, they practically threw themselves at Joe. About fifteen minutes later, the new waitress, Caitlin, went on break and joined the others in vying for this guy's attention. By the time I had finished my third cup of coffee and was about ready to go, no less than five divinely attractive ladies had clustered themselves around him, cooing and giggling at his every comment. When I got back from the necessary, another knockout had come in and was about to fall into Joe's orbit.

I just had to know. Hat in hand, I asked him what his secret was. In response, he just laughed, starting with a tittering giggle and quickly turning into choking sobs as he started to cry. It was the damnedest thing I had ever seen. The louder his sobs got, the closer the girls pressed, trying to comfort him, and the more women who came in to find out what was going on. The more women there were trying to get close to him, and doing everything in their womanly power to make him feel better, the louder his crying got.

Eventually, he managed to duck into the john, thereby escaping his adoring public for a time. He had calmed down by the time I came to check on him and was grimly chuckling to himself. He looked up at me with bloodshot and tear-filled eyes, and promised to tell me the whole lurid story if I took him as far as my next stop, and got him away from all those teeming women outside. I'll admit, for a minute there I was afraid he was queer and trying to hit on me. But that whole "girl-magnet" thing was just too damn strange, and I was pretty confident that this guy couldn't rape me if he had to.

With a little help from Ted, the owner, we snuck on out back, and got back on the road without further incident. Once we were in my rig, I asked him what the story was. That's how I learned the tale I'm about to tell you, and I'll try to tell you exactly the way he told me.

"Let's start this with Once Upon a Time," he said, "because that's the easiest way to start a story.

"Once upon a time, Coyote took a nap. The naps that Coyote takes can last for hundreds of years, because Coyote is as old as the world, and he needs his beauty sleep. This time, however, he couldn't sleep properly. Wouldn't you know it, right as he found a particularly good dream, he heard someone calling his name. He rolled over and tried to go back to sleep, but someone else called his name, from a different quarter of the world. Over and over again, they kept calling his name, and they just wouldn't let him sleep. So finally Coyote got up, and took a look around, trying to find out what the hullabaloo was about.

"The World was very different from what Coyote remembered. When he had gone to bed, his Contrary warriors had just kicked Custer's little blond butt all over Little Big Horn (with a little help from a few others). Now, white women were sitting in prefabricated sweat lodges, singing to their Ancestors in poorly learned and badly pronounced Navajo, and invoking his name while praying for miracles.

"The very thought!!

"Yawning, and putting on a new appearance, Coyote went out to have a look around. He went from store to store, and found books about Coyote and Coyote magic in the strangest places. Old Man Coyote saw these things, and a strange thought occurred to him. If anybody were going to market his name as a guiding spirit in this New Age, it would be Coyote himself. Especially since a lot of people were making a fast buck off of it.

"Coyote can be a shrewd businessman when he puts his mind to it, and he quickly became a rising star in the self-help spirituality movement. One day, after unsuccessfully trying to seduce a couple of young ladies, it occurred to him that Kokopelli was taking a nap under the western mountains, and wasn't likely to awake any time this century. So Coyote took the flying saucer that he had built for himself in his spare time, and flew over to Kokopelli's home. Very quietly, so as not to wake his host, Coyote snuck into the mountain, and put a pair of earplugs in Kokopelli's ears. 'It would be very rude,' he thought to himself, 'if I awoke my guest from his well-deserved nap. These earplugs will help him sleep better.'

"Coyote is nothing if not a gracious houseguest.

"Coyote then went over to Kokopelli's closet, and borrowed some of the Dancing Spirit's finest clothes. In case you didn't know, Kokopelli has a spell, which he sings into his raiment. That spell is his charm of ultimate seduction, which he uses to lure beautiful women away from the dances with him. Coyote had long desired the secret of that charm for himself, because he has never been as lucky with the ladies as he would have liked.

"Coyote then dressed himself as Kokopelli, and snuck out with the secret charm. In order to use the clothing, however, he had to trick everybody into thinking that he, Coyote, was indeed Kokopelli. Quickly Coyote went on tour again, telling tales of Kokopelli the Spirit Dancer, Kokopelli who opened the way between worlds. Coyote went from here to there, there to here, dressed as a white-skinned shaman, offering to teach people the way of singing to Kokopelli. But because of Coyote's thoughtful gift, Kokopelli could not hear the songs that the white people sang.

"Kokopelli is as old as the world too. Coyote couldn't bear to look himself in the mirror if he caused his friend to lose any sleep.

"Kokopelli soon became as popular as Coyote. Everywhere you went, you could find portraits of Kokopelli for sale to trendy white people. But everywhere that Coyote could reach to sell himself as Kokopelli, there was someone else who didn't like what was going on.

"Old Man Missionary was a dour and cantankerous spirit who had been walking the Indian lands ever since the first Spaniard explorers came here hundreds of years ago. Now, Coyote knew about Old Man Missionary, but didn't realize how important he was to the ways of the newcomers. Coyote just thought that he was this funny old man who wouldn't let his children have any fun. What Coyote didn't realize was that he got woken up by all these people, because they were very afraid of the Old Man's heavy-handed ways. They were afraid enough to call on the Trickster, which any wise person will tell you is playing with fire.

"Now, Old Man Missionary couldn't stop Coyote from pretending to be Kokopelli, but he could keep it from being any fun. Whenever Coyote sold someone a portrait of Kokopelli, the Old Man would whisper into the person's ear, telling them that such a thing wasn't decent, and then would helpfully make the image more marketable by removing that 'oh so vulgar' erection. How could anybody dance when they were in that condition, anyway?

"This is how Coyote's plan backfired. Because the People of the Nightlands are People of Dreams, the dreams that people have will shape them. Around the world, people dreamed of meeting Coyote in Kokopelli's clothing. But because of Old Man Missionary, this new Kokopelli didn't have any manhood. He would sing and dance, he would play his flute, and he would take you into the Nightlands on vision quests.

"Nobody ever dreamed of Kokopelli seducing them.

"From that day onward, Coyote had the secret of ultimate seduction, but he couldn't use it. All these beautiful women would throw themselves at him, everywhere he went, but there was no way that Coyote could make good on the offer, because the trick that he had played had taken all his sexual characteristics. And to be quite honest, Old Coyote's tired of it. If you'll just let me out here, I can make it the rest of the way on foot."

Now, what I'm about to tell you is God's own gospel, unless Ted's put a new ingredient into his "secret sauce." When I stopped the truck for Joe to get out, this mangy dog wearing Joe's beaten-up old Stetson hat hopped out of the cab. The dog—or coyote, I guess—scratched his ear with a back paw, thanked me for my hospitality, and went loping off into the Arizona desert.

And lady, that's why the charm dangling from my windshield has a novelty penis glued to it.

CAROLYN DUNN

Fishing

HE HEARD THE VOICES OF THE OLD ONES SPEAK TO HIM ACROSS his brother's lifetime, Paul's dark eyes shining, calling from a pond of clear water and glass, black stones holding him at the bottom of a deep, clean grave of clear water. In this dream, Stephen stood on the soft silt edge of a river, and when he looked down he could see Paul's face and hear Paul's voice. When he woke, Stephen was not surprised to hear the sound of water rushing underneath the bed and that there were tears streaming down his face. Half asleep still, he moved toward Carlisle, slid his arm under her breast, and buried his face against the soft cascades of her hair upon her back. Tears were streaming down his face, and he opened his eyes to her wet, soft hair filling him. When he woke, grieving, he knew where his brother was.

A call to home told him the police had found nothing. Both the state police, who on "foul play" investigations always called in the FBI, and the sheriff's office found nothing out of the ordinary; because Paul was last seen at home, the main investigators were his cousin Joe Burns and Sela's new husband, (Cecil) Cee Benally, tribal police. There had been no evidence of foul play, and although it was not uncommon for Paul to be seen in the company of the police, Stephen had felt a little uneasy about the turn of events leading up to his dream. It wasn't unusual for Paul to disappear for weeks at a time, but Stephen knew this time something was different. Something was wrong.

Stephen thought of the ties that bound Paul to him, the binding over the years that always connected Paul to him. His brother was not of this world. It was as though he could breathe water instead of air. When they were younger, their father had lost them at the Indian Market in Santa Fe; finding them, he had bound the boys wrist to wrist with some fishing line he'd found in his pocket, then wrapped the line around his own arm to keep them together. Bound by that thin line, the boys never lost each other again. Stephen never allowed the line to go slack; he kept it taut and Paul within close range; even if he couldn't see his brother he could feel him. And the line had been taut those weeks before Paul had disappeared; Stephen had felt it snap and Paul had swum away.

Five weeks Paul had been gone. He left his cabin in Garberville, walked down the road without his thick, Coke bottle–lensed glasses, and had not been seen since. All he had talked about in the last weeks before he left was going home: talked about seeing Sela's baby for the first time, talked about standing out in the wind upon the mesa, red rock and dust and ash crunching underneath his feet, feeling the bones of his ancestors and feeling like he was at home. Peace had not come to Paul easily; there was too much hurt and sorrow and dispossession in his heart to know peace. What his drinking didn't kill, the heroin numbed. They had tried to save Paul—his brother, Stephen, and their circle of women warriors: Carlisle Emmanuel, the fierce-tempered city girl who had loved them both; sister Sela with her voice and passion that could forge alliances and protect the hungry and weak; and Annalee Hayne, Deer Clan cowgirl extraordinaire who lived in the fringes of the Indian world, picking up the scraps and gruel of the leftovers of the American Dream, making a meal of it and feeding it to her circle of warriors. A dream of a real life in a real world for a healthy Indian world, but Annalee would soon know how short life could be. Her dreams, although having not died, had taken a temporary respite to the battle she had waged against alcoholism and liver failure; and there was hardly time to dream a false dream when fighting the battle for life and death in the real world.

Stephen's dreams were all he could hold on to in the search for Paul. In his dreams Paul was speaking to him, calling his name. He was alive. But Stephen knew the consequences of water rushing between them. His brother was dead and lost to him, this time for good. It wasn't Paul's eyes staring at him through thick Coke-bottle lenses; it was Paul's eyes staring at him through clear running water, eyes that wanted to be closed, water that was both cold and warm. Leaves lifted on the current and up around him, flowing past his open eyes, whispering upon the shadowless current, dark and deep, that he was safe, that he could rest now, if only Stephen and Sela and the others would let him. Rest. Easy. Resting forever in the cold arms of the clearest desert lake, the current still and deep but moving, always changing, ever flowing.

Resting was not easy for a man who ran a lot. Ran from home to find Dad. Ran from home to find love. Ran from home to find a bottle, or a needle. Ran from home to fill the need his father could never have for him. For some reason Paul adored his father, a man whose absences while the kids were growing up were too numerous to count. Patty Burns had held her family together on religion alone, long having abandoned the Mormon faith of her childhood after she became pregnant with Sela. Her own brand of Native teachings and her tirades against Christianity held them together much stronger than the fishing line Pete Cragg had tied to his sons' wrists. Patty had given up on the Mormon church for good, had gone back to her father's house and spoke the language of the Old Ones once again. But there was something still that spoke to Patty through the stars—the angel Moroni spoke to her too—but from a space ship in Galactic Central somewhere in northern Arizona. Joseph Smith was a man—a white one at that—and no matter how much his dogmatic descendants believed Indians were the Lost Tribe of Israel, no Indian woman could ever ascend to the ranks of prophet because she was just that. Indian. Woman. Prophet. Yippy yay ki yi yippy ki yi yay.

So Patty went back to the faith of her mother and father, learned the Beauty songs, heard the voice of Changing Woman and her sisters, and held her family together because she was determined her sons and daughter would not suffer the humiliation of Haskell Indian School, or so the angel Moroni and Changing Woman told her.

It wasn't that Pete was a bad father, per se, but a virtual absentee during his sons' formative years and Sela's first baby at sixteen. Stephen was never dependent on anything in his life, learned how to cook and clean up after himself by the time he was seven, and never took anything for granted because things like the wind and his father, Pete, could never be counted on to remain the same. But that was all right because things changed, always moving. The next most constant thing to the stars at night and those desert rattlers and the long houseboats attached to trailers all along the interstate heading up to the lake was his mother Patty and his brother, Paul.

They were old Navajos, those Burns kids, many of the Old Ones said. They weren't small like their grandma Natcheni (who some said was part Apache, but that's a whole other story) or their grandpa Nelson, but tall, lean, slim waisted and long legged; with straight thin noses and long cheekbones. Spirits, some had whispered, look like those half-white Burns kids. There was laughter behind that statement, that Dine spirits looked like a white man's three children with their mother's last name. Spirits spoke the language of dreams, and when those Burns boys opened their mouths someone was dreamt into being.

Days passed Stephen by with no word of his brother's whereabouts. He began to dream of home, of Changing Woman and the night sky out of which she had borne the stars. He dreamt of the Old Ones and their language that came to him only in dreams, of the night skies and smoke of prayers rising to the stars. At night, moon sung of desert flowers blooming in the spring heat, dark desert storm clouds forming in the middle of nowhere. Every night Stephen saw those clouds, heard the song of the storm as it slithered across the mesas and into the valley. Every night Stephen saw the two-room house he'd lived in for so long, saw Patty's long dark hair swept up into a mass of sweat-soaked dark mats, heard her voice as she alternately hummed, "See the pyramids along the Nile/see the sunset in a tropic isle/just remember darlin,' all the while/you belong to me . . ." and "I'm in love with a Navajo boy . . ." She turns suddenly, and she's not Patty any more but Paul, his eyes not covered by bits of broken and bruised Coke-bottle glass but the clear green water of home.

Stephen woke on the fourth night from the same dream, Paul's name just a whisper on the night wind in the City, just a sparkle in the thousand-year-old light of stars. Nighttime is a time of magic, of myth, and of memory; the stars calling out our names. As he had done all the nights before, Stephen closes his eyes, and sometimes a drop or two of water is squeezed out from the outside corners of his eyes, rolling down his temples to the hard, foam-filled pillow, barely leaving a tiny drop on the white case upon which his dark hair, so like his mother's, falls feather light and free, sweat soaked in a mass of dark mats upon the pillow. His eyes close again, and he dreams of his grandmother Natseni, of the House of the Sun, and of Nanyehi, and whispers across the cold clear water of home to his brother's open eyes, "I will never forget you . . . ," and of Dine spirits dancing across the mesas and mountaintops, making their way to the river and in the language of the Old Ones singing a song of crossing over.

◆•✦•◆

Another six weeks went by before Stephen had told Annalee the truth about Paul. He didn't want to shock her, since Annalee had just gotten out of the hospital and since her husband, David, had taken her back and they were living only ten miles up the road from Stephen's place where he and Carlisle had been living since they moved from the City up north. Annalee's son Bryan was old enough now to remember that his mother had been gone for awhile, and any mention of Annalee's life in the City and during the time she had left them was pretty much still a sore spot.

Annalee was ecstatic when Carlisle got the teaching job at the university, and through the community center in town had gotten a two-day teaching program started up at the high school in comparative literature, preparing the high school kids for the rigors of Western classical literature. That meant Carlisle would be back with them, and even though Sela had returned home to Arizona, Annalee's little community would be strong once again. And being in and out of the hospital with various liver disease–related ailments put Annalee in need of her friends and community around her.

"We've got to tell Annalee about Paul," Carlisle had told Stephen one night over dinner. "She's got a right to know. I mean what happened was a long time ago, Stevie, but she still loves him." Like Stephen, Annalee had loved and lost Paul to the trickery of the bottle, to the witchery of the needle, and there was no bringing him back. All the pain and suffering and hurt Annalee and Paul had been through together had somehow made Annalee stronger, made her heart and her mind and her vision clear so she could heal herself and steel herself for the fight of her life.

So Stephen got in the truck and drove ten miles up the road to Annalee's house. He thought maybe she could tell him the truth about Paul. Maybe she could go to the water, find out what Paul was trying to say or to do, then that would be the end of it. Then Stephen would call Sela and they would finally lay Paul to rest.

Stephen drove up the narrow, redwood-lined dirt road and up to the house. David had done some work on it since the last time Stephen had been up to see them. The front porch had been redone, and it looked like the garage had been converted from an old storage space to David's new studio. The dogs lay in the dirt, under the shade of the oaks that surrounded the house, set against the dark green of the redwoods, pushed up against the timberline. It seemed quiet to him, and his feet touched the earth, springy and bouncing back. The pond David had put in a few years back was quiet, with the occasional jumping of trout that were never fished for breaking the silence, barely enough for Stephen to notice. The dogs watched him, waited for some sign of recognition, and when Stephen whistled they all rose and came to greet him. "Hey, dogs," he said, and patted as many of the black heads he could before reaching the walkway up to the front porch. A few Coke cans were crushed into small aluminum circles and lay in a box beside the trash cans. Stephen reached the front door and knocked. It was a new door, he noticed, the frosted glass and etched flowers the only break on the pale oak lines.

He heard some scuffling inside, and soon the door opened. Annalee Walker Hayne stood, thin, frail, bent slightly, her eyes sunken, darkened orbs in her head. Smaller than he'd ever seen her, half the strong, resilient, hearty Creek-Cherokee-white woman from Oklahoma who wore cowboy boots and Wrangler jeans nearly every day of her life, who drank and swore and drove a 1970 white Mustang convertible with the top down even when it fog-rained a fine mist covering the San Francisco nights and wetting the white vinyl interior until they slid across the seats with wet clothing, she looked up at him, a tiny thing of bones and eyes and hair enmeshed in a black sweater that seemed to hang off her, and she smiled. When she smiled, her eyes lit and for a few seconds, a slight moment, she reminded him of the woman he held so close to his heart for many years. "Hey," she said, and opened the door wider, "I was wondering when you'd get around to visiting. You spend too much time at home with your Beloved Woman." Her voice was hard, filled with a Southern twang that would have been insulted had it been called a drawl.

Stephen smiled his half smile, a man's smile, and moved past her as she closed the door behind him. The house was bright, in spite of the darkness from the fog and the trees outside. Orange candles graced nearly every corner of the room, and Stephen's eyes drifted to the sprig of cedar tied in a bunch on the coffee table, its embered and glowing ends shining bright against the pale smoke that rose from them, moving up toward the ceiling and to the sky. Stephen moved across the wood floor of the dining room and into the living room. Brightly colored afghans draped the dark couches, and the TV was on but muted. Annalee's ever-present pad of legal lined paper sat on the table next to bottles of prescription pills, a box of Kleenex, and a large clear glass filled with water. A coffee cup graced the table as well, filled halfway with the black sludge Annalee drank daily. Motor oil, Stephen used to call it at home, and many times during their years in San Francisco they sat at the table, drinking cup after cup. Sometimes Annalee would sneak a couple of shots of whiskey, sometimes brandy, late into the night.

Stephen picked the pillow off the floor, and propped it against the others before Annalee sat down, leaning on them. "Thanks," she said, and closed her eyes for a second, then opened them with a sigh.

"You look good," Stephen lied; well, not really lying but comparing Annalee to the last time he'd seen her in the hospital two months earlier.

"Fuck you; I look like shit," was Annalee's answer, as she covered herself with one of the afghans. "You been drinking?" she asked.

Stephen shook his head. "Not unless I have to."

"Dr. Sayles said you looked pretty good. How's your liver?"

He smiled. "Okay, I guess. Probably some damage done from all the partying I did when I was younger."

She nodded. "Good. Go lay down on the floor so I can cut it out. The sooner I get one, the better I'll be for standing on my own two feet."

Stephen grinned. "Annalee, you know I love you but I ain't gonna give you my liver. I need mine now, thanks."

"Oh well," Annalee sighed, "you can't blame a girl for asking." She reached across her legs to the table and picked up her coffee cup. "I saw Carlisle yesterday. She said things are still as crazy down there as they always have been. With all the things she's done you'd think they'd kill to have a full professor in the department, but they keep saying there's no money. Story of our lives, huh? No money."

Stephen leaned his head against the couch. "House looks good. David's been doing a lot of work, ay?"

"Those paintings he did downriver sold in the City, so he and Bryan are gonna put a new bathtub in upstairs. I'm so damn weak I can hardly stand up, Stevie, and they're gonna put in a bathtub I'll damn near drown in. The size of a hot tub, for Christ's sake. David always told me he'd kill me, and I guess this is how he'll send me downriver."

"Bryan'll fish you out."

"I hardly ever see the damn kid now he started playing baseball. He's talking about going into the big leagues, you know. A kid of mine playing the all-American sport."

"He turned out to be a good kid, Annalee. You should be proud of him no matter what he does."

She laughed. "He's good too, Stevie. Plays shortstop. He's quick, and David said they want him for the All Star team and the season's barely started."

"What is he now, eight . . . nine?"

She gave him a look. "Thank you, sonny boy, you make me feel younger already. Twelve in January."

Stephen shook his head. "Twelve." His eyes met with hers across the table. Behind her head, sitting on the sill in a large glass bay window, an orange candle glowed, dripping wax onto the saucer it was in. Her eyes were the only thing of her that remained. But Stephen knew there would be good times as well as bad in this long illness, and he hated seeing her like this, but Annalee was determined to get better. "I didn't tell you everything about Paul," he said suddenly, and at that moment, he knew she already knew.

"Carlisle told me you still hadn't heard anything," Annalee said, settling once again against the pillows at her back and neck.

"Last time I saw you, in the hospital, I just heard something from him that wasn't good. He didn't want anybody to know, so I didn't tell anybody. I was gonna tell you, Annalee, but you were pretty bad last time I saw you. I didn't want to upset you, and besides David was there."

Annalee closed her eyes.

"He'd been real sick up until then, he had had stomach problems that they thought may have been an intestinal parasite. And his eyes was gettin' worse and worse. It was a virus, they said. Normally, the doctors told Sela, the things are fought off when your immune system is working right. So they put him in the hospital and ran all kinds of tests. His immune system . . . wasn't working right at all."

"He got it from the needle," she said, her voice quiet. It was the voice that reassured Stephen when he was most desperate, all those years ago when his life was coming apart, unraveling the very fabric that he had fought so hard to weave. It was a woman's task, to weave, but his mother had taught him how when he was a little boy, so he could take care of himself when he had to, and it was one of those things he would never forget. And he would never forget the tone in Annalee's voice then, just as he would never forget it now, "Didn't he?"

"Yeah," Stephen answered, his eyes not leaving her face. He watched her, and remembered how she was when he first saw her, beautiful, strong-willed Annalee Walker from Oklahoma, with enough strength to keep them all glued together, dying now of liver disease and wasting away amongst the strength and resilience of the redwoods that covered her backyard. He never wanted to tell her about Paul, about the doctors' diagnosis, especially after all that she and Paul had been through together, especially after all that she and Stephen had been through, but he needed to tell her. The whole tale. "He didn't want to die wasting away somewhere in a hospital where no one cared about him, Anna. He wanted to die while he still had the strength to do it."

"He didn't want to die like me," she said in that same voice.

Stephen shook his head. "Anna, you're too mean to die."

She smiled. "I know. I just wanted you to think I was dying." She shifted slightly, and turned toward him. "Can't find a goddamned gold candle anywhere anymore, Stevie. These orange ones give off a nice light. You think anyone lit an orange candle for Paul?"

He shook his head. "I don't know."

"He still needs it, to light his way to the Land of the Dead. He can't find his way, Stevie, until you let him go."

"Sela doesn't even think he's dead. She refuses to believe it."

Annalee nodded. "She knows deep down. You've seen it in your dreams, haven't you?"

"Yeah," his gaze drifted out the window. "But I want to know for sure."

"There's a way, you know, it's spirit magic. Through the eyes of a deer, old Yemisa would say. She could tell you about Paul, all the way until the end." She moved to sit up, and Stephen thought it looked briefly painful, but Annalee stood anyway. She was looking old for a thirty-six-year-old woman, but when she finally stood Stephen understood something about grace and agility that alcohol could never kill. He followed her through the house and to the front door, where she moved past the porch to the pond. She touched her hand to the water, dropping some cedar and tobacco that she had rolled into a ball with her fingers. Rings rippled from the offering, then settled, as if the offering had never been made. Annalee watched the steady and silent water for a long time, standing there, gathering strength, pulling her power around her like a coat. She breathed in, and a smile crossed her face. "It's true. He's gone, Stevie. He can't find his way back home. He's there, isn't he? On your rez. At Lake Powell."

Stephen nodded.

"My dad taught me how to fly-fish for trout when I was maybe eight or nine. We put on those big canvas pants and suspenders, and then he'd pull out his fishing hat—Cleveland Indians, with that screaming face all teeth and eyebrows—and cast out. Over and over again. You've got to draw them out, he'd say, make 'em think there's something worth coming to the surface for. Make 'em think there's a whole swarm of things out here for them to eat, things that look good. It takes a long time. And he'd stand there, casting out, over and over, until finally, one of those big old fish would come to the surface. One, then another, and another. And then we'd have trout for dinner." She turned and looked at him, the fog-enshrouded sky framing in soft gray around her black hair. "You need to go home, Stevie, and stand at the edge of the lake with your pole and cast out until you catch him. Bring him back home, 'cause right now he's lost. Too much in this world for one little Burns boy to take."

Tears shimmered in Stephen's night sky eyes. He began humming, ". . . See the pyramids across the Nile/see the sunset on a tropic isle/just remember darlin', all the while/you belong to me . . ."

Annalee slipped her arm through Stephen's. "David put this pond in for me, you know. He never fishes. I guess I'm gonna have to hang on long enough to teach Bryan about fly-fishing."

Stephen smiled. "How come you never taught me to fly-fish?"

"You're not my son, Stevie."

Stephen smiled. "But you've always been like a mama to me."

Annalee sighed. "And I will always be just a little in love with a Navajo boy . . ." she sang, ever so softly, under her breath to the cool surface of the pond. The wind had died down a little, and the needles fell from the trees in perfect flying arcs, hitting the ground in silence.

The pond was clear for about two or three inches, then turned muddy and dark, and no shadows escaped or entered it. But for a few seconds, a few moments when there was no wind and no sounds coming from the trees or the fog as it fell silently onto Annalee's hair, raising tiny water drops on the blackness there, Stephen could see clearly, in water as clear as glass; there was a deep, clear grave of water, and two dark eyes peering from below, open and looking for a light from an orange candle that would lead them home.

"I wish I could swim, Stevie. But if I got in there now I'd drown in a second. And David wants me to have this goddamned bathtub."

"What should we do about Paul?"

She laid her head on his shoulder. "It would make it easier for Sela if we had a little butterfly magic, so she'd see his transformation. Paul's gone, Stevie. We all saw that coming from the beginning. He never had your strength." She stopped speaking and listened. The sound of gravel and dirt under tires was making its way up the hill. "We'll bring him out and then he can go. Too much shit to put up with in the world for one little Burns boy to take."

A truck pulled up the dirt driveway at that moment. Annalee's husband, David Hayne, pulled the truck to a stop. Out of the back bed, a big white dog with black eyes and a curling tail jumped down and ran toward Annalee and Stephen. The other dogs started barking, but this white one turned on them, and then they were silent. "How do you feel, honey?" David called over as he jumped out of the truck, his long hair tied back in a tight ponytail down his back. He reached for long pieces of stretched white canvas out of the bed, and moved toward Annalee and Stephen standing reed thin and strong against the line of water and black silt.

"Like shit," Annalee answered, but she smiled.

"Well," David said as he walked up the path, "you look like shit too." He glanced up at Stephen. "Wanna throw her in, Stephen?"

Stephen's laugh echoed from the trees and back. "Thought about it," he answered.

"Stephen and me, we're fishing, honey," Annalee said, calling after David as he moved into the house. "Don't you knock over any of my candles now."

"Okay!"

The dog moved over to Annalee's side and sat, her tongue hanging out of her mouth. "I had a white dog that looked just like that when I was a kid," Stephen said. The dog watched them with eyes darkest onyx and shiny light. She sniffed at the hand Stephen held out, then licked him.

"Let's go in and drink some motor oil, Stevie. I'm getting awfully tired just standing here."

Stephen led Annalee to the driveway, their steps slow and careful. From the corner of his eye Stephen could see the water rippling, and a trout leapt up, watched the sky, and landed back below the darkness and absence of shadow. "That was a big one," he said, and for a moment, the water cleared, and light entered it. And there, on the surface, a shadow appeared, looking like a Dine spirit with a white man's last name, shaking off the water and rising ascendant on the smoke of prayers and light, drinking in the trees and sending a shower of cold clear stones back to the bottom of the pond that had held him below the surface. Stephen said, "It is finished."

DAWN KARIMA PETTIGREW

Loaves and Fishes

I. THE REMARKABLE NATURE OF MIRACLES

MANNA REDPAINT FORAGES FOR FOOD. SHE TEARS THROUGH the cardboard boxes of Tide under the sink, sending sandy powder across the tile floor. She shakes the box of sponges, which usually stores her dollar bills and food coupons. A box of Brillo, Manna's hiding place for her beloved deviled ham, contains only the pads themselves. Manna hurls the pads over her slim shoulder. Nothing. Not one of her canned treasures remains.

Gallup has been cruel to Manna. She fled here, hitched a ride with a total stranger, to escape her domineering mother and forget a flute player named Thomas Crow. She has ended up with hunger pangs, indigo bruises, and a baby, well a toddler really, left behind by one of the stranger's intoxicated party guests. Now she and the baby will starve if Manna cannot find the money or the canned goods she has hidden throughout the house.

Manna opens the refrigerator. The bulb lights timidly. One egg sits forlornly among thirteen red and white cans of Budweiser. Manna, who already has strong teeth and bones, gave the last of the milk to the baby yesterday. She prays that calcium is cumulative.

Manna shuts the cool door. Shaking the hunger from her head, she tries to think. The commodity butter and powdered milk are missing. The stranger must have taken them to trade for more beer down the road. *Loaves and fishes gone haywire*, Manna muses. Good sign. If she can joke, her mind must be working. As long as her mind functions, she can create a solution, stay one hunger pang ahead of starvation. She and the baby could eat grass, if they can find any in Gallup's dry heat. Sheep eat grass and they seem healthy. They can eat sheep, if they find an untended flock. No, sheep are too big to steal. They can walk to where sheep live and eat what they eat. They might find real sheep food. Sheep Chow probably tastes like corn flakes or farina.

She could give the baby the egg before hiking New Mexico's desert roads in search of a Good Samaritan.

Blessed is he who considers the poor, remembers Manna. Perhaps she should eat the egg, then bear the baby the three miles to the nearest neighbors. *They could consider us. We are the poor and they could be blessed.*

Manna likes her plan until she tries her legs. Quivering, they convince her that walking anywhere will end tragically. Manna opens the cupboard again and removes a compact that has doubled as her personal safe since she arrived in Gallup. She lifts the puff and prays for a crumpled portrait of Thomas Jefferson to fall from the layers of pressed powder. No use. The stranger has discovered her hidden food stamps. He has stolen them and the rest of her going-away money.

The compact clatters into the sink. Fragile grains float into the ever present drip of water and disappear. Lifting the smooth compact, Manna drops it again. It clatters against the chrome, losing slices of powder.

"No! No! No!" Manna roars. She strikes the sink with the side of her hand. The compact leaps, landing with a shattering sound. Wrapping her slim fingers around the compact, Manna lifts it above the sink and brings it down against the scratched chrome. She screams, long and loud, crashing the compact repeatedly, willing the return of her food and her hope of escape.

Slivers of glass prick her wrist as the lid surrenders, scattering over Manna's knuckles. Tiny droplets of blood, flowing crimson, mark her fingers.

Manna reaches for a dish towel, wincing at its sourness. She turns on the faucet, flooding her own blood away with the opal powder. Shaking her hand free of blood and water, she wraps it in the rag. Her scream transforms itself into sobs and she sinks to the floor.

Manna cries for her hand. She sobs for her heart, for Thomas Crow, and for her mother, whose fault all this is. Tears for the loss of her freedom, her stolen stash of money, the missing treasures of deviled ham and tuna fish stream from her eyes, over her cheeks. Wailing, keening, Manna weeps for her lost groceries and for the baby whose mother she is not but temporarily is. She is this baby's only friend and she cannot even feed her.

Manna's tears have produced no miracles. When she raises her head, the baby is watching her from the doorway. Her peaked face convicts Manna, who has left the baby unattended while crushing compacts and feeling sorry for herself. Manna wipes at her wet eyes with her good hand. "Oh, Baby. I am so sorry." The baby stares at Manna. Her eyes widen as she notices the blood seeping onto Manna's skirt through the dish towel.

"Hurt?"

"Honey, it's just a scratch or two. It hurts a whole lot more on the inside than on the out."

"Ouch?"

"Yes, ouch, but not too bad. I'm sorry if I scared you." She is not only letting this baby starve into the next world, but terrifying her in the process. "My temper got away from me for a minute, but I chased it down and brought it back." Another joke. She has not lost her entire mind. "I'm fine, honey. Manna's okay."

"Mama, okay?"

Manna has no idea. She can hardly keep up with herself without worrying about this baby's missing mother. "I don't know, sweet pea. I don't even know who your mama is. But I'm fine. Manna's fine."

The baby considers this gravely. "Mama okay." She smiles at Manna, who realizes that her tiny jaw is moving. Chewing.

"Is there something in your mouth?"

The baby nods in reply.

"Are you eating?"

Another nod. Food. Manna hopes whatever it is is non-toxic and plentiful. She forces calmness into her voice as she reaches toward the child.

"Can you show me what you're eating?"

Nodding again, the baby draws a sheet of paper from behind her small back. The paper is the color of tired goldenrods. The corners and a fair part of the middle are missing.

"Oh Good Lord." Manna's heart grows more exhausted by the minute. The baby places the paper in Manna's palm. "Thank you, honey." Manna closes her weak fingers around the colorful sheet. She hopes that paper can be considered fiber. Maybe there are minerals in the dye. The baby swallows. Manna's head hurts.

An eagle and the profile of a Dog Soldier sprawl across the sheet. The title of the event is missing, but the baby has been gracious enough not to eat the date or the location.

"The VA . . ." Manna reads the date again. Tonight, in downtown Gallup. "It's probably a powwow or something for veterans," she tells the baby, who lunges for the flyer. Manna holds it out of her reach. "Hold your horses, little lady. If this is what I think it is, you might not have to eat paper after all. They have fry bread at powwows and we're pretty enough to get somebody to share some with us. Might even throw in some red Kool-Aid if you smile at 'em in just the right way." The baby reaches again. Manna continues to read.

"Mama!" shouts the baby.

Manna's eyes find slim letters at the bottom of the page. ADMISSION: 2 CANNED GOODS, the creased letters read. Canned goods. If people gave canned goods, they'd need someone to get them. Manna catches her breath at the promise of pasteurized heaven.

"Food!" Manna clasps the flyer. She can walk far enough to find a ride into town and to the VA. "Canned goods!" Manna drops to her knees in front of the baby. "We are going to get dressed up and go get our fair share of food, little lady." Inspired, she squeezes the small body. "We may even take them a few cans of our own."

Manna kisses the baby and heads for the fridge.

II. THE ALLURE OF SPIRITS

Manna and the baby know how to wait. They sit patiently beside the road. Manna feels less like a bad example for hitchhiking since they are only doing it to find food. Besides, they are going to a powwow full of veterans, who have to be better role models than the staggering party guests that surrounded the baby earlier.

Manna decides that the VA is a good place for the baby. If the flyer fails them, she will leave the baby at the VA. Veterans like babies. TV news always shows them rescuing infants from firefights and carrying toddlers piggyback toward democracy. A veteran may keep the baby or find someone who can prevent the Mormons from claiming her tiny soul.

Maybe an elder woman will raise her to replace a daughter she lost years ago. If the flyer lies, if there is no food, Manna will observe the old women, looking for one who dances Southern-cloth and laughs at the M.C.'s jokes.

"If there is no food, I will give you up," Manna whispers into the baby's ear. "I promise you will not starve." The baby sighs and sucks on the fringe of Manna's dance shawl. Manna has had enough. A struggling mother and child may not halt the sporadic traffic, but unattended Budweiser is another story.

Manna leaves a six-pack in the middle of the desolate highway. In minutes, the drivers of a crimson Ford pickup stop to claim the windfall of apparently deserted beer. When they pull away, they do not notice that Manna and the baby have made themselves small in the bed of their vehicle. When they arrive in the VA parking lot, they have no way of knowing that, every so often, spirits are currency.

III. THE WITHERING OF FIGS

"These are not canned goods."

The woman guarding the door to the VA glares over her glasses. She is a small woman, the color of newsprint. She thrusts her hands deep into the pockets of her denim dress.

"Ma'am." Manna shifts the baby to her other hip. Her eyes meet the woman's and hold them. After a lifetime of her mother's withering stare, it will take more than a scowl to deter Manna from her pursuit of packaged food.

"I said," the woman says sharply, "these are not canned goods." She is a white woman, made of odd angles and wrinkles. Manna pities her for defending the door to the dance like Cerberus instead of enjoying the pow-wow. Coyote versus Cerberus. Manna likes the matchup.

"Ma'am," Manna speaks slowly. "These are canned goods. Goods in cans. B-vitamins, yeast, it's all pasteurized even."

Manna points to the sheet of golden paper on the table, next to a box of creased one-dollar bills and VA insurance forms. "Your flyer says two canned goods per person for admission to this powwow. We have six cans here." Manna taps a can in time with the beat of the drum inside.

"That's six cans in exchange for me and a baby, who really ought to be one canned good in the first place." Manna waves her own furrowed flyer, creating a slight breeze across the baby's face. The baby reaches for the paper, and Manna lets her have it. "You're almost making a profit here."

"This is a *sobriety powwow.*" The Cerberus woman stretches "sobriety" into a snake of sinister syllables. "Sobriety is practiced here."

"Well, I can appreciate that Ma'am, but you see, the title of the event was missing from our flyer. I didn't know." Manna smiles sweetly. "Both the baby and I are sober."

Pursing her hips in disapproval, the Cerberus lady frowns. "Two canned goods or five dollars." Her eyes narrow as she stares at the baby. "Is your daughter eating that paper?"

"Oh, God. Honey, give that here." Manna envies the baby's goat stomach. She feels cruel, demanding that the baby spit out her only sure source of nourishment. She squeezes the plump cheeks. The baby continues chewing.

"Ma'am, we don't have five dollars. We don't have any dollars. To tell you true, all we have is this beer here and we're . . . " The baby swallows the paper noisily. Manna leans over the table and whispers. "We're hungry."

The Cerberus woman sits silently. Inside the VA, the drums are playing a sneak-up. Manna misses Cherokee, longs for Thomas Crow, sochan greens, and trout. She should never have fled to Gallup to starve, trying to make miracles out of spirits. The baby bites into the paper again. Manna does nothing to stop her.

The woman looks at the baby and turns her gray face toward Manna. "Maybe, young lady, if you spent your welfare checks on food instead of on liquor," she pronounces it "lick-or," giving it a prudish, self-righteous sound, "you and your daughter would not go hungry and have to eat paper."

Manna's face burns. She straightens, raises her chin. Her tongue forks and points as she pounds the table in front of the Cerberus woman. "We are hungry, now. We will not always be hungry, though. But you, three-headed-dog-woman-guarding-instead-of-dancing, you will always be narrow-minded and mean." Manna snatches several sheets of paper from the table and hands them to the baby. Gesturing, the Cerberus woman opens her mouth to protest. "Blessed is she who considers the poor," Manna tells her. Then she carries the beer and the baby away from the VA.

IV. THE MERCY OF PATRIOTS

Someone is shouting at Manna. Manna stands straight, ignores the noise, figures it must be the Cerberus woman demanding her flyers. She crosses the parking lot, heading for the road. The baby rings Manna's neck with her chubby arms. She smells like vanilla extract from her bath and Manna forgets her promise to give her up.

"Hey, lady," a teenage grass dancer grabs Manna's upper arm. Red fringes rise and fall as he breathes raggedly. Manna turns to face him, and he grins at her, showing egg-white teeth.

"My uncle, there, he wants to pay for you to get in. He heard them give you a hard time and he gave them money for you guys, too." The grass dancer points with his lips, motioning toward the VA.

Manna sees a peanut butter–colored man sitting in a wheelchair. Pewter hair flows over his shoulders, stopping above a salad of colorful ribbons over his heart. The teenage grass dancer nods at her.

"He ain't no crazy, lady. He's a veteran. He's okay. What do you want me to carry? The beer or the baby?" Manna hands him the beer. "Okay," the grass dancer declares, "come on. It's powwow time for you guys after all."

"Thank you, God," Manna utters under her breath. When she looks up, the man in the wheelchair is waving at her. Manna promises herself that once she has eaten, she will lift her hands and sidestep wildly, to every veteran's honor song.

STEVE RUSSELL

Six O'Clock News

THE WIDOW SWIMMER LIVED ALONE BY CHOICE. SHE WAS A Cherokee-tall woman with straight and shiny black hair that showed no hint of gray well into her fifties. Lots of *Tsalagi* and even a few *yonega* had paid her court only to be left in the tinkling glass showers of her laughter—harmless, oblivious merriment that anyone would be interested in *her*. She was the Widow Swimmer as long as I had known her, but not for lack of opportunities. Outside of Deer Clan—her relatives—only old Ray Sixkiller ever got invited for meals.

Except for kids, of course. According to my grandparents, Mrs. Swimmer had lost her only son in the Korean War, but she always had kids around her house. When we were small she used to read to us until it got dark and then tell us stories until we had to go home: funny stories like Rabbit and Coyote, serious stories like Grandmother Corn, and even scary stories like Ravenmocker. Her stories often came with other treats: pies, cookies, and even strawberry shortcake in season.

Ray Sixkiller was a professional brush hog. With an ancient International Harvester pickup of indeterminate color and an assortment of tools collected over years of making do, Ray could do anything: clear the land, plow the land, harrow and plant, bless and harvest, build anything, repair anything.

For all Ray's odd collection of tools, the *yonega* would say he lacked any visible means of support. I never saw him work for a paycheck, but he was always working. Hiring him by the hour was a lost cause. He would not show up for the sake of working. Working was a means rather than an end. But he would build a toolshed, lay a new sewer pipe, pour a concrete foundation—just about anything but punch a time clock. I once watched him change out one of those big fuses the size of M2 firecrackers without even turning the electricity off.

First time I saw Ray up close was after the tornado in 1954 split the big elm tree in my grandparents' front yard. The wind just about took the roof off our house. Grampa got some asphalt shingles on credit at Oklahoma Tire & Supply and tried to repair the roof. It was slow going. In his seventies, he was too old to climb; aged in single digits, I was too young to do roofing.

Grampa managed to crawl up to the peak of the roof, and I scampered up the rickety wooden ladder with shingles, then with nails, and finally with the hammer. He got the top row done and crawled back to the starting point, hands and feet straddling the peak. Grampa turned and moved down the damaged section of the roof on his knees. I watched from the top of the ladder, directly below him. He was wheezing and sweating, and as he pulled out his handkerchief, his feet slipped.

Everything came sliding toward me at once: the hammer, the nails, a stack of shingles . . . but I let them all fall and tried to grab Grampa. As Grampa hit the top of the ladder, I remember thinking that for once I was glad to be a fat kid. The ladder pushed back from the house but my weight was just enough to keep it from falling backward. Grampa was caught with one arm over my back and the other scraping along the roof, his feet pushing vainly for a hold. There we hung, off balance, unable to go up or down. I yelled for help knowing there was no help and the phone lines were still out on the Indian side of town.

Next thing I knew, there was this six-foot-plus Cherokee with a big toothy grin and a torn T-shirt coming up the ladder behind me. Ray reached over me with his right arm and steadied Grampa as he grabbed the roof with his left and pulled the ladder close. I smelled the sweet odor of ceremonial tobacco overpowering our sweat and fear. It seemed odd to see the tattoos on his biceps from inches away.

"Nice catch, young sprout," boomed a voice behind my ear. "Now let's see if we can get down." Ray directed me to take a couple of steps down and swing to the inside of the ladder. While I came down that way, he got Grampa's feet turned to the ladder.

Safe on the ground, Ray suggested that he ought to finish the roofing after he got done sawing the tree up on the 12th Street hill, the job he had interrupted when he saw our predicament.

Grampa looked at the ground. "It will be awhile before I can pay you."

"Aw, we'll work something out."

Ray had the roof done by dark. Granma invited him in for supper. She killed a chicken for the occasion and fried it in commodity lard after coating it with commodity flour. She made corn bread and opened some of the green beans she put up from the last garden and a jar of wonderfully sweet peaches.

Over the meal, Ray learned that my grandparents were raising me on Social Security and Grampa's pension from the Spanish-American War. Granma told him how lucky she had been to be able to can several bushels of peaches this year, in addition to the pears from the tree in the backyard. So it was that Ray left out that night with Ball jars of green beans, peaches, and pears, and he called the roofing job even.

Five years or so later, I was one of the kids who skipped school to hang out with Ray, to the distress of the authorities. He used to take us night hunting. The only seat belts his International Harvester pickup had were on the front fenders, one on each side to keep teenage butts affixed during the tooth-crunching chase as Ray whooped and hollered like a sure enough three-D 'skin and tried to keep some terrorized cottontail in the headlights long enough for us to get a shot. Rabbit, squirrel, anything good to eat—we hunted more at night than by day. But not deer; Ray had a thing about deer.

"It's not a fair question," he would say.

Ray followed the old ways, as much as he could in the fifties. Before setting out to jacklight rabbits, he walked seven circuits around the truck for the seven clans while mumbling in Cherokee, puffing his hand-rolled smokes the whole way. And it was wrong, Ray told us, to take a deer without the deer's permission.

Now Ray Sixkiller was not hung up on taking deer out of season—just ask the game warden—but he would not use a light. The deer, mesmerized in the light, would agree to anything. "It's not a fair question."

In the daytime, plenty of deer gave Ray permission to take them, and often as not he would be seen taking a quarter of venison down to the Widow Swimmer's place. We were too polite to notice what time he left or if he left. Plenty of women gave Ray permission to take them too, or so people said, but he kept coming back to the Swimmer place to eat venison and roasting ears and listen to the Tulsa Oilers' games on her shiny black plastic Philco.

The radio at our place was older, bigger, and made of wood. We were convinced that plastic was a sign of quality that would pull in radio waves from farther away. Mrs. Swimmer was kind enough to let us use her plastic Philco on some clear nights when we could get WKY in Oklahoma City. WKY played Elvis.

WKY also had a newsline where they would pay one hundred dollars for the best news tip called in by listeners every month. There was very little news in the Nation and even if there was we couldn't get WKY often enough to keep track of the competition. But that didn't stop the fantastic thoughts of what one hundred dollars would buy, not to mention having your name said on the radio in the City.

One night the Widow Swimmer retired early and left us listening to the Hillbilly Cat on her shiny black Philco. It was the usual gang of would-be rock 'n' rollers: myself, my clan relative Tommy Plum (we are of the Longhair Clan), and our Muscogee pal Randy Harjo. Mrs. Swimmer had no neighbors on either side and a pretty good pasture in back, and I guess the music didn't bother her, because all she asked was that we turn the radio off as we left and shut the door to keep Bushyhead inside. Bushyhead was her cat, and also the name of one of her relatives who used to be involved in the tribal government.

We got to arguing about which Sun Records act should have taken over the world and once again bemoaning the sale of Elvis to RCA so heavy that we didn't hardly notice Ray Sixkiller's old Harvester clattering gravel and raising clouds of red dust on the dirt road out front. Ray must've missed the driveway because we heard an awful scraping noise and a cloud of red dust came wafting in the front screen door.

Ray was close behind. He gave us a goofy grin and shuffled through the living room and off down the hall without exchanging a word. The sour smell of old beer followed him. A couple of beats later, the radio was drowned out by some loud thumps.

"RAY SIXKILLER, DON'T YOU DARE COME TO ME WHEN YOU BEEN DRINKING!" I had never heard Mrs. Swimmer raise her voice before. Neither had Bushyhead, who made himself scarce.

There was some mumbling and stumbling and Ray came down the hall holding the back of his head. I started to make some wisecrack to Randy, but all of a sudden I could see the whites of his eyes and the look on his face made me turn to see Mrs. Swimmer emerge from the hallway in her nightgown and slippers, brandishing a shotgun. "Out!" she hollered, "OUT!" Ray sailed off the Swimmer front porch, legs still pumping, and came down for a perfect three-point landing, one point being his nose.

Halfway to the street, Ray must've remembered that his truck was high-centered in the ditch. He turned at the fence and walked back toward the porch, open palms up in a gesture of placation.

I couldn't hear what he said, but Mrs. Swimmer was in no mood to be placated. "I told you I'd never have another drunk Injun around this place! Now take your sorry drunk ass out of here before I blow if off! Right now!"

Ray took another step. Mrs. Swimmer lowered the shotgun from the level of his chest and fired.

Funny sound. I've heard a shutgun many times before and since, fired them myself. But a shotgun fired at a human being has a funny sound, soft and distant but at once loud and immediately present in my marrow, like I always imagined the call of the Cherokee ravenmocker, the last sound before death's endless silence.

Everything all runs together after the sound of that shot. Mrs. Swimmer running back inside, tears flowing. Grampa running from across the street, cutting off Ray's pants leg and trying to stop the blood with his hands. And the blood.

They told us in school that our skin was red and I thought the dirt street was red and I'd seen the red in a stoplight and in the pencils that checked our homework, but I never saw red, bright red like the blood spurting out of Ray Sixkiller's leg. He passed out.

I ran across the street and told Granma: "Mrs. Swimmer shot Ray Sixkiller and he's dying!" I turned her old wooden radio to WKY and hunted frantically for the telephone number. "This is news! This is really news!"

After Granma called the ambulance and we could hear the siren coming, I talked her into calling WKY. "Ray will need the money," I pointed out. "It's too far for the ambulance to take him to Indian Health Service." I knew instinctively then and learned for sure later that even dead people have bills.

She talked through the long distance call with the operator. When someone answered she made me turn the radio way down. She told the story in plain English without my breathlessness.

"I see," she said, and let the telephone dangle at the end of her arm. She looked at me, eyes glistening. "They say it's not news. Another shot Indian is not news."

"It is so news! Look, the ambulance is here, the one from the *yonega* hospital! Ray might die! It is so news!"

◆ ◆◆◆◆ ◆

It was so news, all over the Nation, but it was people news rather than radio news, and knowing it firsthand conferred a status that almost made up for the one hundred dollars I would not win.

Ray did not die and he refused to press charges against Mrs. Swimmer.

Ray's Paint Clan relatives put on a hog fry and raised the money to take care of his bill at the *yonega* hospital, and I organized Ray's hunting buddies to pull his truck out of the ditch.

Mrs. Swimmer took Ray a fresh baked cake while he was in the hospital. When she got back, I asked if Ray would still be listening to the Oilers at her place. "Yes," she said, "I suppose we will have the ballgame on. We agreed that I ought to cook for him until he is back on his feet, so he is coming here for awhile. . . ." She paused. "To visit. Until his leg heals."

The radio station never did learn why the Widow Swimmer lived alone by choice.

KAREN WALLACE

Alyssa's Father

KEN WAS SITTING IN HIS BIG WING CHAIR WHEN I OPENED THE
door. His eyes were closed. The TV was on with the sound turned down
and the radio was blasting rock and roll. The floor was littered with every
kind of beer container imaginable.

He was sitting literally in a mound of green and brown glass, aluminum
cans, and empty potato chip bags. He had a brown liter bottle of cheap beer
in his left hand. I thought that the mess on the floor was almost beautiful, if I
sort of squinted. That way the overhead fluorescent lights, flickering slightly,
reflected off of the metal cans and different-colored glass and made a sort of
eerie glow that obliterated the absolute hideousness of the apartment.

I knocked again as I peered into the room, but Ken was totally oblivious. I closed the front door behind me and walked in. I watched as Ken
slowly brought his right hand to his mouth and took a huge drag off of the
joint he'd been smoking. He gulped the smoke deep into his lungs and held
his breath. Just when I thought that he wouldn't remember to breathe
again, or would get a rush from approaching unconsciousness and decide
that he liked it, Ken finally opened his eyes and let the smoke out. His eyes
were red and watery. I was pretty sure he couldn't see me.

"KEN!!" I yelled over the blaring music. He was leaning back in the deep chair, his eyes open now and on the ceiling.

"WHERE'S THE BABY, KEN??" I screamed as loud as I could.

After a few seconds, like he was moving through water or was sitting in something soft and sticky, Ken brought the big brown bottle to his lips and drained the last of the beer. With the same slow movements, he gently dropped the bottle onto the filthy carpet, then leaned over and flicked some ashes from the fat cigarette to the floor next to it. He still didn't answer and closed his eyes again. I waded through the trash, past him and into the bedroom.

The two windows were closed and the room reeked of cigarette smoke. There were bottles here too, and empty cartons of Marlboro Reds. There were a couple of full ashtrays in one corner, surrounded by dirty jeans and T-shirts. At my feet, there were dozens of dirty dishes and a huge mug half full of coffee. Mold was thick on the surface. The only furniture in the room, a big mattress on the floor, was unmade and had several big dark stains around the edges. I think Ken found it on the sidewalk a few blocks away after he'd moved in.

There were a bunch of dirty, discolored sheets balled up in the middle together with a blanket, which, if I did that thing with my eyes again, was almost white. I think.

Lying in the center of this unpleasant mess, barely visible in the dim light, was Ken's daughter. Alyssa.

Ken is a big Indian guy from South Dakota. Where all the real Indians are, he tells me. Ken likes to say he's a full blood, but he admitted to me one day that he's really three-quarters. Like it really makes a difference. He looks like the warrior on an Indian head nickel or like one of those wooden cigar-store chiefs. You couldn't mistake him for anything else.

He has dark skin and straight black hair that hangs to just below his shoulder blades, the kind that looks blue sometimes in the sun. He was trying to grow it to his waist, but it's too fine. He's also going bald, so he wears a decrepit old cowboy hat with a turkey feather stuck in it all the time. He's got a big beer belly and a bad limp from a car accident he'd been in back home. He's about six-two and wears glasses. I used to have a crush on him.

Ken's also an addict. He keeps trying to get sober, but life is just too much for him most of the time. He told me that he left the rez to get a college education so that he would feel competent to run for tribal council. Instead, he's alienated himself from all of the people he was trying so hard to impress.

They say he's too white now.

So, Ken just drinks and smokes and snorts and shoots up. He says he likes to get high. That it gives him a unique perspective.

Yeah, right.

He gets high almost every day, except now it takes a lot more to actually make him pass out, which seems to be his goal. I think that he's probably addicted to so many different things, he loses track of what he's trying to quit at any given time. The last time he checked himself out of the local Indian residential rehab center, he was out looking for pot an hour later. It's not addictive, he told me. At least he didn't have his first beer until the next day.

Standing in Ken's tiny one-bedroom apartment, surrounded by trash and dirty clothes, I found myself staring down at this little girl in a dirty blue sweatshirt and pink socks. I picked Alyssa up from the foul mess that was masquerading as a bed and carried her back to the living room. I cleared a space on the couch and sat down with her on my lap. She looked up at me and waved. I think she fell asleep then, but she could have just been faking. Already she knows that life is easier when you're asleep.

Ken had opened his eyes again and was looking up. His place is one of those cheap apartments from the seventies that is furnished in puke green and has weird glittery stuff stuck on the ceiling. Ken thinks it's pretty.

The joint he was holding slipped from his fingers and fell onto his thigh. He yelped when it burned through to his skin, then finally picked it up. He went back to contemplating the ceiling. I sat and stared at him for a long time.

◆━◆➤◆━◆

Ken and I had first hooked up because he likes women. A lot. There's always some girl hanging around who wants to know what it's like to be Indian, who strokes his hair and tells him about her trip one summer to Mount Rushmore. He and I were both in school at the time and had a class together. Ken dropped out the semester before he graduated.

I don't think he would have talked to me if he thought that I was actually Indian too. Three-quarters of me. He doesn't like Indian girls. They're too tough, he says. And mean. He's always hanging around with blondes instead. Especially if they have nice cars. He keeps trying to marry the ones who can't ever remember how much cash they're carrying.

Most of the girls that are interested in Ken love to listen to his stories about the rez and the strange people he knows. They think he's very mysterious and treat him like an exotic toy. I think he likes it. I've heard a lot of his stories myself and think that some of them are probably true. Which is unfortunate.

———◆•∗•◆———

I discovered Alyssa by accident. I found Ken drunk outside of my apartment building a couple of weeks after we met and took him home. Ken is a mean drunk and I was worried that he would hurt someone. He tends to pick fights with men who are at least as big as he is and only half as drunk. He denies that he has a death wish. He was still mostly conscious and I managed to stuff him into my little rusty Dodge and then help him up three flights of stairs and into his living room.

Just as he collapsed into his chair, I happened to look down near my foot. There she was. Alyssa. She was sitting next to his chair, dressed in a dirty pair of overalls. She was holding an empty beer can. Coors, I think. She just looked at me, then held up the can for me to take. She smiled. That was three years ago. Alyssa and I are good friends now.

I've only seen Alyssa's mom a few times. Samantha's small and blonde and too young to have a baby. She lived with Ken for six months and then got pregnant. He left and they didn't talk again until the baby was almost a year old. Now, she's decided she's not ready to be a mother, so Ken took Alyssa.

Sam comes and goes and almost always threatens to take the baby away if Ken doesn't get sober. She comes to the apartment every once in awhile with a friend or two, a cigarette usually hanging from her lips. She'll yell at Ken for awhile, then leave. She doesn't always remember to say hello to Alyssa.

I don't know if she has a family, but I think she's living with some guy now. Ken hasn't seen her for three weeks. Alyssa has the same black hair as Ken, but looks a lot like her mom, with beautiful clear skin and huge brown eyes. She's gorgeous, but Ken is afraid she doesn't look right. He thinks that her skin is too fair and her eyes are too light.

He wants her to be a real Indian.

Ken doesn't have anything to worry about. I've been noticing that Alyssa is already a little too Indian. At least a little too much like Ken. When she stays over at my place, she likes to watch TV. She sits on my couch wrapped in an old Navajo blanket I have and drinks apple juice out of her bottle. She has a little brown paper bag that she keeps in her pocket and wraps it around the bottle before she'll drink.

Just like her daddy.

Sometimes, when I go to check on them, Ken starts talking about the rez. He only does this when he's drunk. When he's sober, he doesn't have anything to say at all. He gets more and more talkative the more he drinks. Most people get nervous when he gets that way. I have no idea how many times he's been left alone, sitting with his third or fourth pitcher of cheap beer in front of him. When he gets really smashed, just before he actually passes out, Ken likes to talk about home and his friends. They were real close and used to get into a lot of trouble together.

Ken says that his best friend was killed in the accident that wrecked his knee. He's never talked about it when he was sober, so I'm still not sure if it's true. I think it is. He also tells me that he stabbed a white man in a bar with a bowie knife and spent a couple of years in jail. I can't tell what to think about that one.

The night that he told me those two stories, we were at the Firefly, an Indian bar around the corner from my apartment. Ken had just finished a pitcher of beer and he started to cry. He told me all about his mom and his sisters and then told me about the night of the accident and the man that he almost killed. He drank another pitcher after that. I think he scared himself. Then he asked about me for the first time. I think he just wanted to stop talking about himself. And he likes to tease me because I have green eyes and brown hair. When I first told him I was Indian, he laughed. He said I was probably Cherokee.

Just like every other girl he meets.

When I look at Alyssa now, I think of that conversation. Watching Ken cry. I wish I could warn her and tell her not to be sad. Sometimes it's fun to be Indian, but not often. Especially if you don't look like Geronimo. Or Ken. When I was little, my dad used to take me to the Indian center. Since he was a dancer, everyone was pretty nice to me. Probably they would have been anyway. I remember though that there was a girl there who had pale, pale skin and bright red hair. She was a good dancer (she had a beautiful blue jingle dress), but she was still just the little white girl.

After my dad left, my mom wouldn't take me to my dance classes because she felt uncomfortable at the center. She doesn't know how all the gear works and isn't friends with any of the other mothers. She's only been to one powwow and the piece of fry bread she ate there made her sick. I didn't go to a powwow again until I had been on my own for a couple of years. I don't dance anymore.

When I told Ken about all this, he told me I was a wanna-be. He showed me his BIA card and bragged about growing up on the rez. I couldn't get too mad because he was so drunk and I didn't think he would remember anything the next day anyway. He did. That was right before he went back home too.

I don't think I've ever seen anyone look so sad as Ken did when he came back and told me about the trip. He'd already been at college for two years before he'd gotten enough money to travel anywhere, even home. When he arrived, his friends acted like he didn't know anything about the rez or the people on it. He said they were suspicious of him, and defensive, and said he didn't have any right to judge them. They told him that he talked and acted like a white man and that he couldn't do anything for them. I think that they actually told him to leave.

Now, when Ken thinks back on that trip, or looks at Alyssa, his own flesh and blood who doesn't speak Lakota and has never set foot outside of California, he tells me that I'm okay. I don't know if he really believes it.

After Ken nearly set himself on fire with the joint, he finally spoke.

"Do you want to know the secret of life?" he slurred.

Of course I told him that I did. He didn't say anything for at least a minute. Alyssa and I waited quietly. Then he licked his lips and took a deep breath.

"Don't park in front of someone else's driveway and don't name any living thing Bertha. That's all. You'll be okay then." He nodded emphatically as he spoke. I think he was dead serious. Then he passed out.

I took the roach from his hand and put it out. I left it on the plate with the rest of his roaches. AC/DC was blaring from the radio. "Highway to Hell." I had to laugh. I turned the TV off and the music down. Ken gets nervous if he wakes up and there's no noise. The whole apartment smelled like cigarette smoke and pot. Ken's mouth was hanging open and spit was dripping down his chin now. He started to snore. I took some of Alyssa's clothes and stuffed them in a dirty pillow case. She already has a couple of bottles at my place. I had even bought her some new paper bags.

I turned off most of the lights and then we left.

That was three days ago. I think Ken is gone. Alyssa sleeps in my room in a crib that we found at the Salvation Army. She's been staying at my neighbor's apartment when I'm at work and goes with me to class. I don't know where to look for Ken or her mom. I left a note on Ken's door and told the landlord that I had the baby. He didn't care, but said he would tell Ken when he comes back. If he does.

I called my mom to find out how to take care of Alyssa. She thinks I should call social services and tell them that Ken was neglecting her. Let them take care of it, she told me. I don't think I'll be talking to my mom again any time soon.

Alyssa's too big for the crib that we bought, but when we went shopping, it was what she liked best. She sleeps with the Navajo blanket and a big stuffed Snoopy. We've been to the grocery store once together. She likes to eat bologna. Ken used to fry it for her in the morning for breakfast and then give it to her in a sandwich for lunch too. Every day. We're working on that.

But other than the bologna problem, she's a great roommate. We like the same TV shows and music and we both like going down to the beach to watch the ocean. And she loves going to school with me. Alyssa trusts everyone and, every once in awhile, she'll grab someone's hand, whoever's closest, to walk over to the student store to buy some candy or more apple juice.

Alyssa never cries and rarely talks. She seems happy to me. She's still pretty little to know what's going on, so I don't know if she realizes her dad is gone. She hasn't asked about him.

I went down to the Indian Center yesterday to find out about day care. It turns out they have all kinds of programs for single parents. Alyssa could even take swimming lessons. There's a powwow there next week and I met a lady who still has a little jingle dress that her daughter outgrew. It looks great on Alyssa.

We'll be okay.

RAVEN HAIL

The Crystal Cave

THE WHIR OF THE WINDOW AIR CONDITIONER WAS ENOUGH to lull anyone to sleep. David sat at his desk and tried to concentrate, but it was no use. He finally gave it up, shuffled a few papers on his desk, and walked out. He thought he had made it past the reception desk, but his secretary spied him. Practically nothing ever got past Miss Jamieson.

She would never ask, but her raised eyebrows indicated her curiosity.

"I thought I might leave a little early and take my son down to the riverbank. He's anxious to try out his new fishing pole."

"Well, watch yourself so you don't get sidetracked by that new widder Mankiller's house on the way."

"The name is Sixkiller," he patiently pointed out.

"Oh, excuse me. It's just that everyone seems to have business over that way ever since she moved in. You'd think no one had ever seen a Cherokee Indian before."

"Well," he grinned, "I think I should do the neighborly thing and drop in and borrow a cup of bourbon."

"It's a cup of sugar," she corrected him.

"You borrow what you like, I'll borrow what I like. I can do more with a cup of bourbon," was his parting shot as he went out to his car.

It was a perfect day for driving along the countryside. He hadn't really meant to stop, but he wasn't in any particular hurry, and he saw Robin Sixkiller in the front yard pulling weeds.

"How's the weed business?" he greeted her. "I hear you've got a weed for every need!"

"What do you need?"

"I'll take a pound of marijuana," he said. "That's the 'in' thing at the moment, isn't it?"

"I'm fresh out."

"Then what do you have that's good on the market?"

"Oh, there's some sage, and that's rosemary," she pointed out.

"What's the rosemary good for?"

"It's good for making tea," she explained. "Would you like to try some rosemary tea?"

"Sounds good—if it's not too much trouble." He followed her into the house and settled down in an easy chair, making himself comfortably at home. Before he had time to finish his first cigarette, she reappeared with two frosty glasses of a somewhat cloudy liquid, complete with ice cubes.

"Looks like lemonade." He sampled it. "Tastes like lemonade, too. It's delicious."

"I added some lemon and honey. Most people like it that way."

"Then would you call it rosemary tea with lemon, or lemonade flavored with rosemary?"

She laughed. "I hadn't thought of it that way."

"Will it make me healthy, wealthy, or wise?"

"Rosemary is for remembrance. It's not supposed to give you any more knowledge, but to allow you to remember what you already know. Of course, too much of it might remember you right out of this world."

"Already I remember something," he said, "that I hadn't thought of in years. It was somewhere right in this area, too. They used to say that there was an old cave hidden somewhere—a long time ago. Full of gold and silver and all kinds of treasure. When I was a kid I used to spend whole afternoons looking for it. Found lots of wonderful treasures, too, like big fat bullfrogs, and shells, and arrowheads, and juicy blackberries. I combed the countryside, far and wide. But of course there was no cave. It was just a wonderful fantasy to think and dream about."

There was a comfortable silence as if both withdrew into individual thought. Then, as if reaching a decision, she said, "There is a cave. I know where it is."

He wondered if she could possibly be serious. "Where is it?"

"Next to the springs."

He shook his head. "I looked there." Then, as an afterthought, "How did you find it?"

"There is an old Indian legend that people originally came to Earth from the Pleiades Star Cluster. They traveled through space by the use of solar energy. When their mission was completed, they went back to the Pleiades. While those first people were here, they lived underground. That's why I am here—because the cave is here."

"Of course, you know I don't believe you. Will you show it to me?"

"Yes."

"Right now? Today?"

"No, not today. But one day I will show it to you."

"Oh, someday," he countered. "That's what they always say. Always someday—but never today."

"You don't believe me."

"I'll believe it when I see it." He settled back into the chair, as if that ended the matter.

To his surprise, she slipped on her moccasins, stood up, and started for the door. "Come on."

He had a comfortable feeling of lethargy, as if he were about to doze off sitting in the chair. When he stood up he felt a tingling sensation at the tips of his fingers and toes as if they had gone to sleep while he was sitting there. He roused himself and followed her through the open door and down along the path. The sun was a great round ball of flame as it hovered over the horizon.

"It's a little late in the day to go poking around caves," he observed. "Or is it dark in the daytime, too? I didn't think to bring my flashlight."

"We'll be able to see," she assured him. "We won't go all the way through—not today. It wouldn't be a good idea. Some other time we'll start earlier and take the grand tour. But now we can just satisfy your curiosity that it's there."

They reached the springs and she walked a few feet past. She lifted aside the lush growth of wild grapes and waited for him to come alongside. He could see nothing, and wondered if she had been only teasing after all.

"Take my hand," she cautioned, "and don't let go of it until we get back out here."

"Why?"

"We might get separated and you don't want to go wandering around a strange cave all by yourself."

"Think I might panic?" He smiled at the idea.

"No, I just wanted to hold your hand, and that's the best excuse I could think of."

"You don't need an excuse."

"Well, then—ask a silly question and you get a silly answer."

She took his hand and went behind the vines, pulling him after her. He couldn't see a thing and the leaves and tendrils brushed along his face and arms. Then she came to a full stop, and in the smothering darkness he felt something crawling along the back of his neck. Thinking it must be a spider or some creepy-crawly thing, he slapped at it and it squashed in his hand. He brought his hand around in front of him and felt the frustration of not being able to see it. The sudden light gave him the impression that it was blood and goo. But it was only purple grape juice. He had caught a grape and squashed it. Only then did he realize that they were in the cave and there was light. He looked for the source but could not find it. It was not bright; he realized it had only appeared so at first because of the contrast from complete darkness. It was a hazy, diffused light everywhere, except for a shining crystal stone near the entrance.

The walls were perfectly straight—too straight to be natural formation. And all the way around were figures of animals and birds and people, possibly—or partially. He started around the walls to examine them more closely, and she followed along. In the muted light he couldn't tell whether it was painting or carving. The cavern was not very large, but it seemed larger because there was nothing in it but a large stone table with a bowl on it and a stool behind it. The bowl was large and ornate. It looked like copper. It was carved like a coiled snake, with the head extending outward from the rim at the top. With two shining eyes staring straight into his eyes.

It looked so real that he reached out to feel of it to make sure. He had the distinct feeling that the head was moving forward to meet his hand, when suddenly the light went out. It so startled him that he jumped away, tripped over the stool, and fell flat on the floor. In the complete silence and darkness he lay perfectly still and tried to think what to do next. Then there was a faint sound, like a dried leaf scraping over stone. He crawled frantically in the opposite direction to get away, until his head bumped against the wall. He was stunned, and hesitated until the pain subsided, and then realized that he had lost his bearings and had no idea which way was out. He lay there, petrified with pain and fright, while the scraping sound came closer and closer. Then her hand touched his shoulder and followed it down to take his hand. She helped him to his feet and guided him gently to the entrance, through the vines, and out into the open air.

The sun had set and through the gathering twilight they walked silently back to the house. Not a word had been spoken since they first entered the cave. The evening noises of the birds and little forest animals settling in for the night were a welcome normal sound. A bullfrog called out, "rivet," and another answered back.

By the time they reached the back door, he was feeling a little foolish.

"Well," he said, "you do put on a good show."

"Would you like another cup of tea?"

"Tea? No, thanks. I think I'll stick to Scotch and soda from now on. It may give me delusions and hallucinations, but they're the kind I'm used to."

"Scotch and soda it is, then. I think I'll have some coffee, though, because I have much to do tonight and I'll be up until all hours."

"Where did the light come from?" he asked. "Did you just say 'Let there be light' and there it was?"

"No," she smiled. "It isn't quite that simple—but really no great mystery after all. Did you notice the crystal stone at the entrance? There is an opening to the outside on the opposite wall. You don't notice it outside because it's near the springs. When the sun is at a certain spot near the horizon, and the stone is placed in the right position, it catches the light directly from the sun and the facets of the stone reflect the light throughout the cavern. So—I push the stone, and the lights go on!"

"Not magic, huh?" he mused. "Then why did the lights go out? There's no way you could have pushed that stone again."

"That's right," she agreed. "But don't be a button-down mind. Just because I turned on the light doesn't mean that I also turned it off."

"It turned itself off?"

"Well, you might say that—in a way. You see, the sun disappeared below the horizon. And the moment there was no more sun—no more light."

He thought about it while he sipped his drink. "You know, I must have panicked. I heard a noise and thought it was that snake coming after me."

"Like this?" She slid her moccasin across the bare floor. "That was me looking for you. It's a good thing you bumped your head and stayed put, or we might be there yet, playing follow-the-leader around and around and around."

"It all sounds so natural and reasonable, the way you explain it." He put down his empty glass and went to the front door.

"Do you always leave your doors open—even when you're out?"

"Only on Midsummer's Eve," she admitted.

"Is that one of your holidays? Were you expecting someone?"

"Not really. It's just an old superstition, so old nobody knows how it started. Midsummer's Eve, they say, is when the Little People walk along their paths to get to—wherever it is that Little People go; and if a house is on their path and the doors are open, they walk right through and go on about their business. But if the doors are closed, they tear the house down or burn it up, or push it out of the way."

"And this house is on the fairy path?"

"I can't say that it is," she said. "But on the other hand, I can't say for sure that it isn't."

"Do you really believe that stuff?"

"I like to. I understand that these old superstitions work just the same, whether you believe them or not." She shrugged. "Anyway, the breeze is wonderful on a hot night. And what could I possibly have here that anyone would bother to steal?"

"You. You could be murdered in your bed, you know."

"Do people murder people around here?"

"Only witches on Midsummer's Eve," he said. Then he waved goodbye and walked away into the summer night.

He had reached his own front door and was fumbling for the key when a thought struck him. He had completely forgotten to borrow the cup of bourbon. Oh well, he'd just have to go back for another visit. Things were certainly looking up for the rest of the long hot summer.

LYNDA MARTINEZ FOLEY

Night of the Radishes

The "Night of the Radishes" festival is held on the zocalo in front of the government palace in Oaxaca, Mexico. Booths are arranged to display scenes from history, the Bible, or folklore created from carved radishes of all sizes and colors. The most inventive and original receive prizes. Held on December 23rd of each year, it is a night known for magic, mystery, and mayhem...

MANUELA SIGHED AGAIN AS SHE DREW THE FINELY WOVEN blanket over her naked body. It was long past midnight and her husband, Juan, still had not returned to their home in the town of Cuilapan nestled at the base of the western Oaxacan mountains. She had waited patiently, then impatiently, then resignedly as she lay in the huge featherbed, watching the hours tick by on the gold timepiece that had been a wedding gift from the mayor.

She reached under the soft, luxurious covers and poked ashamedly at her firm flat belly. Earlier tonight she had prayed to change that belly, asking the gods to convince Juan to give her a child. She had almost everything she had ever dreamed of: the finest home in town, household items no other townspeople could afford, clothes and jewelry befitting the woman belonging to the local tribute collector. She had been a dutiful wife since their marriage a year ago in the great city of Oaxaca. After being appointed *cacique*, Juan had no problem arranging for their nuptials to take place in the courtyard of the regional governor's palace.

Manuela had been a typical sixteen-year-old bride full of romantic innocence, until she discovered she merely satisfied her husband's growing need for control and wealth. He went elsewhere for sexual fulfillment, except when he forced Manuela to obey his strange sexaual demands that never included regular intercourse. She was clinically still a virgin, and her husband reveled in the infamy he gained by having an "untouched bride." None doubted his manhood, but all respected the authority and power that allowed him to keep such a beautiful young bride "unridden yet tamed."

Until this moment, Manuela had believed that she wanted a child more than anything in the world. But now a new ache, deep inside her, caused her body to sweat and shiver. She blushed at this sudden need to understand the rapture and mysteries of womanhood. She no longer desired to procreate. She was no longer satisfied playing with baubles and finery; instead she hungered for pleasure and fulfillment.

Manuela stared out the expensive glass window of her bedroom and watched the full moon set behind the fragrant flowering trees. Juan had promised to stay home on this quiet, warm December night, for tomorrow he would journey to the city to celebrate the Night of the Radishes, then *Noche Buena* and the rest of the *Navidad* festivals at the governor's estate. Her husband wouldn't allow his young bride to attend the festivities, so he had agreed to be with her this night instead of nuzzling the cheaply dressed whores at the town cantina. But he had lied again, and she meekly accepted his betrayal, just as she had accepted his betrayals throughout their marriage.

Manuela's loins ached with a strange emptiness. She felt hollow and powerless as she waited for the morning light. But when the cock finally crowed and she heard Juan stumbling through the front door, Manuela experienced surprise as her soul refilled with new strength and purpose.

Some small part of her wondered if perhaps Juan deserved another chance. Perhaps if she were somehow a better wife. . . .

Her drunken husband entered the bedroom and laughed loudly. He waved a half-empty bottle of expensive mescal at her and shouted, "Drink with me! I am going to be a proud papa!" He fell onto their bed, still balancing the blue glass bottle.

Manuela was stunned at first. As she reached out to grab the bottle, she wondered if Juan was actually admitting he wanted to make a baby with her. But her soaring heart lost its wings when he sat up and roughly groped her, calling her "Elena, *bonita* Elena." She now realized exactly what her drunken husband was celebrating: he must have gotten his favorite whore, Elena, pregnant. He called out "Elena!" one last time before he fell across Manuela and passed out.

Manuela pushed Juan's inert form off of her. The bottle of mescal rolled off the bed and clanked onto the tile floor, spilling its precious contents. Manuela didn't care. She sobbed as she cursed Juan's unconscious form. She no longer knew what she wanted, but she knew what she did not want: to bring a new life into her terrible world.

She dressed quickly and walked through the main living quarters, pausing to look at her lovely home. The living area was clean and welcoming, due to Manuela's hard work and effort. She refused to hire a servant or buy a slave when she could easily keep house for her and her husband.

She walked into her bright blue tiled kitchen and breathed in the scent of honey from the fresh waxcomb she had located and taken the previous day. She dipped one forefinger into the gooey mess and avidly licked the sweetness, the only breakfast she had time for today. After gulping cool water from a pewter pitcher, she grabbed her most prized possession from its hiding place under the cooking stones: the crystal necklace her mother had given her before she had died. This one piece of jewelry, with its rumored magical stones, meant more to her than any of the gifts and jewelry showered upon her by Juan. Manuela wrapped the necklace like a shiny bracelet on her right arm, then left her house and headed up the dirt road toward the trail to the mountain home of Yolanda the dark witch, or *bruja*.

The morning sun had barely risen, but by the time she reached the trail, Manuela's carefully embroidered clothing began to stick to her body. Though tired from lack of sleep, Manuela continued the arduous climb up the craggy hillside toward the witch's home. Her strength came from her determination that since her husband would not give her any of the pleasures of womanhood, she would find a way to make sure he could not receive the pleasures of manhood. The *bruja* would help decide the appropriate revenge.

Finally, she reached the small opening between two enormous boulders that served as the gateway to the witch. Although overheated and panting from exertion, Manuela hesitated at the entrance to the old woman's dwelling place. She shuddered as she felt an uncommon chill, her resolve wavering. She remembered her mother's sharp warnings about "old Yolanda and her evil ways."

Manuela's mother, Raquela, had been *curandera* of the village before she died. Her mother had used magic to heal the villagers instead of curse them. Unfortunately, Manuela had shown no sign of her mother's healing gift, so the village no longer had the services of a *curandera*. The villagers were forced to utilize the services of the dark witch, just as Manuela was prepared to do.

Manuela pushed her sweaty dark locks away from her sun-browned face and forced her body through the gateway to the magically corrupt *brujeria* of old Yolanda.

The passageway opened into a small grassy glade with two leafy green jacaranda trees forming a roof over a small thatched hovel built against the mountain. Manuela could hear but not see burbling water from a brook or spring. She saw no sign of any living creature.

"Old Yolanda!" she cried out as she approached the small dwelling. "Old Yolanda! I, Manuela, daughter of Raquela, have come to ask a favor."

"I give no favors," a raspy old voice said from behind Manuela. She whirled around instantly. There stood the village *bruja* known as old Yolanda, her gnarled hands clutching a snake-shaped cane, and her long gray hair an untidy mass of tangles that covered her shoulders. She wore layered patchwork clothing that was surprisingly clean, though threadbare. She reeked of strange exotic scents that almost made Manuela gag.

"And I have no need for fine possessions purchased with tax money taken from the peasants," the *bruja* said.

Manuela didn't deny the old crone's accusations. Instead she bravely faced the dark witch and slowly removed the crystal jewelry from her arm. The *bruja*'s hooded eyes glittered as she recognized the fabled gems. Manuela thought the hag would snatch the necklace away, but the old woman slowly extended her palm and waited for Manuela to drop the crystals into her hand.

The *bruja* closed her fingers and nodded appreciatively. "You can buy many favors from me with some crystals from your mother's necklace. Come inside." She stiffly staggered toward the thatch hut. Manuela followed.

Upon entering the small dwelling, Manuela realized she had only entered an anteroom. The hovel provided an entrance to a huge cavern in the mountain. The cavern's walls glistened from water reflecting hundreds of burning candles that littered the floor. Manuela gasped at the strange, flickering beauty of the cave. She breathed cool clean air, not the smoky remnants of the burning candles. Either Yolanda used great magics to purify the air or there were other openings that provided ventilation.

Old Yolanda stiffly picked her way through the burning candles and stopped at a formation of rocks that seemed to be carved into a rough table and chair. The *bruja* sat down and placed her snake-headed cane across her knees. She indicated that Manuela should stand across the table from her.

Manuela timidly stepped around the burning candles until she stood facing the dark witch across the table.

The *bruja* placed the crystal necklace, an obsidian knife, and an enormous white radish on the stone table. She mumbled a few words and looked up at Manuela with a kind, sad look.

"Little daughter," she whispered, and Manuela flinched at her use of the familiar endearment. "Little daughter, you know I cannot give the power of life to you. Only a *curandera* can help you to conceive. So are you here to request a darker favor of me?"

Manuela ignored the *bruja*'s question and stared at the amazingly large, pale radish, thinking how perfect a carving it would make for tonight's celebration of radish images in the city. She saw part of a brow and a square chin in the white radish's shape. Even someone with little skill like her could shape it into a representation of a man's face, perhaps even her husband's face, she thought as she stared.

"What do you want?" the *bruja's* gravelly voice whispered.

"To punish my husband," Manuela said without taking her eyes off of the radish.

"Are you sure?" the *bruja* asked.

Manuela thought of the intensely powerful aches that had gathered deep in her body the previous night. She pondered her choices: revenge or fulfillment. She decided on the former.

"Yes, I am sure that is what I want."

"Hmmmm," the *bruja* said. "The chicken can only obey the rooster for so long. And what would you have me do to this rooster of yours?" she asked with a gap-toothed smirk.

There was a long silence as the aged witch and young woman eyed each other.

"I want to take his manhood," Manuela said bitterly.

Yolanda pushed the shiny black knife toward the angry woman. "Here. This will do the job while he is sleeping."

"No!" Manuela shouted, but not in horror. "No," she said more calmly. "I want something more subtle, something that will deny him as he denied me. Something that will hurt him deeply as he has hurt me. Do that, and I will give you not just a few crystals, but the entire necklace!"

The *bruja* hissed her pleasure. "*Si, si si.* A worthy revenge is warranted." The old woman stood and used her strange cane to hobble around the cavern. She gathered candles, plants, and other strange items as Manuela waited patiently. Finally, the *bruja* finished her preparations and approached the table to sit once more.

"Does your husband wear something like this?" the old woman asked, while shoving a small silver talisman at Manuela. Manuela carefully examined the exquisite silver form of a butterfly hanging from a rough brown cord. The wings of the creature seemed to be made of flames.

"No, my husband wears nothing like this. Why would he?"

"This charm protects the wearer from curses," the dark witch cackled. "Perhaps you would like to purchase it?"

Manuela shook her head and handed the silver butterfly back to the *bruja*. The old woman quickly shoved the talisman back into the folds of cloth near her cleavage, then grabbed the dark knife. She slit her left palm and slapped the bleeding cut against the large white radish. She gently placed the bloodied knife on the table and began to chant and throw herbs and plant stalks into the candle fire surrounding her.

As the cavern grew hazy, Manuela began to feel dizzy. She breathed in strange-smelling smoke and coughed twice. She stared at the old woman's hands and watched the blood-tinged radish begin to move out from the *bruja*'s hand and cross the table of its own accord. It writhed in a lifelike manner as it crawled toward Manuela.

"Say his name!" the *bruja* cried between gritted teeth. "Before you pick it up you must say his name, say who he is!"

Manuela shrank away from the large root as it neared the edge of her side of the table. But once again her resolve for revenge won out over her fear.

"Juan!" she cried. "The mayor's *cacique*, Juan Mendoza!" As she reached out to grab the radish it almost leaped up to meet her fingers. She stared at the now pink radish, lying still and lifeless in her hands.

"He must eat of that radish tonight, *La Noche de las Rabanos*, the Night of the Radishes," the *bruja* instructed. "If you do as I say he will receive greater punishment than you can imagine."

Manuela nodded and turned to leave, purposefully giving no thanks. Her mother had warned her that to thank evil was to welcome it into one's heart.

"One last thing, Manuela, daughter of Raquela," the crone cried out. "You cannot change your mind. Once he has tasted the root, you cannot change your mind."

Manuela hurried across the cavern floor, her hands firmly clutching the strange root. The candles on the floor flickered out as she rushed past. She ran back through the thatch hut and across the grassy glade. She quickly squeezed through the boulder gateway, ignoring the pain as her elbows scraped against the rocks. Stopping to catch her breath, she tucked the magic radish into her bosom and began the long climb down the mountain to her small village, oblivious to the heat of the noonday sun.

Manuela smiled as she remembered how much Juan loved spicy radish soup and tortillas. She would cook a very special snack for him to take to the city festival tonight.

For a brief moment she contemplated following her husband into the city, so that she might observe the culmination of her revenge. Instead, she decided to wait at home as usual, until Juan returned and begged for her help.

Once again Manuela sat perched on the edge of the huge featherbed, waiting for her husband to return home. However, the moon had barely set when she heard Juan open the front door and cry out her name.

"Manuela! Manuela! Please help me," he sobbed as he staggered into the house. He rushed into their bedroom and fell to his knees, pressing his tear-stained face against her legs.

"Forgive me. Forgive me," he begged. "I've been cursed and I need you to help me."

Manuela was surprised she felt no joy as the seeds of her revenge began to blossom. Her husband sat devastated and powerless at her feet, yet all she wanted to know was exactly how the curse had manifested.

"Please, my husband. Be calm. Tell me what happened," she soothed as she stroked the slick dark hair on his head.

Juan held her soft hands in his coarse ones and explained. "The gods have cursed me. I cannot lay with a woman ever again! There must be some way you can help me."

"If I am to help you," Manuela said in a calm, no-nonsense voice, "I must know exactly what occurred. Do not lie or I myself will curse you," she threatened, ignoring her conscience.

She could tell Juan was embarrassed, so she knelt on the cold floor beside him, embracing his shoulders and leaning her cheek against his. "Tell me, my husband."

Juan choked back a sob and spoke of his uneventful trip to the city. He admitted he had been accompanied by Elena, and had even offered to share his snack with her on the way. She had refused.

He and Elena had arrived in Oaxaca City and entered the grounds of the governor's palace to celebrate *La Noche de las Rabanos*. However, when the revelry had barely begun, he found himself consumed with passion for his glowing, pregnant mistress, Elena. As he stroked her long black hair, kissed her neck, he found himself growing erect with excitement. But when he reached out to her chin and turned her head to face his, Elena had transformed into a rotting, skeletal corpse. Juan had screamed and tried to push her away, but she had clung to him, her maggot-infested mouth asking, "What's wrong? What's wrong?"

Juan had shoved her aside and run away through the *zocalo,* knocking over displays and booths. He ran straight into the arms of a thirteen-year-old girl, dressed in her festival finery. She tried to help him, calm him, treat his injuries. She had reminded him of his Manuela, her smile sweetly innocent as she pressed a cool wet cloth against his forehead. She had smelled of honey and gardenias.

Juan couldn't help himself. He grew excited in her arms, but when he looked at her, she too turned into a putrescent corpse with sunken eyes and flayed skin. Once again he had scrambled away in confused fear.

A colleague of Elena's named Jade had found him, huddled and sobbing in a heap of refuse. She had taken him back to her poor but clean room, sponged him off, and given him a fresh shirt. Juan had offered her money in return, and she had misunderstood.

Jade had disrobed and began to kiss Juan, but he had lost all interest in the sexual act. She had continued to kiss him, and he had politely responded without fervor. But her professional hands had touched and caressed Juan until he began to kiss her back in earnest. He softly bit at her lips as he felt desire stirring in his loins.

Suddenly he had reeled back, gagging as Jade's fleshy lower lip seemingly came off into his mouth. Once again a woman who had aroused him had become a stinking carcass whose rotting arms reached out to hold him.

Juan had fled the demons in the city, vomiting twice before he caught a ride on a farmer's cart back to the village.

"Imagine me, Juan Mendoza, leader of men, lying sick for an hour in the stinking hay of a farmer's wagon." He gave an anguished laugh. "The gods have spoken to me. They directed me here, to you." Juan continued, as he kissed Manuela's hands. "I promise never to lust for another woman. I promise to treat you with the love you deserve. I believe you are the only one who can help me."

He stood and picked her up and laid her gently on the opulent bed.

Manuela sat stunned as her husband carefully undressed her. He stroked her body tenderly and kissed her, his eyes open and wary. But soon desire overcame him. He looked upon Manuela's face and screamed, leaping off the bed. Manuela knew she had turned into a corpse in her husband's mind.

Juan crouched in the corner of their small bedroom, naked and moaning. She walked over to him and touched his hair. He bleated like a small frightened animal. She saw that his diminished passion had caused his sex to hang flaccidly.

"Look at me!" Manuela commanded, surprised at the strength of her voice.

Juan opened one eye and sighed. "You are yourself," he said simply. He kneeled at her feet and plaintively looked up at her, like a dog waiting for a bone.

Manuela happily instructed him. "Put on some night clothes. Come to the bed. We will deal with this in the morning."

Juan obeyed her as if used to it and crawled into their bed. He begged her not to tell anyone of his strange affliction. He thanked her over and over again, pathetically promising that he would take care of her, be faithful to her, if only she would continue to be his wife. His fear of losing his community standing and dominance was nearly palpable.

Manuela felt nothing but pity for him and for herself. She ached with unfulfilled desire. Her revenge was meaningless. She had gotten what she wanted, but had now realized she needed so much more.

She shook Juan lightly and whispered, "Tomorrow I will visit old Yolanda on your behalf to see if there is something she can do for you. I will take good care of you, my husband," she lied. They fell asleep with arms entwined, together in body, but separate in soul.

Early the next morning Manuela once again made the long trek up to old Yolanda's *brujeria*. The dark witch sat quietly on a stone in the grassy glade.

Manuela skipped the pleasantries. "I've changed my mind," she bluntly told Yolanda.

The *bruja* cackled and shook her head. "I warned you, little daughter. You cannot change your mind. The curse stays no matter what you feel or believe."

Manuela gave a strange half-smile as she played with the lace on her skirt. "No, I've changed my mind about the talisman. I'd like to buy the butterfly charm to protect myself from curses." She bravely stared at the *bruja*. "I plan to enjoy myself for awhile and don't want Juan or anyone else to interfere."

Old Yolanda solemnly pulled the butterfly charm from a pocket and handed it to Manuela.

"Thank you," Manuela said deliberately. The *bruja's* eyes opened wide with delight.

"What is the charge?" Manuela asked.

The *bruja* grinned as she said, "No charge." One of her rheumy eyes winked at Manuela. "I'm sure I will see you again, *si*?"

Manuela nodded and placed the necklace over her head and around her neck. The silver charm burned for a moment when it touched her skin, but she hardly noticed. She numbly walked out of the *bruja's* domain and climbed back down the mountain to face the even darker, twisted world that awaited her, a world she could manipulate and finally enjoy.

M. L. SMOKER

Twins' Story

TIME AND TIME AGAIN NO ONE TOLD HIM TO STOP DRINKING.
Over the long years no one could stop themselves from not telling him that
he would die from it. They all knew. In fact, they saw it every single day.
Everyone just sat back and waited for that moment mixed with alcohol that
would end it all. Then, they could finally sit back on their creaky porches
with a speck of satisfaction and say they knew it all along.

At the big basketball tournament in Glasgow he drank a pint of
whiskey, alone in his car in the parking lot and then tumbled in to sit on the
players' bench. His sons, the twins, who could make shots with style and
grace from the three-point line even when there was no such thing as a three-
point line yet, hung their heads almost down to their ankles they were so
ashamed. Ashamed in front of all the white spectators at least. Their dad,
Old Spotted Wolf, sat there on that bench and every time the coach called
a time-out, he'd jump up and scream plays at them like it was nobody's business. Too bad all he could remember were moves from his long lost quarter-
back days. His boys just ignored those intoxicated attempts to have them
run off left tackle. And those white folks, who could forget about them?
They sat in the bleachers, shoulders slouched over, all crowded in the steamy

gymnasium to watch their farm boys who would soon take over the family businesses. When they saw Old Spotted Wolf they laughed and tossed disgusted looks into heaps on the court. What was that old drunk Indian doing down there anyway? Didn't someone have the decency to kick him out of the gym? Didn't someone have the decency to kick him out of town?

By the time the twins reached the rez and dragged him off the yellow bus and into the house they had forgotten all about it and suddenly he became just like everyone else again. They weren't so ashamed anymore. There, mixed with all his relations, he stumbled and fell and cut open his head or wrecked his car into a tree just like all the rest. Their dad, Old Spotted Wolf, could drink with the best of them at the tavern bar, they'd say with laughter. Sometimes all they could do was laugh.

They lost the game that night in Glasgow, 79–75. It all fell apart in that second half. That's what usually happened when Old Spotted Wolf got those urges of a proud father and decided to drive to Havre or Scobey or wherever to watch those two boys of his. August and Austin could sense his drunken arrival as the humiliation would carefully creep up into their bellies like the moves of a grass dancer. They wouldn't even have to look at each other to know that their magic, the only thing they could say they owned, was gone as soon as they smelled him. That horrible aroma filled with despair and pride and whiskey.

Now that magic, it was real and it was powerful. It was just about the only thing their mom bothered to give them besides their breath. That and too much candy so that they lost most of their teeth by the time they were fourteen. She hadn't meant for it to happen, it was just that when all the commodity cheese and beans and flour were devoured by her two growing boys she'd feel so guilty she'd scrounge up enough change to manage to buy them half the shelf of candy at the smoke shack. Sometime between packs of Bubble Yum and Three Musketeers they lost a few teeth because of her attempts to make up for the rumbles in their stomach late at night. She left right around then. Maybe she couldn't stand to see those gaps or maybe she didn't like to look in those four eyes that were just like their dad's anymore. She walked out of the broken front door and down the empty street one midnight, black hair slipping out of a loose braid. Probably didn't even know where she was headed. August and Austin watched from the window of the bedroom they shared that night as she walked away from them forever without even saying good-bye. They called out to her in their silences, saying that they needed her still, loved her fry bread, would always laugh at her dumb jokes, but she pretended not to hear them because it just hurt too much to know that they belonged to her and would always look like a spotted wolf. Damn all the spotted wolves she had ever known, football fans even, she should have known from the beginning. Her boys would play basketball. She whispered that to them in the moonlight as she turned the corner and disappeared.

They never saw her again, and they never talked about her again. Took the one photograph they had of her leaning up against an old Buick out by the mission school and burned it unceremoniously in the backyard without saying a word but all the while worshipping that ash that wiped her from their existence. But no matter how hard they tried they could still feel her magic from deep within their chests whenever they picked up a basketball. Maybe because she loved the Celtics so much. They couldn't answer any of the whys or hows, but they knew it was because of her they were co-captains of the Frazer Bearcubs and co-MVPs of the league ever since they were sophomores in high school. They had the touch that she had given them. No one could beat them on the court, all except for their dad. Probably because the same was true for their mom: no one could beat her except for that Old Spotted Wolf.

They were famous on the rez. Even more famous than any movie star on the TV because they were real flesh and blood who still managed to seem unearthly from the stands of a basketball court. For a season, kids idolized them like they were Magic Johnsons. Even the big city papers wrote an article on the unstoppable Spotted Wolf twins. They knew that the only one who could really stop them was their dad. For days on end they sweated it out, wondering whether or not he would make the drive to Helena in a couple of weeks for the state tournament. His whiskey- or vodka- or gin-filled presence meant they would lose for sure. They realized just how desperate they were one night after another reporter had called the neighbor's place to get an interview with them since they hadn't had a

phone in three years at their house. Realizing that this was their big, perhaps one and only chance at something, anything, they decided to sabotage
the old station wagon—that damn dependable piece of junk that always
managed to carry their dad to all those away games like a real warrior. With
just a few pulled plugs here, a cut wire there, they felt assured of the state
championship.

Their day arrived and they found themselves standing in the biggest
gymnasium they had ever seen. August and Austin stood center court in
their baby blue jerseys and shook hands with two players from North
Billings High—the two white kids hadn't ever even heard of Frazer and
didn't even know what an Assiniboine was for that matter. The twins felt
all of that in just the millisecond that they touched their opponents' hands
and wanted to win more than anything else they could ever have in the
world. Their world wasn't all that big anyway and nothing could be more
huge within it than the next two hours. Two hours that they prayed their
dad would miss. He could always hitchhike, they thought simultaneously.

First quarter. Combined they scored fourteen of the Bearcubs' nineteen
points. At half time, up by seven, the twins walked into the locker room with
the taste of a championship and their mother's cooking in their mouths. She
was there, in their hands, in their movements. Her memory wandered
silently into the room and for the first time in years neither of them bothered to push and shove her away. Her memory was warm and alive.

Sometime into the third quarter it began to happen. Their hearts
began beating a little faster. Austin missed two free throws and then they
knew for sure. Old Spotted Wolf would walk in any second and make his
grandest debut ever. They thought that they could see him out of the corner of their eye, turn to look, and then miss an easy pass to the other. Their
frustration tore into their shins and ankles as they ran harder and dribbled
faster in the only attempt for something they might ever be able to say they
earned in his life.

Thirty seven and a half minutes, the same exact amount of time it took
Old Spotted Wolf to get picked up on Highway 2 by a truck driver headed
to Helena. Thirty-seven and a half dizzying, heart-wrenching minutes
later they sank to their knees as they begged for the sound of the buzzer to

make them go deaf or blind, anything painful just so that this other pain would not seem like their death.

They remained there in that same spot, huddled on the floor side by side until the stands had cleared and their teammates were already long off to the showers. When they looked up, he was still standing there, watching the only two things he had left in the world sob so hard their tears created a puddle that seemed to swallow them up. When they finally looked up into his eyes, he knew. He had single-handedly managed to take away from them the only thing that could matter, all after he had already taken away from them the only other thing that had ever mattered. He knew they hated him, and he understood why she had hated him too.

Some time later when the snow had melted and the weather was warm enough for mosquitoes, the twins walked up, one after the other, and received the only other thing they would achieve in their lives, a high school diploma. It's just a piece of paper, they thought together as they got in their dusty brown Nova and drove out of the parking lot toward the bridge with the dried-up riverbed. The bridge was the next best place for a bunch of underage kids to party and guzzle down cheap beer when their parents and aunts and uncles and cousins would probably already be passing out in their own living rooms. On their way out of town, Austin and August crossed the old railroad tracks, never even bothering to notice the new white metal cross on the red post stuck there, right on the side of the road, just waiting to turn rusty and orange. . . .

The look in their eyes had told him enough the night of the game. They wanted him gone, and he knew that no distance one could ever travel would be far enough for them or her. He simply nodded and pushed the exit door open with his back and stepped into the night already filled with sorrow. The boys looked at each other and found no regret in the other's eyes.

How many miles he walked that night he never knew. Somewhere down the road from Helena someone from the rez, he couldn't remember their face, picked him up and drove him home. He didn't even bother to go inside. Instead he hopped into the old wagon and turned the key that was always there and wasn't surprised at all that she started this time. She must know she's carrying a real warrior now, he thought. A real warrior who had the courage to park them both right there on the road and wait. Wait for the sound of heavy metal on metal in the distance. Wait for the glowing eye bulging in the darkness of early morning. Wait for the loud horrible and beautiful crash that would take away his pain, his sons' pain, her pain.

Right in that very last moment he almost smiled when he thought they would all think he was just another dumb drunk Indian. And he hadn't even touched a bottle in twenty-four hours, the longest sober stint he could ever remember having.

Compatriots

LUCY HEARD THE CAR'S MOTOR WIND DOWN BEFORE IT TURNED off the gravel road a quarter of a mile west of the house. Maybe it was Bunky. She hurried and left the outhouse. She couldn't run if she wanted to. It would be such a relief to have this pregnancy over with. She couldn't see the color of the vehicle, for the slab fence was between the house and the road. That was just as well. She'd been caught in the outhouse a few times, and it still embarrassed her to have a car approach while she was in there.

She got inside the house just as the car came into view. It was her aunt, Flora. Lucy looked at the clock. It was seven-thirty. She wondered what was going on so early in the morning. Flora and a young white woman approached the house. Bob barked furiously at them. Lucy opened the door and yelled at him. "I don't know what's wrong with Bob; he never barks at me," said Flora.

"He's probably barking at her," explained Lucy. "Not many whites come here."

"Oh, this is Hilda Afferbach. She's from Germany," began Flora. "Remember? I told you I met her at the Calgary Stampede? Well, she got off the seven o'clock bus, and I don't have time to drive her all the way down to my house. I took her over to my mother's, but she's getting ready to go to Lethbridge. Can she stay with you till I get off work?"

Lucy smiled. She knew she was boxed in. "Yeah, but I've got no running water in the house. You have to go outside to use the toilet," she said, looking at Hilda.

"Oh, that's okay," her aunt answered. "She's studying about Indians, anyway. Might as well get the true picture, right? Oh, Hilda, this is my niece, Lucy." Flora lowered her voice and asked, "Where's Bunky?"

"He never came home last night. I was hoping it was him coming home. He's not supposed to miss any more work. I've got his lunch fixed in case he shows up." Lucy poured some water from a blue plastic water jug into a white enamel basin and washed her hands and face. "I haven't even had time to make coffee. I couldn't sleep waiting for him to come home." She poured water into a coffeemaker and measured out the coffee into the paper filter.

"I'd have some coffee if it was ready, but I think I'd better get to work. We have to punch in now; it's a new rule. Can't travel on Indian time anymore," said Flora. She opened the door and stepped out, then turned to say, "I think the lost has returned," and continued down the steps.

The squeak of the dusty truck's brakes signaled Bunky's arrival. He strode toward the door, barely acknowledging Flora's presence. He came in and took the lunch pail Lucy had. "I stayed at Herbie's," was all he said before he turned and went out. He started the truck and beeped the horn.

"I'll go see what he wants." She motioned to Flora to wait.

When Bunky left, she went to Flora: "Maybe it's a good thing you came here. Bunky didn't want to go to work 'cause he had a hangover. When he found out Hilda was going to be here all day, he decided he'd rather go to work."

"If I don't have to leave the office this afternoon, I'll bring the car over and you can drive Hilda around to look at the reserve, okay?"

"Sure, that'll be good. I can go and do my laundry in Spitzee." She surveyed the distant horizon. The Rockies were spectacular, blue and distinct. It would be a nice day for a drive. She hoped it would be a repeat of yesterday, not too hot, but, as she stood there, she noticed tiny heat waves over the wheat fields. Well, maybe it won't be a repeat, she thought. Her baby kicked inside of her, and she said, "Okay, I'd better go tend to the guest." She didn't relish having a white visitor, but Flora had done her a lot of favors and Hilda seemed nice.

And she was. Hilda made friends with the kids, Jason and Melissa, answering their many questions about Germany as Lucy cooked. She ate heartily, complimenting Lucy on her cooking even though it was only the usual scrambled eggs and fried potatoes with toast and coffee. After payday, there'd be sausages or ham, but payday was Friday and today was only Tuesday.

"Have you heard of Helmut Walking Eagle?" Hilda wanted to know.

"Yeah, well, I really don't know him to talk to him, but I know what he looks like. He's from Germany, too. I always see him at Indian dances. He dresses up like an Indian." She had an urge to tell her that most of the Indians wished Helmut would disappear.

"I want to see him," Hilda said. "I heard about him and I read a book he wrote. He seems to know a lot about the Indians, and he's been accepted into their religious society. I hope he can tell me things I can take home. People in Germany are really interested in Indians. They even have clubs."

Lucy's baby kicked, and she held her hand over the spot. "My baby kicks if I sit too long. I guess he wants to do the dishes."

Hilda got up quickly and said, "Let me do the dishes. You can take care of the laundry."

"No, you're the visitor. I can do them," Lucy countered. But Hilda was persistent, and Lucy gave in.

Flora showed up just after twelve with the information that there was a sun-dance going on on the north side of the reserve. "They're already camping. Let's go there after work. Pick me up around four."

"I can't wait to go to the sun-dance! Do you go to them often?" Hilda asked Lucy.

"No, I never have. I don't know much about them," Lucy said.

"But why? Don't you believe in it? It's your culture!" Hilda's face showed concern.

"Well, they never had sun-dances here—in my whole life there's never been a sun-dance here."

"Really, is that true? But I thought you have them every year here."

"Not here. Over on the Blood Reserve they do and some places in the States. But not here."

"But don't you want to go to a sun-dance? I think it's so exciting!" Hilda moved forward in her seat and looked hopefully at Lucy.

Lucy smiled at her eagerness. "No, I don't care to go. It's mostly those mixed-up people who are in it. You see, Indian religion just came back here on the reserve a little while ago, and there are different groups who all quarrel over which way to practice it. Some use Sioux ways, and others use Cree. It's just a big mess," she said, shaking her head.

Hilda looked at Lucy, and Lucy got the feeling she was telling her things she didn't want to hear.

Lucy had chosen this time of day to do her wash. The Happy Suds Laundromat would be empty. As a rule, the Indians didn't show up till after lunch with their endless garbage bags of laundry.

After they had deposited their laundry in the machines, Lucy, Hilda, and the kids sauntered down the main street to a cafe for lunch. An unkempt Indian man dogged them, talking in Blackfoot.

"Do you know what he's saying?" asked Hilda.

"He wants money. He's related to my husband. Don't pay any attention to him. He always does this," said Lucy. "I used to give him money, but he just drinks it up."

The cafe was a cool respite from the heat outside, and the cushioned seats in the booth felt good. They sat by the window and ordered hamburgers, fries, and lemonade. The waitress brought tall, frosted glasses, and beads of water dripped from them.

"Hello, Lucy," a man's shaky voice said, just when they were really enjoying their lunch. They turned to look at the Indian standing behind Hilda. He was definitely ill. His eyes held pain, and he looked as though he might collapse from whatever ailed him. His hands shook, perspiration covered his face, and his eyes roamed the room constantly.

Lucy moved over to make room for him, but he kept standing and asked her, "Could you give me a ride down to Badger? The cops said I have to leave town. I don't want to stay 'cause they might beat me up."

"Yeah, we're doing laundry. I've got Flora's car. This is her friend, Hilda. She's from Germany."

The sick man barely nodded at her, then, turning back to Lucy, he asked her, "Do you have enough to get me some soup. I'm really hungry."

Lucy nodded and the man said, "I'll just sit in the next booth."

"He's my uncle," Lucy explained to Hilda as she motioned to the waitress. "His name is Sonny."

"Order some clear soup or you'll get sick," Lucy suggested to her uncle.

He nodded, as he pulled some paper napkins out of a chrome container on the table and wiped his face.

The women and children left Sonny with his broth and returned to the Laundromat. As they were folding the clothes, he came in. "Here, I'll take these," he said, taking the bags from Lucy. His hands shook, and the effort of lifting the bags was clearly too much for him. "That's okay," protested Lucy, attempting to take them from him, "they're not that heavy. Clothes are always lighter after they've been washed."

"Hey, Lucy, I can manage. You're not supposed to be carrying big things around in your condition." Lucy let him take the plastic bags, which he dropped several times before he got to the car. The cops had probably tired of putting him in jail and sending him out each morning. She believed the cops did beat up Indians, although none was ever brought to court over it. She'd take Sonny home, and he'd straighten out for a few weeks till he got thirsty again, and he'd disappear as soon as he got money. It was no use to hope he'd stop drinking. Sonny wouldn't quit drinking till he quit living.

As they were pulling out of town, Lucy remembered she had to get some Kool-Aid and turned the car into the Stop-n-Go Mart. Hilda got out with her and noticed the man who had followed them through the street sitting in the shade of a stack of old tires.

"Hey, *tamohpomaat sikaohki*," he told Lucy on her way into the store.

"What did he say? *Sikaohki*?" queried Hilda.

The Kool-Aid was next to the cash register and she picked up a few packages, and laid them on the counter with the money. When the cashier turned to the register, Lucy poked Hilda with her elbow and nodded her head toward the sign behind the counter. Scrawled unevenly in big, black letters, it said, "Ask for Lysol, vanilla, and shaving lotion at the counter."

They ignored the man on the way to the car. "That's what he wants; he's not allowed to go into the stores 'cause he steals it. He wanted vanilla. The Indians call it 'sikaohki'; it means 'black water.'"

Although the car didn't have air-conditioning, Lucy hurried toward it to escape the blistering heat. When she got on the highway, she asked her uncle, "Did you hear anything about a sun-dance?"

At first he grunted a negative "Huh-uh," then, "Oh, yeah, it's across the river, but I don't know where. George Many Robes is camping there. Saw him this morning. Are you going there?"

"Flora and Hilda are. Hilda wants to meet that German guy, Helmut Walking Eagle. You know, that guy who turned Indian?"

"Oh yeah, is he here?" he said indifferently, closing his eyes.

"Probably. He's always in the middle of Indian doings," said Lucy.

"Shit, that guy's just a phony. How could anybody turn into something else? Huh? I don't think I could turn into a white man if I tried all my life. They wouldn't let me, so how does that German think he can be an Indian. White people think they can do anything—turn into Chinese or Indian— they're crazy!"

Sonny laid his head back on the seat and didn't say another word. Lucy felt embarrassed, but she had to agree with him; it seemed that Indians had come into focus lately. She'd read in the papers how some white woman in Hollywood became a medicine woman. She was selling her book on her life as a medicine woman. Maybe some white person or other person who wasn't Indian would get fooled by that book, but not an Indian. She herself didn't practice Indian religion, but she knew enough about it to know that one didn't just join an Indian religious group if one were not raised with it. That was a lot of the conflict going on among those people who were involved in it. They used sacred practices from other tribes, Navajo and Sioux, or whatever pleased them.

The heat of the day had reached its peak, and trails of dust hung suspended in the air wherever cars or trucks traveled the gravel roads on the reserve. Sonny fashioned a shade behind the house underneath the clothesline in the deep grass, spread a blanket, and filled a gallon jar from the pump. He covered the water with some old coats, lay down, and began to sweat the booze out.

The heat waves from this morning's forecast were accurate. It was just too hot. "Lordy, it's hot," exclaimed Lucy to Hilda as they brought the laundry in. "It must be close to ninety-five or one hundred. Let's go up to Badger to my other aunt's house. She's got a tap by her house and the kids can cool off in her sprinkler. Come on, you kids. Do you want to go run in the sprinkler?"

The women covered the windows on the west side where the sun would shine. "I'm going to leave all the windows open to let the air in," said Lucy, as she walked around the house pushing them up.

Lucy's aunt's house sat amongst a clutter of junk. "Excuse the mess," she smiled at Hilda, waving her arm over her yard. "Don't wanna throw it away, it might come in handy." There were thick grass and weeds criss-crossed with paths to and from the clothesline, the outhouse, the wood-stove. Lucy's aunt led them to an arbor shaded with huge spruce branches.

"This is nice," cooed Hilda, admiring the branches. Lucy's aunt beamed, "Yes, I told my old man, 'Henry, you get me some branches that's not gonna dry up and blow away,' and he did. He knows what's good for him. You sit down right here, and I'll get us some drinks." She disappeared and soon returned with a large thermos and some plastic tumblers.

They spent the afternoon hearing about Henry, as they watched the kids run through the sprinkler that sprayed the water back and forth. Once in awhile, a suggestion of a breeze would touch the women, but it was more as if they imagined it.

Before four, they left to pick Flora up and headed back to Lucy's. "It's so hot after being in that cool cement building all day!" exclaimed Flora, as she settled herself into the car's stifling interior. "One thing for sure, I'm not going home to cook anything. Lucy, do you think Bunky would mind if you came with us? I'll get us some Kentucky Fried Chicken and stuff in town so you don't have to cook. It's too hot to cook, anyway." She rolled up a newspaper and fanned her face, which was already beginning to flush.

"No, he won't care. He'll probably want to sleep. We picked Sonny up in town. Both of them can lie around and get better. The kids would bother them if we were there."

It was a long ride across the Napi River toward the Porcupine Hills. A few miles from the Hills, they veered off until they were almost by the river. "Let's get off," said Flora.

Hilda gasped at what she saw before her. There was a circle of tepees and tents with a large open area in the middle. Exactly in the center of the opening was a circular structure covered with branches around the sides. Next to this was a solitary unpainted tepee. Some of the tepees were painted with lines around the bottom; others had orbs bordering them, and yet others had animal figures painted on them. Smoke rose from stoves outside the tepees as people prepared their evening meals. Groups of horses stood languidly in the waning heat of the day, their heads resting on one another's backs and their tails occasionally flicking insects away. The sound of bantering children and yapping dogs carried to where they stood.

"Let's eat here," the kids said, poking their head to look in the bags of food. Flora and Lucy spread a blanket on the ground, while Hilda continued to stand where she was, surveying the encampment. Flora pointed out the central leafy structure as the sacred area of prayer and dance.

"The tepee next to it is the sacred tepee. That's where the holy woman who is putting up the sun-dance stays the entire time. That's where they have the ceremonies."

"How many sun-dances have you been to?" asked Hilda.

"This is my first time, but I know all about this from books," said Flora. "Helmut Walking Eagle wrote a book about it, too. I could try to get you one. He sells them cheaper to Indians."

Hilda didn't eat much and kept looking down at the camp. "It's really beautiful," she said, as if to herself.

"Well, you better eat something before you get left out," advised Lucy. "These kids don't know when to stop eating chicken."

"Yeah," agreed Flora. "Then we can go down and see who's all there."

Hilda had something to eat, and then they got back into the car and headed down toward the encampment. They drove around the edge of the camp and stopped by Flora's cousin's tent. "Hi, Delphine," said Flora, "I didn't know you were camping here."

Lucy knew Flora and Delphine were not especially close. Their fathers were half-brothers, which made them half-cousins. Delphine had grown up Mormon and had recently turned to Indian religion, just as Flora had grown up Catholic and was now exploring traditional beliefs. The same could be said about many of the people here. To top things off, there was some bad feeling between the cousins about a man, some guy they both had been involved with in the past.

"Can anybody camp here? I've got a tepee. How about if I camp next to you."

Delphine bridled. "You're supposed to camp with your own clan."

Flora looked around the camp. "I wonder who's my clan. Say, there's George Many Robes, he's my relation on my dad's side. Maybe I'll ask him if I can camp next to him."

Delphine didn't say anything but busied herself with splitting kindling from a box of sawn wood she kept hidden underneath a piece of tarp. Jason spied a thermos under the tarp and asked for a drink of water.

"I have to haul water, and nobody pays for my gas," grumbled Delphine, as she filled a cup halfway with water.

"Oh, say," inquired Flora, "do you know if Helmut Walking Eagle is coming here? This girl is from Germany, and she wants to see him."

"Over there, that big tepee with a Winnebago beside it. That's his camp," Delphine answered, without looking at them.

"Is she mad at you?" Jason asked Flora.

"Yeah, it must be the heat," Flora told him with a little laugh.

Elsie Walking Eagle was cooking the evening meal on a camp stove outside the tepee. She had some folding chairs that Lucy would've liked to sit down in, but Elsie didn't ask any of them to sit down though she was friendly enough.

"Is your husband here?" asked Flora.

"No, he's over in the sacred tepee," answered Elsie.

"How long is he going to take?"

"Oh, he should be home pretty soon," Elsie said, tending her cooking.

"Do you mind if we just wait? I brought this girl to see him. She's from Germany, too," Flora said.

Lucy had never seen Helmut in anything other than Indian regalia. He was a smallish man with blond hair, a broad face, and a large thin nose. He wore his hair in braids and always wore round, pink shell earrings. Whenever Lucy saw him, she was reminded of the Plains Indian Museum across the line.

Helmut didn't even glance at the company but went directly inside the tepee. Flora asked Elsie, "Would you tell him we'd like to see him?"

"Just wait here. I'll go talk to him," Elsie said, and followed her husband inside. Finally, she came out and invited them in. "He doesn't have much time to talk with you, so . . ." Her voice trailed off.

The inside of the tepee was stunning. It was roomy, and the floor was covered with buffalo hides. Backrests, wall hangings, parfleche bags, and numerous artifacts were magnificently displayed. Helmut Walking Eagle sat resplendent amidst his wealth. The women were dazzled. Lucy felt herself gaping and had to shush her children from asking any questions.

Helmut looked at them intently and rested his haze on Hilda. Hilda walked toward him, her hand extended in greeting, but Helmut ignored it. Helmut turned to his wife and asked in Blackfoot, "Who is this?"

"She says she's from Germany," was all Elsie said, before making a quick move toward the door.

"Wait!" he barked in Blackfoot, and Elsie stopped where she was.

"I only wanted to know if you're familiar with my home town Weisbaden?" said Hilda.

"Do you know what she's talking about?" Helmut asked Elsie in Blackfoot. Elsie shook her head in a shamed manner.

"Why don't you ask *her* questions about Germany?" He hurled the words at Hilda, then, looking meanly at his wife, he added, "She's been there." Elsie flinched, and, forcing a smile, waved weakly at the intruders and asked them in a kind voice to come outside. As Lucy waited to leave, she looked at Helmut whose jaw twitched with resentment. His anger seemed to be tangibly reaching out to them.

"Wow!" whispered Hilda in Lucy's ear.

Outside, Flora touched a book on the fold-out table. Its title read *Indian Medicine* and in smaller letters, *A Revival of Ancient Cures and Ceremonies*. There was a picture of Helmut and Elsie on the cover. Flora asked, "Is this for sale?"

"No, that one's for someone here at camp, but you can get them in the bookstores."

"How much are they?" Flora asked, turning the book over.

"They're twenty-seven dollars. A lot of work went into it," Elsie replied.

Helmut, in Blackfoot, called out his wife's name, and Elsie said to her unwelcome callers, "I don't have time to visit. We have a lot of things to do." She left them and went into her husband.

"Do you think she wrote that book?" Lucy asked Flora.

"He's the brains; she's the source," Flora said. "Let's go. My kids are probably wondering what happened to me."

"I'm sorry I upset her husband. I didn't mean to," said Hilda. "I thought he would be willing to teach me something, because we're both German."

"Maybe you could buy his book," suggested Lucy.

"Look," said Flora, "if you're going to be around for a while, I'm going to a sun-dance this next weekend. I'm taking a few days off work. I have a friend up north who can teach you about Indian religion. She's a medicine woman. She's been to Germany. Maybe she even went to your home town."

"Oh, really!" gushed Hilda. "Of course, I'll be around. I'd love to go with you and meet your friends."

"You can come into the sweat with us. First, you'll need to buy four square yards of cotton . . ." began Flora.

But Hilda wasn't really listening to her. She looked as if she were already miles and miles away in the north country. Now, a sweat, she thought, would be real Indian.

DEBRA EARLING

Jules Bart, Giving Too Much– August 1946

I ALMOST COULDN'T LIFT HER FROM THE WATER. SHE WAS SO heavy and I thought to myself I had to, that somehow it was all part of finishing the job, lifting her up from the water, carrying her back to her mother. My legs were shaking like my bones were bending and I said to myself a hundred times while I was carrying her that she was only a young skinny girl. Hell, I've lifted calves from drowning out of sucking mud and I never felt like they were heavy enough to break me, to pull the muscles in my back tight as a hoist tilting an engine. But she was heavy and unmoving. She was dead. And not in the way my mother was dead, like there was a measure of good peace. This girl was hard dead. She was a nightmare waiting to be dreamt. She was someone that just might be standing here by the river in the early morning dark of a good fishing day. And I thought to myself, even a lot of hard work, even a good many late hours in the barn dust couldn't chase the memory of her from me.

And I think it's funny when I'm in a room full of porch ranchers who are impressed by the fact that I'm a damn good cowboy, a cowboy who could rope a cow fart if I wanted, and I joke and laugh with them and they never know I get spooked by things. None of them know. I laugh with them at myself because of the crazy son of a bitch I really am when the cowboy hat comes off. Truth is, I once took a woman home with me and not because I wanted to rattle my balls. I had had a shit-the-bed nightmare three nights in a row and I was scared. And I'd never tell them, deny it on a long day until the dark comes and I'm walking home alone with a few beers in my belly like courage, my shoulders huddled up around my ears, my teeth chattering.

I've seen my face in the window, a reflection from a bare bulb, and I've jumped. I think that's why I get along well with horses. It never bothers me to hop a bronc that can butt my balls so far up my throat you'd think they were my Adam's apple. I can grab on. I can hold the fear to me like a good drink. But bad dreams make my muscles twitch. I know the meaning of spooked. I know how hard it is to let go of the day when you're living alone. I've seen a mean night come out of nowhere, a bad dream that stinks in your nostrils like a snort of cow shit. I've heard my dead mother calling from the other room on a calm night. And I have to breathe slow. Calm down. Light a smoke. I see things out of the corner of my eye and it scares the shit right out of me.

It's not always that way. Sometimes I go along for months not noticing the house settling or the sounds the barn animals make on a winter night. But just like some ornery horses are always looking around for a good scare, I guess I'm looking for a thrill. My mother used to say it was the sign of a restless heart always to be a little scared of things. "You're not telling the world what your heart's desire is," she would say. And deep down I know she was a little right and it embarrasses me. Still, I'm content to work hard and to sit out on my porch in the evening. Sometimes I pull my bed out there, out under the stars. A few nights back I counted seven falling stars. I wished on every one of them for a quick kiss and a good piece of ass. I had me a few smokes, wished that I played the guitar like Gene Autry.

———◆•◆•◆———

I got drunk, shit-faced, ploughed, nozzled, stoned, tight, staggering, three-legged drunk not too long ago when I got a little jumpy. Some gal was telling me, Norma Lipscomb it was, that I was so drunk I unzipped my pants and pissed off the barstool. She said I was so drunk I tried to pick her up and that I showed her my dick. She said I promised to give her the meat from my best calf and that I said I would come chop all her wood and lay her right through the winter of next year. But I don't remember any of that. Don't remember saying a damn thing like that, think she was lying. Anyways I think when a man gets a little drunk he speaks the partial truth. And the truth is I'd never screw Norma Lipscomb not even if you paid me. The woman has tits she belts at the waist. She's got two mud moles with long whiskers on her chin. And besides that, you can see up her nostrils. I wouldn't dip water from her trough if I was dying a thirst. I wouldn't do a lot of things I thought. But when Antoine Pretty Chief asked me for a light under the neon red of the bar sign outside, something funny happened.

I stepped outside for some air and the summer night felt cool on my temples. I lit a cigarette and smelled small rain on the dry ground. A wind was coming up from the river and I leaned into it, feeling the cold alcohol in my blood swirling. Antoine Pretty Chief stepped from the shadows and I already knew he was close to me but I couldn't focus until he was standing in the light. I turned around and that son of a bitch was so pretty he took my breath. His hair was so black it looked glassy and his eyes were large and wet and he looked like he'd been crying.

"How the hell are you?" I asked.

I spun around a little too fast on my heels and fell on my ass. I sat there for a minute and it felt good to be sitting, to let the world stop spinning, when he reached over and easy pulled me up. I was so close to him I could smell his sweat and he was sweet as dry wood and I sniffed him. I couldn't stand on my own so he propped me up. He had shoulders like a good cowboy and I wanted to laugh because he's an Indian and I knew it wasn't funny. Funny to me drunk, I guess. I laughed anyway. He pulled me up close to him. He had a silver ring on his smallest finger, a ring that caught the light. His nails were white. I was trying to tell him something. Trying to tell him about being scared but I don't think I said a word to him, not a word he could recognize.

Hell, I was so drunk my heart was pounding through my shirt. And I feel sick now to remember I liked the son of a bitch. I liked his power like a horse. I had a hard-on the size of my gearshift but I wasn't sure why. He pulled me up by the waist and I could feel his cock behind me.

"You sick asshole," I said. "Get your hands off me. Get your goddamn hands off me." But he pulled me to the truck and hoisted me in. He didn't say anything. He didn't say a word. He fished in my pants for my keys and I made like I was trying to stop him. He just put me in my truck and drove me home. When we got to the house, he stopped the truck and set the brake. I could smell him. I wanted to get away. I wanted to go in the house. I looked up, feeling the alcohol again. My temples were ice and I looked out the window to the long path round back to the house. I tried to focus my thoughts on opening the door and standing on my own. A wind gust rocked the truck and I turned to him. I saw his neck. I could see his heartbeat in his throat. His heartbeat in his neck. His neck thick as a stallion's. There was a pale blue light. Blue light through his hair from the moon. Shit. I fumbled for the door. I was going to get my ass out of there. I could feel my balls swell. His teeth were so white they were blue as the moon in the darkness. I better get out of here, I kept thinking, but wanted to stay. And before I knew it he had his mouth at my fly and I wanted to kiss him. I wanted to kiss the son of a bitch. I wanted to strip buck-naked and feel his heavy muscles, his cock against my belly. And I never felt that way before, I swear to God. And I puked till there was nothing left in me, then I puked some more. But sometimes I find myself thinking about Antoine Pretty Chief. And I whisper to myself so I can deny it. I love him.

Now Louise comes along and I swear she's the most beautiful woman I've ever seen. I wanted her so many times but she's never noticed me. And the night her sister dies she comes home with me. A bad night for both of us. A hell of a night for me. I take her home and we sleep together. I hold her in my arms and squeeze her. She's so damn beautiful. She's got a mean wound on her left breast but she's tough. She's had a harder ride than most cowboys. I bury my whiskered face in her sweet tits. I've never had it so good. But then she wakes up crying in the middle of the night. And I think about her sister dead and gone. I think about myself alone. The night is strange and I cry too, but I don't let Louise know. In the night she can't see my face. I haven't cried since my own mother died and not so much even then. In the dark we smoke cigarettes. We talk about a lot of things, little things, nothing really, and I don't know what gets into me but I find myself flapping my gums to her about Pretty Chief. I tell her about me and Pretty Chief, what we've done. And it feels good to be talking in the dark, pulling on a smoke, good not to be alone. But in the morning comes gray and the rain stings and I've given myself away.

Tender Street

1

HE WAS GOING SLOWLY THROUGH THE CAFETERIA WHEN SHE noticed him this time, his light eyes flickering unobtrusively over the vacated tables. He was almost colorless except for his eyes, which had faded to ash-gray. This colorlessness made him virtually invisible. She thought that you might see him standing on the other side of a crowded street, but before he had crossed it he might be able to disappear without a trace. This was a mysterious and fascinating idea. She believed that he, with utmost nicety, in some physical manner, shunned the casual observer's glance, although she had never seen how he did it. Think of such secrecy, such timing, such efficiency! She marveled. She imagined he spent the early evenings wandering from one shabby eating establishment to another. Often she had watched him here, and speculated about him. In her endless inner monologue she told herself he was a phenomenon of this society. She recognized him as one of the regulars, the street persons, of this city on the western seaboard of the wealthiest country in the world.

A fiery crown upon the city's fabled hills, entire banks of windows were aglitter with cerise and orange reflections of sunset. But no roseate echo infiltrated the cavernous recesses of Sum Ling's Cafeteria. The no-color man plodded softly along the aisles, which at this hour of seven were shadowed under the dimmest of lightbulbs. The front booths were alive, filled with the noise and motion of the young Asians who made Sum Ling's their night's rendezvous.

More than usual, tonight she relished the cheerful sounds of the young people and the comforting homey clink of china. She was talking on the phone at the cafeteria's mini-booth, when suddenly she saw that the man had seated himself in her abandoned booth, only an arm's length away. She had never been this close to him before. Everything became clear and extraordinarily precise. A button was missing from his earth-colored Burberry. He carefully removed his blurred, bodiless hat with its stained sweatband. He gazed with warm interest at nothing at all, then shifted his look to another empty space. So that is how he avoids looking into our eyes, she thought. She trembled a little and made herself smaller. But he did not notice. He evidently hadn't seen her leave the booth, then, she realized; he didn't know she was the diner whose place he had appropriated. He has successfully erased all of us. How innocent! whispered her mind. How shameful to eavesdrop on him! But she could not stop.

Feeling abysmally surreptitious, she watched him slide toward himself her tray and its leftover heap of Ling's Special Oyster Beef with Rice which she had scraped together in the center of the plate. With a trace of long habitude, he did not look down, but let his right hand fall, grasp the fork between carved-stone fingers, and raise it laden to his lips. The merest hint of apology appeared in his vague eyes, his posture, even the quick return sliding motion of the fork. (I shall have done, and be gone from your sight. The echo in her mind seemed to come from him.)

His sharp profile tweezered; his Adam's apple bobbed with his chewing. The pile of brown-gravied rice vanished rapidly. I should have left him more meat, she thought with a flash of tenderness. Then she proposed to herself brightly: I could go back and sit down and talk with him. At once she was breathless with her bold idea. She started to intone the farewell ritual into her friend's ear. She felt eager, as if she must begin to run.

He pursed his straight mouth, wiped it with fastidious care on her crumpled paper napkin which he laid with a gentle gesture on the worn laminated tabletop. The pale eyes swept a benevolent glance over the adjacent booths. She swerved hers fast away, thinking, He almost caught me! When she looked back, he had risen and was moving at the edge of a crowd of bantering youths. As she bobbed and swayed, peering between them for a glimpse of him, she keened lightly to herself. She raised a hand and fluttered it toward his back in a pleading gesture. At the other end of the telephone wire, her friend began the ritual responses. She heard nothing. Her lips were busy with silent phrases.

Without a sound she cried, "Wait!"

She noticed, even from here, that the seat of his raincoat was very wrinkled; then among the dwindling crowd his shapeless figure became smaller and smaller until he was gone.

2

Jamb didn't know whether it was day or night, or how long he and Satin had been lying there. As soon as his eyes opened he knew he had hit the cement again. He moved his arm and felt the familiar street gritting against his skin. Satin's head came up off his shoulder and he saw her shining fur profiled against a strange building. Her ears turned like a weather-vane in several directions, and she looked questioningly at him.

"Easy, Satin," he croaked. Her ears dipped. He concentrated on her dark eyes, his own a wavering glaze. No movements of his body were possible. He had no idea how long he'd been unconscious. All he knew for sure was that Satin was here; she hadn't been taken away. But where was this? He couldn't move to get up, to find out.

Satin had come down on her elbows again and was scanning the street. He stared at the scintillating wet pores of her nose, black like the rest of her whole massive Labrador shape; about as black as he himself was.

Watching the legs of passers-by, he knew no one would stop. He had plenty of experience in that area. Then he heard the familiar police ambulance siren, coming to take him downtown. Satin would bark and growl to no avail. He'd have to leave her here on the street. Again. A pair of blue-jeaned legs halted in front of them. Jamb tried to lift his head, but it wasn't any use. A face emerged out of the fog that seemed to swarm in front of Jamb, and he saw a shock of uncombed hair over a ragged shirt collar.

"Hey, man, take a slug of this," came the young man's voice. Jamb saw a brown hand, a Styrofoam cup, and a bent plastic straw. The hand came closer and Jamb opened his mouth. The coffee hit his stung dry lips sharply. He tried to drink though, and got a few sips as the coffee cooled down in the chilly 5 A.M. wind. Tried, too, to say something. The young man butted in, "Don't talk, man, rest your face." There was a pause. "The wagon's on its way. I have an idea. I'll take your dog to the SPCA, and see to it that they get your name. What is it?"

"Jamb Roland," he mouthed painfully, as one split tooth knifed an already cut lip. The siren whined closer, and the dipping wail stopped at the nearby curb. Through his ruined ears he heard very little besides the mumble of the van cops and some buzzing words about an ambulance.

The young man's voice was quiet, assertive. "Where will you take him?"

"Emergency, for now." The cops lifted Jamb to a makeshift gurney, and the young man took firm hold of Satin's leash. "Not to worry, Jamb. I'll see that she gets a square right away, and I'll tell them the whole bit at the SPCA. Not to worry, hear."

Jamb couldn't see Satin but he dimly heard her loud complaining barks as the van started up and howled along the street. The barks echoed through his mind over and over, interspersed with the words, "Thanks, thanks, thanks."

"And he didn't know me from nothin'. Oh, God," Jamb thought.

3

Meterologist Pete Giddings sounded as husky as if he was out in this rain himself, Indian Bilijohn thought, twisting his shoulders deeper into his soaked Burberry. "Office workers on the fifty-first floor of Embarcadero Four are watching snow fly past the windows. It's a weird November, traditionally the tag end of Indian Summer in San Francisco."

Inside the St. Anthony Drop In Center Pete's voice rattled away in static and Bilijohn muttered, "Lucky dude, nothin' to do but yak in the warm." Those guys come in before midnight, he thought, and suppose to take turns, but sometimes they stay till daylight 'fore they get run off. He peered into the Center. The figures hulked inside, just lumps of gray. The bare bulb above the doorway came alight, dim orange against the early dark. In out of the slanting rain, four mummy bags lay fanned out like spokes around the center post. Bilijohn's ruined eyes blinked trying to find the guys' faces. Maybe he knew somebody, could scrounge a decent, whole butt for a change. But the faces were muffled. Huh, he said aloud. In Florida, they'd die right away with pneumonia, but here takes 'em least six months to run themselves down enough to get sick. Everybody thinks they got it good since they ripped off them sleepin' bags so they can stay dry this weather. Naw. Just takes 'em a little longer that's all. They ain't so lucky.

He flicked the flying rain from his nose with the back of his hand. Rivers ran down his heavy club of graying hair, soaked his faded blue headband, slithered into the collar of his raincoat, so shiny with age that it felt slick; too old to be warm anymore, like himself. Cold old Indian, he muttered. He stomped his feet. The boots squished. He realized he couldn't feel his feet today. Sure don't help the arthritis, this rain. Gee if I could, I'd go to Fresno. Mike McGarvin would get me a dry place to sleep. Somewhere near the Poverello. Warmer in Fresno, even when it rains. He approached a knot of people having a conference in the street. His lemur-dark eyes focused on them. He noticed they were soaked too. What's keepin' them out here in the streets?

Then he saw the yellow truck parked; two little old gents getting out of it handing out armloads of wax-wrapped packets from the truckbed. Suddenly the street was awash with drenched and tattered street people. The little old gents were just about lost in the surge. Bilijohn inched his way closer until he saw what they were passing out, though it didn't make any difference. Any give-away was better 'n nuthin'. He took his three-pound packet of cheese with a mumbled thanks and moved on down the street.

In half a block he found himself in another line. He craned his head to see where it was leading. He saw a pair of women standing down the curb a ways. They were buying the cheese. Bilijohn's chest wheezed with a sudden sigh. He reasoned that the cheese ought not to go for any less 'n five bucks. And he sure could use a shot of 'Bird. A great wave of spit washed up in his gullet.

When he got to the front of the line, some woman he couldn't look into the eyes of, took his cheese, held out two dollars. His stomach spasmed in an acid drench, and he almost grabbed back the cheese, but he couldn't do it. He wanted to vomit. You thief, he wanted to yell, but he couldn't. The two paper dollars wadded in his fist, he headed down the street to Merrill's Drug. A jug of lousy Thunderbird. Hell, I'm an Indin, man, I can drink Thunderbird in public, he muttered. Us Indins got choices. Two. Thunderbird or Coors.

The cheese could have kept him off the St. Anthony bread line for at least a day if he'd resisted the woman. Lousy mooch, he thought. Naw forget it, he told himself, shrugged and kept putting his soggy feet down, shuffling along Market Street.

He bent to pick up a long butt that wasn't real wet, lying close in under a building's eave. He fished in the pockets of the Burberry. Not a match to my name, he growled. When he came out of Merrill's, the bottle stuck into his pocket, he was still fumbling for a match. He aimed toward the next man passing in the street, then veered away, seeing NO chiseled in the hard lips and granite stare.

"All's I want is a light, man," Bilijohn mumbled at him wagging his hand. Now he felt the good electricity of his first gulp of wine radiate over the ache of his ulcers. The trembling in his legs was getting less. At the corner, standing for a red light, he laid his head back and tossed half the wine down his throat, feeling the stuff zig-zag sharply across the harsh desert of his long thirst. Dude thought I was a derelict, he mouthed, but the swords in his stomach pierced his thought and he winced in pain. Hah! Derelict.

He never seen me ride, did he? But he wouldn't know what to do with a quarter-horse. Naw, he's probably never even stepped in cow shit. Shoo, I wasn't gonna hit on him; all's I wanted was a flame, he reiterated angrily. Then seeing it as a ridiculous joke he let his lips turn up at the corners. His half blind eyes searched the clouds, as if he shared his laughter with the gods.

And the filthy street changed into the long grass of a strangely familiar valley, and Bilijohn was riding. Riding. He didn't hear the high keening screech of brakes, didn't see the lithe swerve of the shining town car. He heard only a distant call: Billy! Billy John! and his own answering holler. Yeah I'm coming as fast as I can! He didn't feel the massy jolt as the sharp hood scooped him skyward, his eyes still measuring the weeping clouds. The half empty gray-green bottle arced into the gutter and tumbled down the torrent of flotsam, the Thunderbird belching out of it. Indian Bilijohn galloped on through the long amber grass, heels pummeling the bright flanks.

ANITA ENDREZZE

The Door in the Mountain

IN AUGUST THE SKY IS A DUSTY BLUE, THE AIR FILLED WITH twirling seeds and bees. On top of the mountain, there were layers of green: blue spruce, light green cedars, wild maples with their shadows of heavy green, the pines with needles shimmering in the heat, and the soft tamaracks the color of limes. Even the sun, filtered through the lacework of leaves, seemed a faded green.

Iris walked behind her aunt. The sky felt so enormous that the child felt safer looking at her own feet, but she couldn't help peeking up at her aunt's swaying hips encased in a pair of loose jeans.

"We're on top of the world," Aunt Pilar had joked just moments before. Iris thought the sky fell around her in dizzy circles. Iris was almost seven but she'd never been to a mountain before.

"Well, then, it's about time," Pilar had laughed before conferring with Iris's mother about the trip.

Aunt Pilar worked at a dry cleaners during the week. On the week-ends she escaped the chemicals and heat by harvesting herbs and botani-cals for natural food stores or florists. In early summer she cut wild baby's breath and sold armloads for bridal flower arrangements. She also collected baskets of juniper berries, wild ginger root, mushrooms, and buckets of tart huckleberries. In winter she created magnificent pine wreaths.

Iris loved to smell her *tia*'s hands. They smelled like dark fresh earth and running water. When Iris looked at her aunt's slim, strong body, she saw bright fish swimming upstream and tiny red deer and blue horses in Pilar's long hair. She drew a picture of what she saw and gave it to her aunt.

Her aunt gasped, then ran to the kitchen where Julia, Pilar's sister and Iris's mother, was fixing dinner. They huddled over the sink, whispering, while Iris jumped up and down.

"What? What?" she screamed. "You don't like it! It's stupid!" She crossed her arms and glared at them.

Pilar turned around. "Ah, no, Iris. It's beautiful. Thank you!"

"You're just saying that!" Tears threatened to spill out of her eyes.

"Calm down, *hija*," said Julia. Her daughter tended to dramatic fits. It was exhausting.

"Really, I love it," assured Pilar. She sat at the kitchen table, motioning Iris to join her.

"I was just so surprised to see your picture," said Pilar, "because this is how I look to myself in my dreams." Her finger tapped the drawing. "You have a special talent for seeing things how they really are."

Iris beamed. Her mother sighed.

"Now, Iris, don't get a swelled head." Julia went back to peeling pota-toes. Her feet ached. She stood all day working as a checker at Safeway.

"Julia, a little praise doesn't hurt." Pilar took a pot out of the cupboard and filled it with water, placing it on the stovetop.

"Nothing is 'a little' with Iris, you know that." Julia plopped the pota-toes in, one by one, and turned on the heat. "If you had kids, you'd know how hard it is."

"Let's not get into that again."

"She's so demanding . . . ," said Julia. "And I'm so tired. I have to do everything around here."

"I know it's not easy raising a kid without a father. Have you heard from . . ." Pilar lowered her voice.

Iris listened to them gently arguing, ignoring her, until finally she stomped out of the room. "You're not supposed to whisper in front of others. That's rude!"

They heard the door slam.

"Now look what you did," said Julia, wiping her hands dry.

"What *I* did?" Pilar rolled her eyes.

But later that night, Pilar explained that Julia needed a little vacation. So Iris and Pilar were going up to a big mountain.

"How big?" asked Iris.

"Bigger than you."

"That's not so big. Everything is bigger than me."

Pilar laughed. "Okay, then. Bigger than all the McDonald arches in the world. Bigger than a sneeze." Pilar teased Iris into a better mood, while Julia sat in front of the blaring TV, too tired to turn it off.

The path was narrow. Pilar stopped to think. Which way to the best huckleberry bushes this side of Canada? They grew best in clearings where the sun could sweeten the berries to perfection.

"Are you lost?" asked Iris.

"Not exactly."

"What does that mean?" Iris looked over her shoulder. She was worried about bears.

Pilar frowned. "I've been coming up here for five years, ever since I moved to Spokane." Pilar had lived in Long Beach, California, before. This last year she finally persuaded Julia to move up north, away from the congestion and dangers of the city. "So I'm not lost, it's just that things change up here. Trees get bigger and meadows disappear. Or a fire burns down my usual landmarks."

"Oh." Iris sat down. "How much farther? I'm tired."

"We're almost there. I was just looking for some bear grass."

Iris shot up. "Bears?"

"It's a type of grass that people put in flower arrangements. I can get a lot of money for it. But you don't have to worry about bears." She started walking again. "At least until we get to the huckleberry patch." She said the last to herself.

They walked in silence for awhile, Pilar carrying the water, a sleeping bag big enough for two, and a backpack of food. Pilar had explained that they weren't actually allowed to sleep overnight in the state park, but she knew a place no one else ever came to, a secret place.

"Here we are." Pilar pointed to the clearing where low bushes stretched across the slope. "Huckleberries!"

"Where?"

The woman kneeled down, carefully brushing aside leaves. Underneath, Iris saw dark blue berries. Her aunt pinched one off the stem, offering it to the little girl.

"Go on, taste it."

"Yum!"

Iris picked the berries eagerly. She noticed that some had a different taste to them.

"You're clever!" laughed Pilar. "There are several varieties of berries. Each has its own flavor."

"How do you know so much about plants and stuff?" Iris's lips were stained blue.

"Someone taught me."

"Who?"

"Just someone I used to know."

"I want to know about plants too."

Her aunt whirled around. She was fierce, her eyebrows knitted together, her mouth a tight line. "I will teach you. No one else! Understand?"

Iris nodded, confused. Her lower lip trembled.

Her aunt took a deep breath. "I'm sorry. I didn't mean to scare you."

They picked berries for another hour. Then they sat down to eat some cheese. Suddenly, her aunt sat up straight. "What's that?"

"What?" asked Iris, looking around nervously.

Pilar listened intently for a moment, then shrugged. "I thought I heard someone calling my name, but it must've been the wind."

"*Tia,* why don't you just grow these plants in your yard?"

Pilar snorted. "That itty bitty patch of concrete the landlord calls a yard? You've got to be joking." She wrapped up the cheese. "Well, I said I'd teach you, so you deserve a real answer."

She took a gulp of water from a bottle. "See, Iris, these plants only grow high up. Everything has its place in this world. If you take it away from its natural home . . . it would wither away and die." Pilar looked sad. She missed the ocean and wild poppies that bloomed in the few undeveloped hills of southern California. She missed the salt air and palm trees. It was hard up here in Washington State during the winter when icicles as long as baseball bats hung from the roof and the cold felt like frozen needles in her bones. If it hadn't been for that surfing and ski bum, Al, she'd never moved up here in the first place. If she hadn't gotten pregnant then got that abortion after he threatened to leave her, maybe things would've turned out better. But then he left her for Cindy, a member of the ski patrol, blonde and cute in her pale blue skintight outfit. If he had stayed with her, maybe Pilar would've been happy. No, she thought, he wasn't a good man. She'd been real stupid to love him. She was better off without him. But she didn't have enough money to move anywhere and somehow the lonely days passed. When she finally talked Julia into moving up here, she'd cried. Now at least she'd have another Yaqui to talk to, even though they tended to fight a lot as sisters sometimes do. Their grandparents had walked on foot two hundred miles from Mexico into southern California in the early 1900s, escaping the terror of the Mexican soldiers who slaughtered their tribe.

Pilar shook away her thoughts, looking at Iris who had flopped down and was gazing at the sky. Pilar smiled and lay down next to her.

"Hey, kiddo, did I ever tell you about the squirrel who gave me gifts?"

"A pet squirrel?"

"No, a wild one who wanted to be friends with me. See, I was living out in the woods one summer, not too far from here." It had been the first summer after Al left her, and Pilar had lived in her old car, squatting in the woods whenever she could get away with it. She was lucky. A month after getting the waitress job at IHOP, her car broke down for good. But by then she had enough money to rent a studio apartment. "Every day this squirrel came over for some bread. I put it on a tree stump."

"Wow."

Pilar turned on her side, propping her head up with one bent arm. Iris had beautiful eyes, wide open with interest.

"The best part was that the squirrel knew I wouldn't hurt it. She trusted me." Pilar smiled. "We had an understanding. I gave her food and she gave me little things she valued."

"Like what?"

"Oh, a pine cone. A mushroom she had dried for winter. And . . ." Pilar paused dramatically. "Once she gave me a ring!"

Iris sat up. "A ring!"

"Yep. It was real old. Someone probably lost it in the woods. Anyway, her greatest gift was her trust. I treasured that more than anything else. When something moved through the forest, she warned me. Squirrels have a very good alert system if you listen carefully. You can learn their language."

"You're kidding me."

"No, and the one time I didn't pay attention it almost cost me my life!"

"What happened?"

"I'll tell you later, back at camp. Now we've got to pick more berries. I've got orders for four gallons and we only have two picked. So up and at 'em!" Pilar rose, dusting off her pants.

Iris looked into her bucket. It was empty. She'd eaten all of Pilar's berries. She promised herself to fill up the whole bucket and not eat a single berry.

◆◆◆◆

That night as Iris snuggled next to Pilar in the sleeping bag, she reminded her aunt about the story she promised to tell.

"That's right," said Pilar. "Are you comfortable?"

"Hmmm." Iris was sleepy but wouldn't admit it. They didn't have a campfire because Pilar didn't want a park ranger ousting them. After all, Pilar said to herself, this was all Indian country at one time. We have a right to be here.

The stars were bright without the campfire. Iris wasn't sure she liked all the darkness around them. The shadows had teeth and eyes. She shivered.

"One day when I was walking in the woods, I heard the squirrels talking but I didn't pay attention. I had other things on my mind." Pilar recalled how she'd heard that James, her brother, had been shot in an attempted car jacking near La Brea Tar Pits. He had been a CPA, the first in her family to graduate with a college degree. She sighed, then continued. "That was a mistake, Iris. Always keep your eyes and ears open in the woods."

"So then what?"

"So, I was just walking along when suddenly . . . I smelled a bear!"

"What does a bear smell like?" Iris sniffed, testing the air.

"Kind of rancid, like old fat." Her aunt wrinkled her nose.

"Yuck!"

"I stood absolutely still. I didn't even breathe. I knew it was behind me. I could hear its teeth clicking. That means it's pretty mad."

"So what did you do?"

"I knew that if I turned around to look at it, the bear would see that as a challenge. So I just kept my back to it and walked slowly away."

"I would've run!" Iris grabbed her aunt's hand.

"No, you shouldn't do that. It'll chase you."

"You were brave. I would've screamed."

Aunt Pilar was quiet for a moment. "Maybe it was courage. I don't know. Mostly, though, I was remembering what I had learned about bears and trusting myself to do the right thing."

"How did you learn what to do?"

Her aunt hesitated. "Someone . . . the summer I spent in the woods . . . I often came to this mountain and one day I met someone who taught me all I know."

"Who?"

"Go to sleep, Iris."

"But . . ."

"No more tonight." Aunt Pilar turned over. Her voice was muffled but strong. "And don't wander away from me tomorrow."

"Bears?"

"Yes," replied her aunt. "And . . . other things too."

The next morning, they spent all their time picking huckleberries. Iris was bored. She peeked over a bush and saw her aunt bending over, picking berries as fast as she could. Iris knelt down. She plucked two leaves and named them Mama and Papa. The Mama leaf was bright green, but the Papa leaf was brittle.

"And the Mama leaf said, 'You spent all our money on drink and women, you lousy no-good bastard!' And the Papa leaf said, 'Take that you, you stupid bitch!'" Iris smashed the leaves together. Uh-oh. The Papa leaf broke. "'You got what you deserve, now get out of our lives.'" Iris threw away the Papa leaf. "'And don't forget to send the support money! Don't you dare drink that up or I'll have them put you in jail,' said the Mama leaf." Iris shook the leaf up and down. Oh, that Mama leaf is mad!

"Then let's put the Papa leaf in jail," Iris said to herself. She broke off little twigs and surrounded the broken Papa leaf. "And here's the baby leaf, that's me. And a dog rock and a cat rock. Now it's one big happy family." She meowed like a cat. "And the Papa leaf says, 'Here's your damn money, it's all I got, so now I can't even buy some smokes. What more do you want from me, blood?'"

Iris squeezed some huckleberry juice over the happy family. Then she looked up. Aunt Pilar was far away, calling her. Iris stood up, grinding the play family into the dirt.

After they ate some salami and bread, Iris felt sleepy. She wanted to go home. She was itchy too.

"When's Mom coming to pick us up?"

"In about three hours. I figure I'll look for the bear grass now, then we'd better head back to camp. We can clean up the site and hike back down to the parking area. Okay?"

"Yeah, but I'm tired. There's nothing to do."

Pilar stared at her. The TV generation expected to be entertained all the time! When she was a girl, her parents took the family into the desert or the High Sierras. She played for hours . . . but then, she had her brothers and sisters. Poor Iris was all alone. No wonder she was a handful. She just wanted some attention.

"Why don't you stay here and take a nap," she suggested.

"No, only babies take naps. And besides, the bears might get me."

"I won't be that far away. You can yell if you get scared." Pilar had a thought. "Why don't you get a sample of every kind of leaf you can find?"

Iris groaned. "That's stupid."

"No, see, we can use them to make rubbings later. You know, with crayons? Or we can dry them and press them between clear contact paper. It's really pretty."

Iris thought about it. "Okay. Just don't go too far."

"I won't."

"If I scream, you'll come?"

"I promise."

"But what if it's a bear?"

"Just remember what I said last night. Trust yourself. What we see and touch is important, but what we know about life deep inside is also what you should trust." She looked thoughtfully at Iris. "I should listen to my own advice. Somehow . . . but I really need the money that bear grass will bring." She rubbed her arms, suddenly feeling a chill. "Listen, Iris, do you know how to get back to camp from here? It's just down that trail."

"Why?"

"Oh, just in case." Pilar was deliberately vague.

But Iris was being her usual persistent self. "In case of what?"

Aunt Pilar sighed. "Well, what if I got lost. It's not going to happen, but if for some reason I don't come back, you got to promise not to look for me. Go back to the camp. When we don't show up at the parking area, your mom will look for you. She knows where we're camping. So, promise? Cross your heart?"

Iris nodded. "Or hope to die."

Pilar shuddered, then forced herself to relax. "Nothing's going to happen. I just get these . . . feelings sometimes. I'll be back in less than an hour."

"Maybe I'll come with you."

Her aunt raised her voice. "No!"

Iris shrunk back. Her aunt squared her shoulders then walked away. Iris didn't understand why her aunt was acting so mean. For a while she pouted. She dug her toe into the dirt and shoved the soil around. She wasn't tired anymore. She was mad. She decided to follow her aunt, quietly, then jump out and yell "Boo!" That'd teach her.

She crept along the trail. It was a faint path, made by deer. She tried to step in the heart-shaped deer tracks, imagining herself with four legs and a long neck. She leaped over granite rocks, pawed the earth, and snorted. Then she noticed a line of ants, following each other one by one. It reminded her that she was following her aunt.

The trail disappeared in a jumble of rocks. Some kind of big mouse poked its head up out of a rocky crevice and piped. Iris smothered a giggle behind her hand. She sat down to watch. A shadow passed over the rocks and the big mouse dived into its hole. When she looked up, she saw a big bird flying overhead. She wondered where her aunt was.

The blue sky stretched its wings. The trees cast longer shadows. She climbed over the rocks. A twig snapped and she paused, walked on tiptoe, her finger over her mouth to remind herself to be quiet.

There in front of her was a flat cliff face of dark granite. She felt silence gathering inside of her and was afraid. She knelt down, peeking around a bush. There were many birds circling in front of the cliff, but Iris was astonished to see their shadows in the sky. On the cliff face, where the shadows *should* have been, were the real birds, soaring. At the base of the cliff stood her aunt, talking to an old woman in a grass skirt.

Around the two figures was a bright light interspersed with the color-ful wings of the birds flying between the two women. Iris crawled closer and heard the old woman talking.

"It's time. You've had your years of richness. Friends. Lovers. Good things to eat. And you have talked with the animals. Now you must touch the rock with your hand."

Pilar shook her head. "All my lovers left me. Remember Al? And there was Martin. He got cancer and died. And Richard. He went back to his wife." She was counting her fingers. "I've been so lonely."

The old woman interrupted. "But you loved them and they loved you. That was the bargain, not what would become of the love. And you must not forget how much you were loved by *him*."

Pilar caught her breath. She wrapped her arms around herself, nod-ding. Then she looked up, half laughing, half in despair.

"Well, I'm certainly not rich!" she protested.

"You have good health and the riches of the earth. With your own hands you have taken the gifts of the earth to bring health and joy to oth-ers. You understand the ways of plants and animals. Are you not blessed, daughter?" The old woman smiled.

"Yes . . . I know what you mean. I am blessed—in the old ways, but . . ." Pilar stopped, confused.

"The old ways are the true ways, the only ways that endure."

Pilar hesitated. She started to reach out to the old woman's out-stretched hand. Iris wanted to jump up, but something held her back. She remained small and hidden.

"Come," urged the old woman. "Remember Cho'oko Baso is waiting for you."

Her aunt's back straightened decisively. She remembered fully, with such a rush of heat that her cheeks flamed, how the young man had loved her. Every curve of her body, every fold of her flesh . . . ah, how he had touched her! Pilar recalled his promise: that he would teach her about plants—their medicines and beauty—and the animals. He helped her deal with the pain of the abortion. She knew he was pure love and life.

"I will give you the riches of life, sweetheart," he whispered. "But when your time is over, then you must leave this life and come into another. You will join me in the Flower World, *Yo Ania*."

She had agreed eagerly, hungry for his love. She brushed aside all thoughts of the future and the payment she would owe.

Now the time had come.

The old woman led her to the rock cliff. Pilar placed her hand on the sun-warmed rock. Instantly, a door appeared and opened, white light streaming out. The birds flew in, gathering their shadows from the sky. A handsome man with long dark hair stepped out and laughed, offering his hand to Pilar.

"At last, my dearest," he said and drew her close. "It's been too long since we talked. I will never leave you again."

They both entered the door, arms wrapped around each other. The old woman turned slowly and looked toward Iris. She smiled, then followed the couple through the doorway.

The door closed and the light leeched into the bright sky. Iris stood up. There was a shadow on the cliff, swaying, bending, singing. It looked like her aunt dancing, but it couldn't be. Iris rubbed her eyes.

◆◆◆◆◆

The park rangers were called out to look for a woman and child lost on the mountain. They found the little girl by a cliff calling for her aunt. When they asked her where the woman was, Iris pointed to the solid cliff face.

"In there."

The ranger looked at her partner. "Head injury?"

The other ranger shrugged. "We'd better call in some paramedics." He looked all around, waving his flashlight in the late summer evening. "Or it could just be the kid's imagination."

"Are you telling us the truth?" Julia asked Iris sternly.

"Mom! She went into the cliff, there was a door and a little old woman and this really cute guy and that's what happened. And lots of birds flying around." Iris started crying in frustration. The rangers shook their heads.

Julia, who stood with her arms wrapped around Iris, spoke up. "Well, even if it is her imagination, that still leaves my sister missing!"

"Yes, ma'am, we're going to call in for more searchers. But it's getting dark. We might have to wait until morning."

"But she might've fallen! Every minute counts. Please!"

"Ma'am, we're doing our best. You might want to take the girl down to our vehicle. Put a blanket around her. She's had a shock."

"Why doesn't anyone believe me?" wailed Iris.

⧫━━━━◆━━━━⧫

Four days later the search was called off when a summer storm threatened the area with lightning and possible forest fires.

"I'm sorry, Mrs. Slade," said Ranger Cole as he stood on Julia's front porch. "We just can't find her. Let's hope she turns up."

Julia shut the door, leaning her head on its smooth surface. Her shoulders trembled.

"Mom?"

Julia started, surprised to find her daughter behind her in the tiny entryway. She explained why the search was called off.

Iris nodded. "She's never coming back anyway. She's with that Cho'oko Baso guy."

Julia's mouth opened. "What did you say? Who?"

"I *told* you a thousand times! Why don't you listen to me? I *said* she went into the cliff with the old woman and that man Cho'oko Baso. That was his name. I heard it all." Iris faced her mother, both hands in tight fists. Her eyes blazed with indignation.

"My god! My god!" Julia staggered into the living room. She dragged Iris with her and they both sat on the old sofa. "You never said his name! You didn't!"

"So? It's a stupid name anyway."

Julia spoke slowly. "When I was a little girl, I heard the same story. It's an old Yaqui story from Sonora. There was a poor young man named Cho'oko Baso. He collected bark for tanning leather. One day, as he searched for wild herbs in the desert, an old man appeared to him. 'Don't work so hard,' said the old man. 'Take this stick and touch that rock.' Cho'oko Baso did that and the rock opened up. A beautiful young woman smiled at him. She taught him many things about the wilderness. About *heka*, the wind and the powers of *hiak viva*, Yaqui tobacco. For many years Cho'oko Baso was a rich man, curing the sick and selling medicinal plants. He had lots of spirit powers. Then one day, he disappeared, just like Pilar. The old people say he had to return to the Enchanted World, *Yo Ania*. It was time to pay his dues."

Iris nodded. "That's what happened."

"But how . . . " Julia shook her head, trying to clear her thoughts. "I thought it was just an old story. It can't be true. And here . . . a thousand miles from the homeland?"

"I saw it, Mom."

"I guess." Julia stood up, dazed. She stared at the TV. People spoke in that small box, danced or fought, and she didn't understand how the images really got there. Something to do with wires and satellites and electricity. Maybe there was another world, beyond her understanding that worked in such mysterious ways. She thought she was too modern to believe in those old stories, but perhaps the Enchanted or Flower World existed in spite of her definition of reality. Who was to know for sure?

But if what Iris said was true, then Pilar knew. She was there with Cho'oko Baso. In his world of enchantment and eternal beauty.

GARY ROBINSON

The Road to Sacred Mountain

IT WAS 6 P.M. ON FRIDAY AS JOANELLE REDHAWK PULLED UP IN front of her one-story L.A. bungalow. It had been another hard week of working office temp jobs trying to make ends meet while she waited for her writing career to take off.

On her way in the house, she checked the mailbox. Along with her "winning letter" from Ed McMahon, she found a long-awaited envelope from Popejoy Publishing. She dropped everything else on the living room coffee table and tore open the letter.

As she read the words "regret to inform you," her face and her spirits fell. She thought it would be different this time. She started throwing things in a suitcase and made a phone call.

"Sandra," she almost cried into the phone. "I can't handle the rejection."

"Joanelle? What are you talking about?" Sandra asked.

"I got another rejection notice on my novel. My agent assured me that this publisher really wanted it. I've got five years of my life wrapped up in that manuscript and not a damn thing to show for it." Joanelle braided her long jet-black hair as she spoke, holding back tears. "And I can't take one more secretary temp job."

"You sound pretty angry and upset," Sandra empathized.

"Yeah, so listen, I've decided to take a little trip," Joanelle continued. "I need to get away, but I don't really wanna go alone. You and Michael wanna come along?"

"I don't know," Sandra responded. "When are you leaving?"

"Tomorrow morning. Sunup," Joanelle said.

"Well, we *are* between projects, but I'll have to talk to Michael. He's out in the studio."

Michael and Sandra were an Indian couple who had been together for several years, struggling with the ups and downs of the acting business and struggling with the ups and downs of just being a couple.

Joanelle didn't have time to wait. "Tell you what," she said. "I'll come by there on my way out of town. If you two wanna go, have your bags packed when I get there. We'll be gone for a few days."

"Where are you going, anyway?" Sandra asked.

"I'll tell you when I get there. It's some place I've been needing to go to for a long time." Joanelee hung up the phone and jumped in the shower for a hot cleansing purge.

So first thing in the morning, she grabbed her suitcase, her guitar, her blue jean jacket with the AIM patch, and her sacred pipe as she headed out the door.

Lakota Sun Dance songs blared from her tape deck as she drove across town in her "Indian car," an old black Chevy van. A large mural on the side depicted an Indian drum group wailing out a powwow song. A bumper sticker on the back declared "Indian Affairs Are The Best."

Joanelle was born on the High Mountain Apache Indian Reservation in southern New Mexico, but her parents moved to Albuquerque when she was nine years old, and then to Los Angeles when she was fifteen. There she had lived most of her life.

She'd always been a fighter—fighting against injustices her people had suffered, fighting against small-mindedness, fighting against those who tried to take away her dreams. As a writer, she had hoped to fight against Indian stereotypes in the media, history books, and everywhere else. It was a hard road.

Michael was just coming out into the front yard with a bedroll and a duffle bag as Joanelle drove up.

"Where are we going?" he asked with a big smile.

"To a place I used to go with my grandmother when I was a little girl," she said. "It was our special place on the rez and I haven't been there in years. White people named it Mount Thomas, but my grandma called it Sacred Mountain. She would go up there when she needed to ask the Creator for something really special. Magic always happened there, and I sure could use some now."

"Cool," Michael said, and they loaded their stuff in the van.

"Bring your drum, your rattles, and your harmonica," Joanelle suggested. "We might wanna make some music on the way."

The three headed east toward the rising sun with a high sense of hope and adventure. Soon they left the tangled freeways of L.A., making good time on the desert highway as the palm trees gave way to scrubby sagebrush.

They made quite a threesome, Indian artisans fighting an uphill battle in what seemed like a foreign country: American pop culture. The trick was to keep your sanity and your identity intact when all that anyone else wanted was for you to help them perpetuate their myths. You know the myths: the Circle-the-Wagons myth, the Noble Savage myth, the Drunken Indian myth, the Medicine Man myth, the Indians-Are-Never-on-Time-for-Anything myth. There are others.

On the California-Arizona border, they stopped to get gas and snacks at one of those roadside convenience stores with the huge red and yellow obnoxious signs. After loading up on junk food and sodas, the van headed back toward the highway on-ramp. Alongside the road was an Indian guy loaded down with a backpack and a bedroll. He was holding a sign that said only: "Indian Country." Joanelle pulled over.

"Where exactly in Indian Country are you going?" Michael yelled out the window.

"Someplace with soul. I'll know when I get there," came the reply.

Michael looked at Joanelle. "What d'ya think?" he asked. "Could be interesting."

Joanelle nodded. Michael opened the door and waved to the hitchhiker. He ran to the van, opened the back door, and climbed in. Off they roared.

His name was Larry. He was in low spirits and had decided to search for the promised land, wherever that was. It seems that his girlfriend had left him, his truck broke down, and his Indian ventriloquist stage act wasn't getting many bookings. Joanelle told him that they were all pilgrims headed to an Apache Sacred Mountain for a little spiritual rejuvenation.

After brief introductions all around, Larry retrieved his Indian dummy "Wind-In-His-Shorts" from his backpack and gave them a sample of his act. They could see why his act wasn't getting too many bookings. It wasn't that he wasn't funny. He had lousy timing. "Timing's the thing," Larry said, "and I just haven't got it . . . yet. But it'll come to me some day, I just know it." Everyone else in the van doubted it, but didn't say so.

Driving cross-country gives a person time to think, time to reflect on life's challenges and that sort of thing. For some reason that long expanse of road in front of you can cause your mind to split into two parts. One part works with your body to keep your car between the white lines, and the other part begins to present you with new possibilities to old problems. Sometimes miles can whiz by while you're in this whole other state of consciousness. That's what usually happened to Joanelle on the road.

But that wasn't happening on this trip. Everyone wanted to talk, all at once, about how fed up they were with their work, their relationships, conditions in tribal communities, politics in tribal communities, politics in the entertainment business, and particularly politics in the Indian art community. And Michael and Larry got into a marathon "Joke-Off" trying to outdo one another with their Indian jokes. Their journey was a portable gab-fest.

The travelers continued eastward down Interstate 40, past the concrete tepees, the fifty-foot Indian man on the sign, the cardboard buffaloes, and the rubber tomahawks: America's cartoon versions of Indian people.

That night, they pulled into a roadside rest area and spread out their bedrolls next to the van. The crisp, clear air provided a stunning view of the star-studded night sky. Larry sang a Lakota prayer song as they drifted off to sleep.

The next day, they pulled into a restaurant in Gallup, New Mexico, for a bite of food. The Turquoise Cafe. The billboard on the highway had bragged of Indian tacos, buffalo burgers, fry bread, and authentic Indian jewelry: open twenty-four hours a day. A somewhat robust Indian waitress came to the table to take their orders. Her name tag read "Elaine." Michael, in his usual way, began joking with Elaine, trying to make her smile, but without much luck. Larry gave it a try, as well. But she told them not to bother. She took their food orders, and when she returned with their drinks, she asked where they were headed.

"Down to Apache country," Joanelle said. "There's a special place there, a mountain I used to go to when I was a kid, and I haven't been back in a long time."

Finally, a grin slowly spread across Elaine's face. "I bet I know that place. I heard about it from my uncle. He used to take special pilgrimages there every four years. It's been a very holy spot to my people, the Zuni, and other tribes in this area, but I've never been there," Elaine said.

The four travelers were impressed that Elaine knew of this place.

"You know there's a powwow this weekend," she continued, "not too far from the mountain. I was kinda wanting to go. Would you guys mind having another passenger?"

Of course no one minded.

"I just live across the street. I'll get my things together while you're eating and be ready by the time you're done."

So the portable gab-fest moved on, with new input from Elaine. She told them her parents' story of relocation to Denver when she was young, to get training and hopefully work. She added her own aspirations and frustrations to the rich mixture of discussion: frustrations with the Indian art scene, the poor quality of health care on the reservation, and the botched cases of Indian land claims caused by the BIA. All the while guitars, harmonicas, and drums provided a sound track to the deliberations.

As the day progressed, everyone noticed that Elaine was definitely attracted to Larry and she tried to sit as close to him as possible. Larry, in turn, welcomed the attention and didn't try to move away.

They arrived at the powwow grounds just before sunset and everybody agreed that they should stay at least for the night. They set up camp, scrounged some firewood, and put a pot of coffee on the fire.

They had arrived in time for the evening's grand entry, so they all went to watch. During the first Intertribal round dance, the pilgrims joined in. The beat of the drum and the songs of the singers were irresistible.

The powwow MC recognized Joanelle across the arena as she was dancing and, after the song was over, he announced over the loudspeaker, "We have a celebrity of sorts with us, the woman who wrote 'My Heroes Have Always Been Indians' a few years ago. Let's give a big hand, everybody, for Joanelle Redhawk: one of our own, making good in the big time."

The crowd applauded enthusiastically as Joanelle smiled and waved real big for everyone. "If they only knew the truth," she whispered to Sandra.

In just a few minutes a voice rang out from across the arena: "Joanelle! Joanelle!"

Joanelle looked around the crowd and found the familiar face of a man she hadn't seen in a long, long time. It was Sonny Two Bulls, an old drinking buddy from Joanelle's early days in L.A. They always managed to see one another every once in awhile somewhere along life's road.

"Hey, girl, you're sure lookin' good for a reformed drunk," Sonny joked.

"I guess all that joy juice I drank in my wild youth helped preserve my fine complexion in my old age," Joanelle replied, striking a pinup pose. Everybody laughed.

"How's the Indian law business these days? Are we winning or losing?" Joanelle asked him.

"Well, up until now it's been about even: cowboys 10, redskins 10," Sonny replied. "But somebody keeps changing the rules of the game, and they seem to own the football. It's all just about to eat my lunch. But it's a long, sad story. That's why I came out here, to drown my sorrows in the sounds of the powwow. And what's your excuse?" he asked Joanelle.

"That, my friend, is a short, sad story," Joanelle moaned. "Come over to the camp with us and we can swap lies, okay?"

The whole group headed over to the camp to drink some coffee and eat Indian tacos. They talked late into the night about things both profound and profane, about the days of old and the good old days.

In the background, the powwow songs and drums echoed through the valley, summoning a racial memory of times when the open sky, the grassy plains, and the towering mountains ruled the lives of their ancestors.

As the conversation and the fire died down, everyone began to settle in for the night. Michael and Sandra spread out their bedrolls near the fire. Larry spread his out beside the van, careful to tuck in "Wind-In-His-Shorts" beside him. Elaine put up a little two-man pup tent nearby and then quietly invited Larry inside. Larry shyly crawled in with Elaine, leaving his dummy outside.

Joanelle was straightening things up inside the van and spreading out her bedding when Sonny approached her.

"Mind if I camp out here with you tonight?" he asked. "I'll behave myself."

Joanelle dug around inside the van for a minute and came up with a spare sleeping bag. "No, I don't mind, Sonny," tossing him the bag. "But you'll have to sleep outside with the others. I need my space."

"I understand," he said with a frown, and walked dejectedly over by the fire.

Joanelle climbed into the van and closed the doors behind her.

She dreamed a puzzling dream that night. She was floating above the ground looking down at her group of friends. They were sitting around a campfire passing her sacred pipe from one person to the next. Michael was singing a pipe song as they smoked the pipe. Joanelle's deceased grandmother came up to them and said, "The road to Sacred Mountain has been moved. You won't find it where it used to be. You have to go a different way."

The next morning the pilgrims packed up the camp and loaded their things in the van. Elaine had a sheepish grin on her face. Larry had an embarrassed grin. Elaine decided to travel on with the pilgrims. Everyone but Sonny piled into the van.

"I wish I was going with you," Sonny said, "but I have some unfinished business to tend to."

As Sonny was saying his good-byes to the troupe, a woman's loud voice rang through the camp: "Sonny. Sonny Two Bulls." An angry but attractive white woman was marching through the camp. She spotted Sonny next to the van. "There you are."

She marched toward Sonny. "You're gonna be Sonny No-Balls when I get through with you," she said. "Where did you spend the night?"

"I told you we were finished, Liz. Now go back to your camp and stop following me around," came Sonny's reply.

"Well, I'm not through with you until I finish giving you a piece of my mind."

Joanelle waved to Sonny and he winked at her.

"You haven't changed, have you, Sonny?" Joanelle commented as the van pulled away. "Who is she, your latest one-night stand?"

"No, she's my wife," he yelled after her. "Know any good divorce attorneys?"

Joanelle pulled out of the campground and onto the open road. As they drove, Joanelle told the pilgrims about her dream.

"What do you think your grandma meant?" Sandra asked. "Was she fond of practical jokes?"

"Yes, she was," Joanelle answered. "She was always joking around and playing little tricks on the people she loved. But she wasn't kidding last night. Well, I guess she was, in a way. She had that little gleam in her eye, like she used to get when she knew something you didn't know and she was trying to make you guess what it was. She was trying to tell me something, but I'm not sure what."

They drove on toward their destination, which was only one day's drive away at this point. Late in the day, they turned off the highway on the road to Sacred Mountain. They noticed a sign that read "High Mountain Ski Resort—10 Miles."

"That's new. I wonder where this resort is," Joanelle pondered out loud.

As the van wound its way up the mountain road, scores of cars passed them going the other way. Finally, Joanelle pulled into the ski resort parking lot and got out of the van. She looked up in disbelief at the resort lodge. Even though it was summer, people were riding the ski lifts and hiking around the mountain.

Michael got out and walked over to Joanelle.

"What's wrong? Why did we stop here?" he asked.

"Because this is Sacred Mountain. Or at least it used to be. I can't believe that something like this could've happened."

Everyone got out of the van and came over to Joanelle. They all stared up at the resort lodge with a blank look on their faces. The sun was setting behind another nearby peak and the sky was filling with hues of brilliant orange and dark magenta.

They were filled with disappointment. Michael drove them back down the mountain because Joanelle was just too paralyzed to function. Back in the lowlands, they headed for the nearest campground for the night.

As night fell, a fog descended in the low-lying areas, so their going was slow and unsure. They drove along a little dirt road for awhile looking for someplace to park the van for the night. Since nothing seemed familiar and no campsite presented itself, they pulled off into a clearing and killed the engine. Fatigue had settled in, so everyone fell asleep where they were.

In a little while, Joanelle was roused from sleep by the sound of someone moaning somewhere out in the fog. She reached over and shook Michael until he woke up too.

"Listen. There's someone out there," she said.

Michael got up and peeked out of the van. There were more noises. It sounded like several people were stumbling through the woods, breathing heavily and moaning.

Joanelle and Michael woke everyone else up in the van. Quietly, they got out and walked toward the sounds. To their astonishment, there was a small band of Indian people dressed in buckskin. Among them was a grandmother and grandfather, a middle-aged man and woman, and a boy and girl. They were all dirty, tired, and hungry.

The man spoke. "We have walked many miles. We have no food or water. Can you help us?"

Michael ran over the van and retrieved some food and water for them.

"What happened to you? Where are you going?" Joanelle asked.

Michael passed out the food as the woman answered.

"We were removed from our homes in the middle of the night by the Bluecoats," she said. "They told us they would kill us if we did not leave. They said that our lands were no longer ours and there was a place they called 'the reservation' that was to be our new home. We ran in fear. Our brothers to the north had already been put on a reservation, given rotten meat to eat and blankets filled with sickness to warm themselves, and left to wither and die."

As the refugee woman spoke, the pilgrims listened in confusion and disbelief. What they were hearing did not make sense to their twentieth-century minds. These were words and actions from the nineteenth-century tragedies among their people.

"How is this happening?" Joanelle asked of no one in particular. "What are we supposed to do?"

"We must keep moving," the refugee man said. "The Bluecoats can't be far behind. If they catch us, they'll kill us."

Feeling the refugees' sense of urgency, and trying to ignore their own sense of disbelief, the pilgrims helped the refugees into the van. The refugees were as confused about the van as the pilgrims were confused about the presence of the refugees. Together, they drove off down the dark, foggy dirt road.

In a little while they came upon another clearing with a single grass hut standing in the middle, illuminated from within by a small cooking fire. A few horses were tied up near the lodge.

They stopped at the edge of the clearing and got out of the van.

"This looks like the lodge of my cousin," the Refugee Man said. "He hid his family away at the first sign of trouble with the white settlers."

Slowly and quietly they crept up to the door of the lodge, following the lead of the Refugee Man. Halfway across the clearing, the horses stirred and a buckskin-clad Indian man came out of the hut to see what was happening. He saw the shadowy figures moving through the fog and moved to pick up a weapon.

The Refugee Man called out to him in their native tongue. The two recognized each other and ran to hug one another. After a few minutes of talking together, the Refugee Man returned to where the group was waiting.

"We are all welcome in my cousin's lodge," the refugee man said. "He has food and warmth for us all for the night."

The curious mixed group of pilgrims and refugees entered the glow of the hut and made themselves at home. With the Refugee Man acting as a translator, they talked on into the night. The man who lived in the hut told them that he had extensively explored the immediate area and he had found a wonderful place where the ancestor spirits came to speak with him. They told him where to find the best game and how to use the herbs that grew in the area for healing.

"They also told me that you were coming," he said to Joanelle in perfect English. "And they asked me to give you a message."

A silence fell over the pilgrims as they listened.

He continued. "They said to tell you that Sacred Mountain is not one single place that you journey to find. Sacred Mountain is all around you. Every place is a sacred place and every mountain is a sacred mountain. Indeed, you carry the sacredness with you wherever you go. Men who are disconnected from themselves and their roots may defile a mountain for their own purposes, but only you can defile the holy mountain in your heart."

The silence became deafening.

Speaking to the whole group, the man continued. "To be sure, there is a time to stand and fight for your family, your life, and your land. But you must learn when to fight and when to save the fight for another day. When it is time to fight, you must use the best weapon for each particular battle. Sometimes it is the bow and the lance. Other times it may be with words and patience. Both require wisdom and courage. Think on it tonight."

With his final words, the man's image began to fade. The pilgrims found themselves getting drowsy. Within minutes, they all fell asleep, enwrapped with the spirit of the evening and the magic of the moment. They were cocooned in a deep, dense sleep all night.

In the morning, Joanelle slowly and almost painfully awoke to find herself not in the hut, but in the van. Her fellow pilgrims were all there too, fast asleep. She peeked out of the van and looked around. They were in the very clearing that, the night before, had held a grass lodge, horses, and other people. Yet, now there was no lodge, no horses, and no other people. Instead, there was a display sign in the clearing at the edge of the dirt road. The sign had a little covering over it.

Joanelle stumbled out of the van with her blanket still wrapped around her. She slowly approached the display to get a better look at it. Near the top it read "Future site of the National Native American Memorial— Dedicated to the generations of Indian people who have been displaced from their homelands. Sponsored by the Sacred Mountain Institute, an Indian-run nonprofit organization."

Under the sign was a little container holding several brochures. As Joanelle reached for one, the rest of the sleepy-eyed, dazed pilgrims arrived beside her.

Rubbing his eyes, Michael asked, "What's going on now?"

Joanelle handed everybody a brochure. The brochure outlined the campaign that was being launched by the Sacred Mountain Institute to get Sacred Mountain returned to the tribe from which it had been taken. Everyone looked at each other with blank stares.

"I don't know about the rest of you guys," Larry said, "but I know where I'm gonna be and what I'm gonna be doing for the next few years."

"What I want to know is where I've been and what I've been doing for the last few days," Sandra said.

"I think we've been traveling in some sort of Indian time warp," said Larry. "Consider, if you will," he said with his best Rod Sterling impression, "five modern-day Indians, confused as hell, and they've just crossed over into . . . The Fry Bread Zone."

Joanelle looked at her friends and laughed a sort of spirit-freeing laugh.

"This is the best trip I've ever been on," she said. "But now I'm starving. Let's go find some breakfast and talk over this battle for Sacred Mountain. I think I have an idea for my next book."

All Michael said was "Cool!" as they walked back toward the van, and the moveable conversation took on new life in search of breakfast.

S. BRUISED HEAD

An Afternoon in Bright Sunlight

AYISSOMAAWA . . .

The Porcupine Hills look soft and brown as we stand gazing out over sunburnt prairie grass.

"Come on, guys. Let's go for a ride," says Hank.

Hank is boss. At least he thinks he is. He is a year older than Anne and me and is the only boy in the family. We let him get away with it, sometimes.

Anne agrees with him. She always agrees with him, especially when we have nothing to do. "We'll ask Mom to make some sandwiches."

"Good idea. Tell her we're going to hunt arrowheads."

Hank decides Anne will ride Brownie, a twelve-year-old bay gelding, same age as Hank. He chooses Hoss for me. Hank says, "Hoss needs some kinks worked out, and this is as good a day as any." He chooses Buck, because Buck is his horse and Buck understands him.

Mom packs enough food to last a week, and, as we make our way back to the corral, she comes to the door and yells, "Don't go too far into the coulee, and watch out for rattlesnakes." She mangles a dish-towel. "Keep an eye open for that bear Jerry saw last week. He says he spotted it down by the old school and later saw it moving toward the hills." She shakes out the towel and waves it. "Get home before dark." She smiles. "Have a good time."

"All right," I yell. "We'll be careful."

"Don't let her worry you." Anne picks up the sack. "There are no rattlesnakes in the coulee, and you know Jerry lies a lot."

"I know Jerry lies. I'm not worried."

Hank has the horses saddled and ready to go. He takes the sack and ties it to the back of his saddle.

A wide streak of dust rises, billows out, and kind of hangs in the air. "There's Dad," says Hank. He pats Buck's neck.

Mom doesn't look too pleased. The dust mushrooms. We hear Dad's loud laughing voice, "Hello Dawlink!" Mom takes a swipe at him with her dish-towel. "I brought company," he says.

"Isn't that old Sam?" says Hank.

Mom shakes hands with Sam; her voice carries on the breeze. "Come in. I'll make you something to eat."

Everybody treats Sam with respect. I remember walking in front of him one time, and, boy, did I ever get it from Dad. I stay out of his way, now.

Hank is all excited. "There's Les!"

Les comes running. We all think Les is the greatest. Dad picks him up whenever he needs help. He trains horses for Dad. He trained Hoss, and helps out during calving season. He travels with Dad, and, sometimes, he even drives. He seems older than fourteen.

"Hey, Les," says Hank. "You can ride Hoss."

"Where you going?" Les lengthens the stirrups.

"Hunting arrowheads."

Anne and I stand there listening. They ignore us. They always ignore us.

"Hey! You kids!" shouts Dad from the house. Hank shoves me and Anne up on Brownie, and we take off. We can hear Dad shouting. We reach the coulee, and Hank reins in. Les looks at him.

"Your dad was calling."

"I know."

"You guys are in trouble."

"He wants us to stay home."

"Well," says Les. "We might as well keep going now. We'll catch heck for one thing or another."

"I know, but maybe if we stay out late, he'll cool off."

"Yeah, he'll get worried," says Anne.

"Yeah, he'll just have more to get mad about," I say.

They just look at me.

We wander into the coulees, stopping every now and then to pick cactus berries. They are green and plump, the size of grapes. Their juice is sweet and sticky. They are easy to find in the short grass, and we go from patch to patch.

As we near an outcropping of rock, Anne says, "Mom said to watch out for rattlesnakes."

"Don't be silly. Everybody knows there are no rattlesnakes in these coulees. Right, Hank?"

Hank and I agree.

"Well, how about that bear Jerry saw?" says Anne.

"Jerry didn't see no bear," laughs Les.

"Are you sure?" Hank licks his lips whenever he's worried. He does it now.

"Sure I'm sure. There hasn't been a bear in these coulees for years."

"Well, a bear could have come down from the hills."

"Look," says Les, "there are no bears in the coulee."

That settles the bear question. We stay away from the rocks. Everybody knows that snakes sun themselves on rocks. None of us likes snakes, especially Hank and Anne.

Hank licks his lips. "Jerry lies a lot."

"You still worried?" says Les.

"I just remembered Dad said he saw something out here."

"I remember, too," says Anne eagerly. "It was the day before Jerry came to visit."

"It was after," I say.

"It was before," says Hank.

Anne smiles at me. "I told you," she says.

"Come to think of it," says Les, "just before we came out, we were at the pool hall in town. Your dad, Sam, and some other men were talking about seeing something out here."

"What did they see?"

"Do you know anything about Sam?"

"Yeah. He's old, and he lives by the school," says Hank.

"You're not supposed to walk in front of him," I say. "Did you know that?"

Anne wants to know more. "What about him?"

Les looks at Hank. "Do you know why he lives there?"

"No."

"He guards the coulees."

We look at Les. He looks back. He isn't smiling. His eyes sweep over us. Then he turns and carefully guides Hoss around a clump of brittle reeds down onto a dry creek bed.

"What do you mean, he guards the coulees?"

"Just that."

"Why should he guard the coulees?" Les has me curious, too.

"Oh," says Les, "there's things out here."

"What kind of things?"

"Animals . . . other things that live in the coulee."

"You've got to be kidding. Only animals live in the coulee." Hank shakes his head and laughs.

"What kind of things?" I insist.

"You don't have to know," Hank cuts in. "What did old Sam have to say?"

In a matter-of-fact tone, Les says, "He thinks a wolverine may have moved in."

"A wolverine? No kidding!" Hank's eyes light up. He moves closer to Les. "Maybe we should forget about arrowheads and go hunting."

"I don't think so."

"But, I've never seen a wolverine. It would be fun."

"We better wait until Sam figures out what to do."

"What does Sam have to do with anything?"

"Sam knows a lot. He says they're dangerous."

I break in—"That's what Emma said."

"Yeah? What did Emma have to say?"

"You're not supposed to listen to Emma," says Anne.

"Well, she says they're dangerous and evil, too."

"Forget about Emma," Hank says, licking his lips. "She's a crazy old lady. Just how dangerous are wolverines?"

"Well, you know that bear?" says Les.

"Yeah?"

"Well, wolverines hunt the hunter."

Hank looks over his shoulder. Anne and I smile.

It is hot. Horse tails switch lazily at slow-moving flies. Saddle leather squeaks. Hooves thud dully on dry grass. An occasional sharp crack echoes down the coulee.

She stands listening to the children's voices. An outcropping of rock hides her den. Inside, it is cool and dry.

Ayissomaawaawa . . . I must be careful, I waited long. Need to grow. Strong. Strong. Strong as when I was young. It was good. Our power was strong. Must be careful. Haste betrays. I must wait. Come, boy. Come alone. Do not fear. There is nothing to fear.

"Hank!" Anne yells. "Look at the chokecherries!"

Low chokecherry bushes grow halfway up to the side of the coulee. Their branches hang with thick clusters of black cherries.

"Let's pick some for Mom," I say.

Hank dismounts. "Good idea, Girlie. Here, you hold the horses."

"Why do I always have to hold the horses?"

"Because I tell you to."

I look down at him. "We can't pick berries, anyway."

"Why not?"

"We have nothing to put them in."

"We can put them in the lunch sack," says Anne.

"Good idea," says Hank. "We can tie the horses up down by those bushes."

I must wait. Cannot hurry. Wait. No strong. Stronger must I get. Soon. Soon. So close.

The bushes are low and evenly spaced. They look as if they were planted by someone. Anne and I fill our hats and empty the berries into the sack. We begin filling our hats again, when Anne spots some raspberries growing near the outcropping of rock.

"Come on, Hank. Let's get some of them, too."

"I'm not going over there."

Anne looks at me. I shake my head.

"Just look at them!"

"Go and get them, then," says Les.

"Yeah." Hank and I agree.

"I don't know." Anne looks at the rocks.

"Nobody's stopping you," says Les.

"There might be snakes."

"Snakes won't kill you. These snakes are just ordinary snakes," says Les.

"Then you go and get them."

"I don't like raspberries."

Ayissomaawa . . . Patience. Must have patience. Soon I will have them. I must have them. Must be careful. Not move. Too soon. Wait. Time. Old woman. Now old woman. Do not frighten.

"Let's go, then. You girls wait for us here. Okay?"

"Why do we have to wait?"

Hank is real nasty. "All right. If you want to walk down, I'm not stopping you."

"I'm not going anyplace." Anne drops to the ground. "You guys can get the horses."

Hank and Les run down the coulee.

"Do you smell something funny?" says Anne.

"Yeah, it smells like sage."

"No. Sage doesn't smell like that."

"Maybe it's dry mint."

"No. Mint doesn't smell like that, either."

"Maybe it's a snake den. Snakes like rocks, you know."

"No. It isn't snakes."

"How do you know?"

"I know," says Anne. "Now quit. You're giving me a headache."

We sit there. The sun is beating down. It is quiet. Flies drone. I feel sleepy. The sun is warm on my back.

Ayissomaawa . . .

"Anne! Girlie! Get over here."

Les and Hank have the horses. They wait while we bring the sack of berries.

"Come on. Hurry up!"

"I don't feel so good, Hank," says Anne. "I have a headache."

"Me too."

Hank and Les look at each other. "So do we."

"Maybe we should just go home."

"We can't let a stupid headache stop us from hunting for arrowheads."

Anne and me stand there, looking at Hank. Nobody says anything. Hank looks at us. "Just around the bend is where we found them last time."

"I wonder if there are any left," says Les.

"There should be plenty."

"What happened to the other ones we found?"

"Mom still has them. She takes them out every once in a while."

Ayissomaawa . . . Horses. Horses know us. Must be careful.

"Are we going to hunt arrowheads or stand around here all day?" I say.

"We're going. Now get on that horse."

Hank lifts Anne and me up on Brownie and ties the sack to his saddle. "Ready to go?"

"Yeah."

The horses walk sideways. Their ears flick back and forth. Their eyes roll, and they jerk their heads up and down. We don't go very far.

"What's that smell?"

"Smells like sage to me."

"No, it doesn't." Anne is emphatic. I agree with her.

"Well, it doesn't smell half bad. It sure is strange, though. Wonder what's causing it." Les looks around.

"What's that?" Anne points to the rocks. I try to see over her shoulder.

"Where?"

"Over there. See?"

"It's just a shadow."

"There's something there," says Anne.

The horses balk. Hoss backs into Brownie.

"Let's go see. Let's find out what it is. Come on, Hank."

Hank licks his lips. "Do you think we should?"

We look at him.

"Well, the horses don't want to go."

Les stands up in his stirrups to get a better view. A surprised look crosses his face.

"It's an old woman."

Brownie whirls. Takes off down the side of the coulee. Anne and I hold on tight. I didn't know Brownie had that much speed. As we hit the bottom of the coulee, I see two riders loom up in front of us. Brownie stumbles, and both of us fall.

"Are you hurt?" Dad sounds worried.

"No," I say, and he pulls me off Anne.

"Anne, Anne, you all right?"

Anne lies there, trying to catch her breath. I look up and see Sam.

"Anne, you all right?"

"Yeah, Dad. I'm okay." Anne lies back and starts to cry.

Before Hank and Les can slide to a stop, Dad is already yelling. "How many times have I told you not to run the horses like that?"

"We didn't do nothing." Hank points back to the rocks. "The horses

. . . they just took off when they saw that old lady in the coulee."

"What are you talking about?"

"An old woman . . . in the coulee." Hank looks at Les.

"She spooked the horses," says Les.

Dad looks back and forth, eyeing each of us. He knows we wouldn't dare lie to him.

"Did you see her?"

"We didn't get a good look," says Les.

Dad looks at us and then at Sam.

"It was near those rocks," says Hank.

"Yeah, and it smelled kinda like sage," says Les.

"You kids get home right now," says Dad. He shoves me and Anne back up on Brownie. "Get going! Stay there till I get back."

We know an order when we hear one.

Too late. Must move. Always moving. He'll come. Tired. Tired. He has power. He will come. No more.

Dad stands at the mouth of the coulee holding the two horses. Sam walks into the coulee.

IRVIN MORRIS

The Hyatt,
the Maori, and
the Yanoama

AFTER SUPPER I CUT A SLICE OF WATERMELON AND SAT ON THE
porch steps, spitting seeds and watching the shadow of the mountains
behind my home stretch across the valley. As they touched the horizon,
there was a final smolder of color. The pale cliffs of Chaco Canyon gleamed
like inlays of mica on the edge of the world. Gray thunderheads tinged with
orange and pink glowed over Torréon and the Sierra Nacimiento. They
were Holy People come from the south, dressed in icy robes of water. They
had come in answer to our prayers once again, bringing nothing less than
life itself.

    Anaasázi. I imagined the canyon sacred with the jingle of copper bells,
vibrant with voices, bright with parrot feathers. The Ancient Ones dancing. Prayer in motion. The plaza at Pueblo Bonito awash with firelight and

the thunder of drums rolling like waves through the canyon. Far to the east, a rainbow glowed in the last light.

Ahaláane, I thought. How better to express the joy and awe?

———◆◆◆———

I sank into the deep cushions of the sofa, and the indigo landscape outside dropped below the cluttered sill. A gilded dragon. Brass elephants. A pair of rosy-cheeked youth, a boy and girl caught in mid-stride, a wooden bucket held between them. They had been on their way back from the well when the ceramist froze them for all time. I aimed the remote and the television came alive, hissing.

Thunderous applause. Hysterical laughter. Then tight faces as Eddie Murphy began talking about black and white. The dog barked. I punched the mute button and the gate hinges squeaked twice. There was a knock on the door. I flicked on the porch light and Frank, my neighbor and in-law, squinted in the sudden glare. He stepped quickly into the room, trailing a faint wake of rain-scented air. His expression was grim.

"Don't tell me," I said. "Is she . . ."

"She is," he nodded. "Again."

While I rummaged for flashlights in the kitchen drawers, he told me that he had just got back from pulling a cow out of the mud at the watering hole. "That took all afternoon, and then I come home to this mess," he said, shaking his head. "Dammit." He'd left the oldest girl in charge, but she'd been too busy gabbing on the phone to notice anything.

The last time the old lady had disappeared, they found her huddled in a clump of saltbush, cold, hungry, and nearly dehydrated.

A knotted cord, images and emotions, slipped through my mind: The old lady—my grandfather's sister—crawling on hands and knees through the furnace heat of a summer day. Over scorching sand, through fields of tumbleweeds, over anthills, under barbed wire fences, across arroyos and the busy bus road. I pictured the thick calluses on her palms, and her face, darkened by the sun, seamed with wrinkles like the eroded foothills to the west. Her failing eyes, clouded and blinking behind thick glasses. Gray hair, once glossy black, in disarray, loosened in wisps from the woolen hair tie. And carrying on conversations with men and women long dead.

One time I had come across her crouching in a shallow ditch, cowering in terror. "*Yíiya, shiyázhí,*" she'd whispered. "*Naakai da shooltse' lágo.*" There hadn't been any Mexican horsemen in the area for over three hundred years.

——◆·❉·◆——

We walked slowly, swinging the beams of our flashlights back and forth. Voices called out now and then. "*Shimásání! Shimásání!*" Grandmother, grandmother. Some of the children whispered and giggled, but an adult voice hushed them. We might not see her, you carrying on like that! It was impossible to see anything besides the stars overhead and the flashlights bobbing in the darkness. In a few minutes, a pair of headlights swung out from the cluster of our houses and bounced toward us. There was no road so the vehicle maneuvered around sand hills and clumps of rabbitbrush. The long beams lit up the rugged slopes of the foothills a mile away.

"There she is!" someone shouted.

"*Shimásání!*"

"You dorks, it's just a piece of roofing paper!"

——◆·❉·◆——

From the top of a low outcrop of clay, the headlights reached across the plain. The vehicle backed up slowly and swept its beams over the land. Then it descended and came toward us. In time, Grace, who was Frank's wife and my aunt, pulled up next to me in their truck. She rolled down her window and motioned to me. I went over, but she didn't say anything for a while. She stared out the windshield.

"You must think I'm awful," she said.

"No, Grace, I don't."

———◆◆◆◆◆———

The truth was that I didn't, really. I understood more than she seemed to suppose. I waited. A burrowing owl called out, predicting more warm weather. A movement to the side caught my eye. "This flashlight of yours burned out," Frank said, handing me the cold object. I clicked it on and the filament in the bulb glowed a dull orange.

"I don't think we'll find her tonight," Frank said. "Best thing's to start again in the morning. Right now, she's holed up somewhere. We won't find her like that."

"You sure?" I asked, but I knew he was right. She would be too afraid to move. She would hide.

Grace sighed and pulled a tissue from the box on the dashboard. "It's sure as hell not easy," she said, her eyes glittering in the dim of the instrument panel. Frank shifted uneasily and looked away. He leaned against the cab. I excused myself to tell the others. As I walked away, I heard the truck door open.

———◆◆◆◆◆———

"Sometimes I feel like quitting my job, but . . . " Grace said back at her house, waving her hand vaguely about the room as she poured coffee. I knew all about their situation and I could sympathize. Splinters and stone—that was rez life. Many families had gone to find better times in the cities, and those who stayed behind were left with the weight of holding things together. Frank and Grace had seven mouths to feed. And if that wasn't enough, the old lady had gone steadily downhill for a couple of years.

She'd cut quite a figure in her youth—a term I once heard her use—the first local woman to pluck her eyebrows and wear lipstick. Faux pearls. In one hand-tinted photograph she wore a fur stole, bobbed hair, and a Garbo-esque hat. Her acid wit had meant her dealings with men went strictly by her terms.

———◆◆◆◆◆———

I once saw a tree fall. The feeling was like that. Within the past year, she had taken to the worrisome habit of leaving her house and crawling about outside, never mind the time or weather. It wasn't that she was deliberately neglected, however. The trouble was that she had to be watched constantly. The minute you turned your back, she was out the door. The responsibility could wear anyone down.

"I'm sick of the hour commute to Gallup, and then *this* happens," Grace said, sitting down across from me at the table. "I suppose I'll have to call in."

"No, don't do that," Frank told her. "I'll saddle up first thing in the morning. I'll find her."

Frank stood in the kitchen doorway, holding their youngest daughter, Faith, who was fast asleep. He carried her into the other room and Grace sighed, looking after them. She glanced at me, and I knew what she was thinking.

Frank had been unemployed for over three years now, ever since the uranium mines had closed. He'd gone around town with references from the employment office, but finally he had stopped knocking on doors. He never said anything about it, but I knew. It was easier to stay away from town than face the humiliation. And you didn't have to see the wealth and the way they treated people.

We walked a razor's edge. What else could we do? Every day we faced the thefts, the lies, and the hate. And there weren't too many things to do about it. Either you smiled and pretended it didn't matter, withdrew to where they couldn't reach you, or kissed ass. Or you went under. Half the boys I'd known in grade school were dead. The list was long: Despair. Self-hate. Alcohol. No work and plenty of time to stew. How would any man feel? He didn't have to tell me why he didn't meet the gaze of the rednecks in town, the tourists who asked to take the picture, or the contemptuous social workers who didn't understand.

"It's totally crazy," Grace said. Frank came back and sat next to her. "They're asleep," he said, indicating the children in the next room with a nod of his head.

"It's a dirty shame," said Frank. "In the old days, old folks stayed with family to the end."

"That's the old days," sighed Grace.

"Dead and buried," said Frank, shaking his head.

"Gone with the buffalo," I said.

Frank looked at me. He grinned. "Belly up," he said, holding out his hand and wiggling his fingers.

"A raw deal," I said.

"A bum steer."

"A crying shame."

"Honestly, you guys," Grace said.

"Just awful," said Frank, and eyed her sideways.

Grace made a funny sound and her shoulders began to jerk up and down. I thought she was crying, but she wasn't. "Utter tragedy," she gasped, and her throaty laugh swept us up. Soon we were whooping and snorting at the absurdity of us flopping helpless as hooked fish in the language.

After we calmed down, Grace brought more coffee and a plate of muffins. "Amazing, isn't it?" she said. "It started with Dick-and-Jane. Now, it's ship-the-old-lady-off-to-a-home."

"The Golden Years," Frank said.

"Shady Pines," I said.

"Okay, you two, that's enough," said Grace. "Let's get serious."

"If your sisters weren't such hang-around-the-fort Indians, you would have some help," Frank said.

"Now, Hon," Grace smiled. "They're making good money. You know they can't get that kind of lab work around here. And they'll help with the cost too, you know."

"I wish I could do something." Frank leaned back and ran his hand through his hair.

"You have the cattle to look after. I don't know what we would do if we didn't have the calves to sell in the fall. Besides, you look after the little ones when there's no sitter. How can I expect you to do all that and watch her, too?"

As I sat listening to them, I smelled the sharp odor of drying roots and wool. I heard the roof creak with the force of the wind. It was mid-winter and I was about five years old. Shimásání stood by the woodstove stirring something in a pot. The room was steamy and warm. She spoke in a quiet voice, describing in our language how her grandmother had told of surviving the forced march to Fort Sumner, three hundred miles to the east. A hundred years after it had happened, the tragedy was fresh in her mind. "It was cold like that," she'd said, pointing with her lips toward the window to indicate the freezing wind outside. "The people walked the whole distance at gunpoint. Many bad things happened. If anyone paused to rest, they were shot. A woman who had stopped to give birth was impaled on a sword. Old people were abandoned and babies were clubbed. Vultures followed them all the way."

I drowsed on her lap, the crackle of the fire inside the iron stove lulling me within the womb-like embrace of her arms. The kerosene lamp cast a soft light on the log walls of her house.

There was a loom by her bed and she spent long hours each day weaving precious inches onto the rugs she made to sell. I played around her, making roads for my toy cars on the dirt floor. I stayed with her while my mother was at the hospital, a mysterious place I knew nothing about. After awhile, she carried me to the bed and covered me with a quilt. Then she blew out the lamp and I went to sleep.

Now, her loom stood idle.

I saw what I had to do. "It's really for the best," I lied. "I mean, it's not doing her any good being out there. Think about winter, the storms, the hot stove. And you won't be the first ones to do it."

The words scraped my throat. Can you believe it, I thought. But these were modern times. The stars had shifted, my grandfather once said, and he didn't know what it meant.

The sink made a gurgling noise. We turned. The small panes of the window above the counter fractured our faces into a strange mosaic.

◆◆◆◆◆

"Remember last month when she almost picked up that baby rattler?" Frank said. "At least she'll be safe in Chinle."

"Safe," Grace sighed. "Who would have thought that one day I would be the one? That she would turn into a child and that I would be the parent?"

"We have to do it, Grace. There's no choice." Frank touched her hand. A surge of anger rose inside me. They would never stop. The changes. The meddling. We were all affected, the men, the women, the children, and now, the elders.

I glanced up and saw Frank and Grace looking at me. I shrugged.

"Dammit," Grace said.

I studied the veins on the back of my hands.

◆◆◆◆◆

The alarm rang at four. I rolled out of bed and quickly got dressed. I went out to greet the dawn with prayer and pollen. Then I put on the coffee and watched the all-night news on TV while I waited for sunrise. In New York City, blacks were protesting the killing of one of their young men by bat-wielding skinheads. The body of an undercover drug agent had been discovered in a shallow grave in Mexico. Outside, the rooster crowed and the clouds to the east slowly turned orange-pink.

The dog gruffed once and the gate hinges squeaked. Frank opened the door and came in. He rubbed his hands together and grinned.

"I found her," he said. "She was in the culvert under the bus road. Hell, I passed by there twice yesterday and didn't think to look inside it. She's home now, sipping coffee and munching warm tortillas like nothing happened." He laughed and shook his head. "That old lady is really something . . ." He looked out the window.

I couldn't help but smile.

I poured two cups of coffee and we watched the rest of the newscast. A suspended walkway in the atrium of the Kansas City Hyatt Regency had collapsed, killing several people and trapping scores of others under tons of steel and concrete. In Brazil, the Yanoama were protesting the destruction of their forest homeland. On the other wide of the world, the Maori were threatening to disrupt a visit by the Queen.

LARRY LITTLEBIRD

The Hunter

MAYBE IT WAS BECAUSE I WAS A CHILD AND SAW IT THAT WAY, or maybe it really is the way I remember it, growing up in my mother's village.

It is fall. There is a special clarity in the way light appears at this time of year. And it gives my memory a sense of another time, a time when my young eyes can see beyond the haze and the world stands out, still, brilliant, and defined. In the fall, all talk and thoughts turn to hunting. As the stories of the deer and the hunter unfold detail by detail, in my child's mind, images of the deer appear and take shape.

They say the deer is a spirit. A creature of God's creation, it needs supplication, understanding, and reverence. It is a blessing, a gift bestowed upon humankind as a remembrance of our own life's interconnected course, an interwoven thread from the beginning of all living time. It is meat for the body and soul.

Endowed with a keen sense of sight, smell, and hearing plus additional uncanny abilities beyond human dimension, this creature cannot be simply slaughtered and used. The deer's realm is the pristine spaces of mountain and plain, its very domain is a sanctuary. Its essence is life; to kill it is to waste it.

This new and wondrous creature begins to occupy me, looming magnificently magnified and imagined in my thoughts as I roam mesas and arroyos playing, as I eat and sleep.

I want to be a hunter, one of the men afield in the fall, gun in hand, bandolier of shiny bullets around my waist, a bright red kerchief about my head. Can I be a man who will endure the rigors of the hunt? The all-night prayer and singing? A man who from daylight till sunset, without food, without drink, will evidence the stamina of a strong people? I wonder.

With a child's anticipation and delight, the fall evenings are spent around the little outdoor fires on the village edge waiting into the night for the signal that will tell everyone a hunter returns. For seeming nights on end, we wait until at last the bright orange spark that lights the shadow of the far southern hill sends me scurrying with the other boys and girls toward the only road by which the hunters will enter. Gathering excitedly at the road's edge, laughing and whispering, speculating about which party of men are returning, our noisy exuberance is suddenly cut silent. A low murmuring sounds from the far deep night. The joyous rise of men's voices singing their songs of the deer coming home to our village reaches us through the darkness.

Someday I will arrive home like these men, my face painted to signify my sacred purpose, greeted reverently by the people, blessed and made welcome. I dream of that day, but how?

One day my grandmother simply tells me, "Day by day, little by little, you will learn. Keep your eyes open, your mouth shut and become obedient to those in authority around you. Life is sacred to us, and you are sacred. You carry it in your heart the best you can. Treat all things as you want to be treated, then some day you will be ready." It is simple and I believe her. But I still want to kill a deer.

With a little boy's forgetfulness, these questions I ponder so seriously easily give way to other equally important concerns as the season passes. Will there be enough snow this year for my homemade sled I've worked so hard to find enough scrap boards to make? Will I ever learn to spin my brightly painted wooden top, whipping it off the tight string as accurately as my older cousin? Will my small frail hand ever grasp the correct grip on the beautiful glass marble that would allow me to win a few more? The seasons come and go, invisibly blending one into another, and even though I still leave more marbles in the ring than fill my pockets, visions of the deer never quite leave me.

During this time I learn to use a home-made inner tube band slingshot until cans, bottles, even objects tossed into the air are accurately and consistently knocked down. After that, proficiency with a rifle comes easily. Even then, something tells me hunting is more than expertise with a weapon. Gradually, I am obsessed by one recurrent thought, "to kill a deer without wasting it."

The year of my first deer hunt, my uncles carefully instruct me on what a man does when he wants to hunt. I do as I am taught; I do it all correctly but I don't kill a deer.

"Killing a deer isn't everything to hunting," my uncles say. "Fasting and praying, a man works hard giving his self to the spirit the deer belongs to. We are only human, we cannot say what our giving should bring. Yes, we want badly to bring home that big buck; we can only work truthfully at doing that. The Creator will see our honesty; we must believe our reward will come about. There should be no disappointment."

Trying not to feel disappointed, I think all this over. I prepared so carefully—my rifle, my bullets, my actions, my thoughts, my prayers. Where am I at fault? Then I remember.

I remember that little boy sitting by the outdoor fires watching for the returning hunters. I remember what he felt in his heart when he saw the stripe-painted faces of the men arriving home from the deer's mountain sanctuary, their beings permeated with invisible blessings, strength, well-being.

I remember water that is made holy as the paint is washed from their faces by the women. I remember the little boy who is told to drink that sacred water. I remember eagerly drinking that murky brown liquid, the taste of sweet sediment in my mouth. The grown-ups laugh and make joking remarks but I drink it anyway because I believe them when they tell me it will make me a strong hunter. I feel my body shudder as the essence touches my young heart that wants only to be a hunter.

It is the desire to be a hunter who will not waste a deer's life that I remember. My feet have touched the mountains where deer live; I have breathed in the same air and drunk of their water. I've gotten close, yet no deer has come to my hungry gun. There is no fault. Had I killed a deer that first year, would I have recalled the little boy who wanted to be a hunter? Or remembered the child who believed the stories old men and old women tell in that other long ago time?

Surely, the deer is a spirit, and I must die if I am to be one. Day by day, little by little, as I embrace and struggle with this gift, my worldly desires must die, my physical needs must die. I must die to the selfish lusts that would entice my body and entrap my soul, until at last, unthinking and clear-eyed, innocent like a child, I am free to believe and know the secret pulsing in the hot flowing blood the hunter hunts. And, somewhere, the red living waters of the pure-eyed deer wait for me.

VEE F. BROWNE

How to Be a Southwest Indigenous Writer

LIVE IN THE SOUTHWEST, NEAR A MESA, BUTTE, OR PLATEAU. Follow the art of the indigenous writer. Talk to the mesa every morning before dawn. Sit on a rock facing the East. Pick up the dirt and let it run through your fingers; throw some to the East, West, South, and North Gods. Be still and stay loose. Learn to watch lambs (*dibe y'zhi*). Plant a tumbleweed garden. Invite a black hair charmer to Navajo tea. Write *yes* with cedar beads. Type *yes!* one full page each day before dawn. Make friends with the deities and coyote. Dream as you drive down the dirt road. Look forward to the female rain, where colorful beads make up the rainbow. Cry during movies—*Thunderheart, Powwow Highway, Dances with Wolves, The Last of the Mohicans, Soldier Blue, Man Called Horse, Little Big Horn,* and *Chief Crazy Horse.* Scream and cheer at the Indian National Finals Rodeo in November. Roll in the snow. Hike as high as you can on the San Francisco Peaks by moonlight. Meet publishers with a smile. Believe you're a damn good writer. Scribble on napkins. Carry broken lead pencils. Wear a turquoise watch. Don't wash your face before you type. Eat buttered popcorn for lunch with Diet Coke. Make friends with liberty and ambiguity. Wear a writer's attitude. Refuse to follow the norm. Refuse to see black and white; see gray. Know there are no definite answers. Do not question your intuition. Nap under a juniper tree. Do it now—begin it and royalties will follow. Laugh often. Sit under the Navajo moon each month. Think possibilities always. Wear moccasins. Write whatever you dream. Let editors correct you. Don't be hurt. Say to yourself, I'll try again. Rewrite and rewrite. Believe in ceremonies. Talk to the stars. Wave to the pink skies and sunset. Sit and talk with the elders. Giggle with kindergartners. Hold babies to the sky in gratitude. Start your mornings with an address to Sunbearer. Wear ghost beads and a turquoise nugget. Let nothing disturb your peace of mind. Stay warm, content, and optimistic. Draw on the canyon walls. Read every other day. Imagine yourself as creator of fiction and nonfiction stories. Jump without fear. Listen to the Wind Gods. Play with words. Tell coyote jokes. Fantasize. Write for your inner child. Build a hoghan with Navajo Pendleton blankets. Hug sand lizards. Share your fried bread with a kangaroo rat. Write romantic letters with poetry of the indigenous people. Take long walks alone. Talk on the phone for seven hours to a dear friend. Ride rams and goats. Talk about the novel. Refuse to be late for Writer's Workshop. Look for characters in your friends. Let it go! Get permission from the Spider People to tell your stories during the winter season. Listen for the first thunder in February. Write to enjoy and weave a rug with words. Listen to what the Coyote has to say. Be honest to one person.

Taa'a kodi ahe'hee!

The End

◆ ACKNOWLEDGMENTS ◆

"The Problem of Old Harjo" and "The Singing Spirit" reprinted from *Voice of the Turtle*, edited by Paula Gunn Allen. Ballantine Books, 1992.

"Bicenti," "Never Quite a Hollywood Star," "Jules Bart, Giving Too Much —August 1946," and "Tender Street" reprinted from *Song of the Turtle*, edited by Paula Gunn Allen. Ballantine Books, 1994.

"The Hunter" reprinted from *Tough Love from Earth Power Coming: Short Fiction in Native American Literature*, edited by Simon Ortiz. Navajo Community College Press, 1983.

"San Lorenzo Day in Laguna," "The Cystal Cave," "The Hyatt, the Maori, and the Yanoama," and "How to Be a Southwest Indigenous Writer" reprinted from *Neon Pow Wow: New Native American Voices of the Southwest*, edited by Anna Lee Walters. Northland Publishing, 1993.

"Compatriots" and "An Afternoon in Bright Sunlight" reprinted from *All My Relations: An Anthology of Contemporary Canadian Native Fiction*, edited by Thomas King. University of Oklahoma Press, 1992.

PAULA GUNN ALLEN (Laguna/Sioux) is a widely published poet, critic, and essayist and regarded as the one of the founding mothers of the formal study of American Indian literature. Her contributions to the field are numerous, including editing the anthologies *Spider Woman's Grand-daughters, Voice of the Turtle,* and *Song of the Turtle; Studies in American Indian Literature;* and the critically acclaimed *The Sacred Hoop.* Recently retired as a professor of English at UCLA, she makes her home in California amongst a host of books, journals, notepads, and best of all, her three children and two grandchildren.

LORENZO BACA (Laguna) received an M.A. in American Indian Studies from UCLA, and says this about his work: "As a visual, performing, and literary artist I draw on traditional forms with the use of modern technology to express contemporary concepts." Currently, he is focusing on performance of poetry, storytelling, and song, with a new compact disc soon to be released.

VEE F. BROWNE (Navajo) is from Cottonwood/Tselani, Arizona and belongs to the Bitter Water and Water Flows Together clans. She is a journalist, educator, Arizona Interscholastic Athletic Association volleyball and basketball referee, and fiction writer. An award-winning author, she has received much acclaim for her children's books, including *Monster Slayer,* winner of the Western Heritage Award, and *Monster Bird.* Browne's short stories have appeared in *Neon Powwow,* 1994, and *Blue Dawn, Red Earth,* 1996. She is also author of *Maria Tallchief* and *Owl Book.*

S. BRUISED HEAD (Blackfoot) was born on the Pegian Reserve in Alberta, Canada, in 1951. Her poetry has appeared in *Firestone* and *Whetstone.* She lives in Alberta.

CAROLYN DUNN (Creek/Seminole/Cherokee) is a poet, fiction writer, essayist, and pastoral minister. Her work has appeared in the anthologies *The Colour of Resistance, Reinventing the Enemy's Language,* and *Through the Eye of the Deer,* which she coedited. She is the author of two volumes of poetry, *Outfoxing Coyote* and *Hidden Creek.* A member of the Mankillers, an all-Native women's drum group, and the Indigenous rock band Red Hawk, she lives in southern California with her husband, son, and mother.

DEBRA EARLING (Flathead) has had her stories published in several collections including *The Last Best Place: A Montana Anthology, Talking Leaves,* and *Reinventing the Enemy's Language.* She makes her home in Poulson, Montana.

CHARLES A. EASTMAN (OHIYESA) (Wahepeton Sioux) was born near Redwood Falls, Minnesota, in 1858. He was educated at Dartmouth College and Boston University School of Medicine, receiving his M.D. in 1890. A highly visible spokesperson and leader during his long life, his major works include *From the Deep Woods to Civilization: Chapters in the Autobiography of an Indian, Indian Boyhood,* and *The Soul of the Indian.* Dr. Eastman died in 1938.

ANITA ENDREZZE (Yaqui) is a poet, writer, and artist. She is half Yaqui Indian and half European (Slovene, German-Romanian, and northern Italian). Her work has been published in ten countries and translated into seven languages. The author of seven books including *At the Helm of Twilight* and most recently *Throwing Fire at the Sun, Water at the Moon,* Endrezze is also an accomplished artist who has exhibited in the United States, Finland, and Denmark. She also teaches part-time university courses in addition to traveling to other states and countries to lecture. She's married, with two children, one still living at home, the other out on his own.

LYNDA MARTINEZ FOLEY (Zapotec) is a wife, mother, and writer who was inspired by the 1994 Northridge earthquake to return to her Zapotec storytelling roots. Her work has been published in the anthologies *Strange New Worlds* and *Through the Eye of the Deer.* She lives in southern California with her husband, sons, dogs, and menagerie of pets.

RAVEN HAIL (Cherokee) was born in 1921 in Washington County, Oklahoma. She spent two years at Oklahoma State University and one at Southern Methodist University. Among the diverse accomplishments of Raven Hail are a recording, *The Raven Sings*, consisting of Native American songs; and *The Raven and the Redbird*, a three-act play about the life of Sam Houston and his Cherokee wife.

LARRY LITTLEBIRD (Laguna/Santa Clara) is a fiction writer, poet, and screenwriter. He's best known for his film adaptation of the Pulitzer Prize–winning novel *House Made of Dawn*, released in the early 1970s.

JOHN M. OSKISON (Cherokee) was born in Vinita, in Indian Territory, in 1874. Journalist, short story writer, and novelist, his works include *Wild Harvest*, *A Texas Titan: The Story of Sam Houston*, and *Tecumseh and His Time*. He died in 1947.

DAWN KARIMA PETTIGREW (Cherokee/Chickasaw/Seminole/Creek/other Native descent) is an ordained minister and president of Wells of Victory Ministries on the Qualla Boundary in Cherokee, North Carolina, and is Pastor of the Cherokee Church in Cherokee, N.C. Reverend Pettigrew's work has appeared in *Wicazo Sa*, *Indian Country Today*, and the anthologies *Under 25: Fiction*, *The Mythic Midwest*, and *Through the Eye of the Deer*.

CARTER REVARD (Osage) was born in Oklahoma and raised on the Osage reservation. After earning his undergraduate degree from the University of Tulsa, he went to England as a Rhodes scholar to study at Oxford University, where he received his master's degree. Dr. Revard received his doctorate in English in 1959 at Yale. He is currently a professor of English at Washington University in St. Louis, Missouri. His Osage name is *Nompehwahteh*, meaning "fear-inspiring."

D. RENVILLE (Dakota/Assiniboine/Gros Ventre) lives on the Lake Traverse Reservation in northeastern South Dakota, and is employed at Sisseton-Wahpehton College. "Siobhan La Rue in Color" is an excerpt from a novel-in-progress, *Siobhan La Rue*.

GARY ROBINSON (Creek) is an Emmy-winning television producer best known for his work on TNT's *The Native Americans*. Currently, he lives in southern California, where he is a producer and writer at Spirit World Productions, an American Indian–owned and –operated production company.

STEVE RUSSELL (Cherokee) is a retired judge and attorney who is currently an assistant professor at the University of Texas, San Antonio School of Social and Public Policy. A member of the Cherokee Nation of Oklahoma, Professor Russell is immediate past president of the Texas Indian Bar Association. He is an active member of the Wordcraft Circle.

SULEIMAN RUSSELL (Laguna/Cherokee) is a poet, humorist, and short story writer who has published extensively online in the science fiction and dark fantasy genres, including *Ex Libris Nocturnis* (www.nocturnis.net) and *The Banner*. He makes his home with his wife, Melissa, in Hayward, California. This is his first offline publication.

JOHNNY RUSTYWIRE (Navajo) is the pen name of a Navajo writer who writes what he knows best: Navajo life and landscapes. The author of an online journal, *Navajo Spaceships, Star Mountain and Life* (www.geocities.com/SoHo/Nook/1574/Starmtn), Johnny is an active member of the Wordcraft Circle.

VICKIE L. SEARS (Cherokee) was a psychiatric social worker and therapist in Washington State. She published a collection of short stories, *Simple Songs,* and many articles on therapeutic issues including multiple personality disorder among American Indians and was active in the Indian Child Welfare movement resulting from the Indian Child Welfare Act. She made her home in Seattle, where she died in 1999, and is survived by her partner, Dr. Linda Lustre, and their dog, Tsalagi.

M.L. SMOKER (Ft. Peck Assiniboine/Sioux) is curently attending the M.A. program in creative writing at the University of Colorado at Boulder. She would like to thank all of her family for their support. The story included in this anthology belongs to her brothers, Austin and August, who are always the stars in her heart.

MARY RANDLE TALLMOUNTAIN (Koyukon/Athabascan) was born in 1918 in Nulato, a village along the Yukon River in Alaska, to a Koyukon/Athabascan mother and a Scottish/Irish father. When her mother became terminally ill, Tallmountain was adopted by a non-Native couple and taken away from her village. Writing was a way of going home, of reclaiming her ancestry, her family, and her homeland, and a way of claiming her own proud Native voice. The author of many works of poetry including *The Light on the Tent Wall, The Way of St. Francis,* and *A Quick Brush of Wings,* she was working on an autobiographical novel, *Doyon,* at the time of her death in 1994.

KAREN WALLACE (Osage) received her Ph.D. in English from UCLA and was an assistant professor at the University of Wisconsin at Osh Kosh. Currently teaching at the American Indian Charter School in Oakland, California, Dr. Wallace's work has appeared in the anthologies *Song of the Turtle* and *Through the Eye of the Deer.* She lives in California.

ANNA LEE WALTERS (Pawnee/Otoe-Missouria) was born in Pawnee, Oklahoma. She obtained her B.A. from Goddard College in Plainfield, Vermont, where she also received an M.F.A. in creative writing. She and her husband, Harry Walters (Navajo), who heads the Ned A. Hatathli Museum at Diné College in Tsaile, Arizona, have two sons. She is currently an instructor in the Humanities Division at Diné College, and is also an independent consultant on American Indian issues.

EMMA LEE WARRIOR (Peigan) is a poet and short story writer whose work has been included in several anthologies including *A Gathering of Spirit, Song of the Turtle,* and *Reinventing the Enemy's Language.*

MARK ROBERT WALDMAN is a writer, editor, and therapist who lives in the mountains near Los Angeles. He is the author of seven books and anthologies, including *Love Games, Inking Through the Soul,* and *Dreamscaping.* Founding editor of *Transpersonal Review* and developmental editor for Tarcher/Putnam, his essays and short stories have been published throughout the world. He looks embarrassingly white.